AF375205

Contents

Preface

This book covers many important segments of British literature. The first part delves into multiple vital dramatic terms. Again two crucial plays from early Elizabethan period and have been dealt with careful manner for better understnding of the students of English literature. The text along with annotations and explanations, important questions and answers of those plays are given to help the students to prepare for their examinations. Further a through study of origin and developement of English drama has been prepared to give a clear picture about drama in general. This book is mainly designed to cater to the needs of under-graduate and post-graduate students.

CHAPTER ONE

Dramatic Terms

Literary Terms (Drama)

1.What is Tragedy?

The word "tragedy" comes from the Greek "he-goat" and aeidein = "to sing" – literally, "the song of a goat." Scholars aren't sure exactly why, but they have a couple theories:

1.) In ancient Athens, where tragedy was first performed on stage. Dionysus, the Greek god to whom the plays were dedicated, was associated with satyrs--a sort of mythological goat.

2.) Goats may have been sacrificed during the performance of tragedies in ancient Athens.

3.) A goat might have been the prize for writing a winning tragedy.

In spite of this mystery, though, we're stuck with the word "tragedy" to refer to a narrative arc in which things start out in order and end in disarray.

In his Poetics, the ancient Greek philosopher Aristotle defined tragedy as a morally ambiguous genre in which a noble hero goes from good fortune to bad. For Aristotle, the tragic hero can't be totally evil or purely good, but instead, must be a "character between these two extremes... whose misfortune is brought about not by vice or depravity, but by some error or frailty, also known as "hamartia," that is, by a fatal flaw. The point of Greek tragedy is to use this morally ambiguous character's death to create an emotional effect in an audience, a purifying sort of emotional release that Aristotle calls catharsis. In Ancient Greece, tragic theater was a ritual performance where the negative emotions of a society could be purged, and the end result had political goals: a better-functioning Athenian democracy.

But Aristotle died over 2000 years ago, and the definition, purpose, and focus of tragedy has changed a bit in that time. In ancient Greece, tragedy was a ritual performance of the downfall of a great man – usually a king or a nobleman – brought low because of some sort of fault. In the medieval period, "tragedy" was concerned with "noble or illustrious men," too, but these tales usually took on a Christian moral valence. In Shakespeare's tragedies, which are some of English literature's most famous, the "tragic action" nearly always focuses on one central character, like Hamlet, King Lear, or Othello, but Shakespeare's tragedies also focus on how broader political consequences follow as a result of a "great man's" death (the fall of Denmark in Hamlet, for instance, or the Ottoman/European political conflict at the heart of Othello).

Modern tragedy is a little different. It doesn't tend to focus on just "great men" and their political actions. Instead, it focuses on the middle class: we might think of Arthur Miller's Death of a Salesman as a good example. Modern tragedies might be ironic or sarcastic, too, playing on two millennia of the idea of "tragedy" to both seriously entertain the drama of life while making light of it, and giving readers of all classes an opportunity to connect with, and share in the emotions and political import of private devastation. When Willy Loman dies in Death of a Salesman, the tragedy is just as much about his failings as it is about the failure of midcentury economic and political systems.

So, just as the origins of the word "tragedy" are ambiguous, so too does a sort of ambiguity and flexibility define the genre of tragedy. However, by and large, if a narrative begins with everything in order and ends in disorder, it can probably be classified as a tragedy.

2.What is Comedy in Literature? Definition, Examples of Literary Comedy

Comedy is a genre in which the goal is to make audiences laugh. Comedy is also a type of dramatic work which employs amusing and satirical tones with a cheerful ending.

The purpose of comedy is to amuse the audience. Usually, this is achieved when characters are able to triumph over negative circumstances with the creation of some sort of comedic effect. In comedies, the endings are uplifting, positive, or successful.

Comedies occur across dramatic and narrative types of literature. In dramatic literature, we see them in plays such as William Shakespeare's A Midsummer Night's Dream and Aristophanes' (known as the Father of Comedy) surviving works. In narrative stories, comedies include the likes of Dav Pilkey's Captain Underpants, a children's book series, and Douglas Adams' The Hitchhiker's Guide to the Galaxy which is widely regarded as one of the best comedic novels.

Types of Comedy

There are several sub-genres of the comedy wheelhouse. Literary comedies differ from how we think of comedy in casual language today. In literature, comedy refers mostly to plays with less of a focus on casual humor.

Romantic comedy deals with themes of love. Relationships are portrayed with their fair share of ups and downs, but true love overcomes obstacles and the ending sees a happy union (or reunion) of the couple.

Shakespeare's As You Like It

Comedy of manners confronts the intrigue of elevated ladies and gentlemen of society. This form of comedy relies on high comedy full of witty dialogue. Usually, complicating characters consist of jealous husbands, witches, cunning wives, and fools. Comedy of Manners is largely satirical.

Oscar Wilde's Lady Windermere's Fan

Sentimental comedy sees middle class characters triumphing over moral indecencies and deal heavily with themes of virtue and overcoming bad influences. Unlike other forms of comedy, sentimental comedy aims to provoke tears more than laughter.

Sir Richard Steele's The Conscious Lovers

Tragicomedy contains elements of both tragedy and comedy. Generally, a tragicomedy is a serious play that has a happy ending.

The Importance of Comedy in Literature

Comedy aims to bring laughter and humor to plays/the theater. Comedy entertains and amuses audiences while also addressing social and personal matters of corruption. For example, comedy uses techniques such as satire and parody in order to poke fun at common human flaws. Often, comedies expose societal and institutional issues in a way that makes the subject less painful to approach.

Comedy types vary from culture to culture, but humor is a universal tool and comedy is an extremely popular method of storytelling. Aside from laughter and humor, comedy brings an awareness to certain truths and important ideas.

Comedy Examples in Literature

Comedy has been used well in literature, particularly dramatic literature, for centuries. Here are several examples ranging from Elizabethan times to contemporary drama:

<u>Twelfth Night</u> by William Shakespeare explores the complications of love which arise from concealment and confusions around identity. Also, this play explores the thin line between love and madness and how carelessly pursuing someone in the name of love can lead to negative outcomes.

Oscar Wilde's <u>The Importance of Being Earnest</u> presents comedy using elements of romance, situational comedy, and farce (exaggeration and over-the-top). The play experiments with confused identities and ultimately everything works out in the best possible way.

3.What is Farce?

A farce is a comedy in which everything is absolutely absurd. This usually involves some kind of deception or miscommunication. When a comedy is based on a case of mistaken identity, for example, you can be sure that it's going to be a farce. Slapstick humor and physical comedy are also common features of a farce.

Although most farces are comedies, there is such a thing as a "tragic farce." In a tragic farce, the humor is always very bleak, but still present – it's a kind of "laugh so you don't cry" situation.

The Importance of Farce

Farcical humor appeals to some of our most basic instincts. People falling down; absurd, outlandish situations; pies to the face: all these things make us laugh for reasons that are somewhat mysterious, and yet somehow universal. Everyone can recognize the comedy of a farce.

Farces are also popular because they develop in a way that seems more or less realistic, despite the fact that the results are highly improbable. That is, the characters make decisions that seem to make some sense given the circumstances, but at every turn things get more and more ridiculous. This slow build-up makes a farce seem somehow believable, in spite of the fact that the plotlines are so improbable and absurd.

This, in the end, is the very simple purpose of a farce: it makes people laugh through broad humor.

Examples of Farce in Literature

Example 1

Oscar Widle's The Importance of Being Earnest is a great example of a farce.

Example 2

Shakespeare, in his sillier moods, loved a good farce. Many of his comedies are based on mistaken identity and the gradual piling-up of confusion and chaos. In *Comedy of Errors*, for instance, there are two sets of identical twins who frequently get confused for one another. (In fact, this play was so influential that "comedy of errors" is sometimes used as a general term to describe farcical stories.)

4.What is a Monologue?

A monologue is a speech given by a single character in a story. In drama, it is the vocalization of a character's thoughts; in literature, the verbalization. It is traditionally a device used in theater—a speech to be given on stage—but nowadays, its use extends to film and television.

Types of Monologues

Soliloquy

A speech that a character gives to himself—as if no one else is listening—which voices his inner thoughts aloud. Basically, a soliloquy captures a character talking to himself at length out loud. Of course, the audience (and sometimes other characters) can hear the speech, but the person talking to himself is unaware of others listening. For example, in comedy, oftentimes a character is pictured giving themselves a lengthy, uplifting speech in the mirror...while a friend is secretly watching them and laughing. The soliloquy is one of the most fundamental dramatic devices used by Shakespeare in his dramas.

Dramatic Monologue

A speech that is given directly to the audience or another character. It can be formal or informal, funny or serious; but it is almost always significant in both length and purpose. For example, a scene that captures a president's speech to a crowd exhibits a dramatic monologue that is both lengthy and important to the story's plotline. In fact, in TV, theater ,and film, all speeches given by a single character—to an audience, the audience, or even just one character—are dramatic monologues.

Related Terms

Aside

An **aside** is when a character briefly pauses to speak directly to the audience, but no other characters are aware of it. It is very similar to a monologue; however, the primary difference between the two is that an **aside** is **very short**; it can be just one word, or a couple of sentences, but it is always brief—monologues are substantial in length. Furthermore, an aside is always said **directly to the audience,** usually accomplished (in film and television) by looking directly into the camera. As an example, asides are a key part of the style of the Netflix series *House of Cards*; the main character Francis Underwood often looks directly into the camera and openly addresses the audience as if they are present, while the other characters do not know that the audience exists.

Dialogue

While a monologue is a given by one character ("mono"=single), a dialogue is a conversation that occurs between two or more characters. Monologues and dialogues are similar in that they both deliver language to the audience. For instance, in a movie, a race winner's speech is a monologue, however, a speech collectively given by several members of a team is dialogue. Both techniques can address the audience, but the difference lies in how many people are speaking.

Importance of Monologues

Monologues give the audience and other characters access to what a particular character is thinking, either through a speech or the vocalization of their thoughts. While the purpose of a speech is obvious, the latter is particularly useful for characterization: it aids the audience in developing an idea about what the character is really thinking, which in turn helps (or can later help) explain their previous (or future) actions and behavior.

Examples of Monologue in Literature

As a technique principally used on the stage (or screen), the best examples of monologues in literature are found in dramatic literature, most notably in Shakespeare's dramas. Below is selection of arguably the most famous monologue in literature—soliloquy, specifically—from Act III Scene I of the tragedy Hamlet. This soliloquy begins with the well-known words "To be, or not to be-that is the question:"

In Mark Twain's short story "The Celebrated Jumping Frog of Calaveras County," the narrator is sent to find a man named Simon Wheeler, who will tell him a story. After the narrator introduces the premise, he explains that he let Wheeler "go on in his own way, and never interrupted him once." He follows with Wheeler's story, told in Wheeler's voice, which he achieves through the shift in the style of speech

Conclusion

In conclusion, monologues (and dialogues) are arguably the most fundamental parts of onstage drama and dramatic literature. Without them, essentially only silent film and theater could exist, as monologues provide the only way for the audience to witness a character's thoughts.

5.What is a Chorus?

A chorus is part of a song or poem that is repeated following each verse. The Chorus of a song or poem is the part where you repeat a verse or a phrase. There are various patterns of repeat. The example of a song with a chorus below has a repeated verse and then a chorus. The example of a poem has just a repeated chorus.

In Greek, the term comes from the word "choros" or a company of dancers or singers who perform in unison. Traditionally, these groups were only composed of men. They participated in festivals, appeared on stage during plays, and held different vital roles for the audience of a performance. Their words might serve as a summary of events as they've so far transpired, or they might provide commentary (of varying degrees) on the story that's playing out.

In some traditional sources, the chorus was more important to the overall work than others. For example, in the work of Greek writer Euripides, the chorus was only lyrical. While in other authors' works, such as later on in the Elizabethan area (the period during which Shakespeare was writing) the chorus was composed of a single actor who recited parts of the text (usually, the prologue and/or the epilogue). Some of the best examples come from William Shakespeare's plays

Examples of Chorus in Literature

In ancient Greek tragedies like Sophocles' 'Antigone,' the chorus in literature plays a multifaceted role, serving as both commentator and participant, offering insights, and moral commentary to the unfolding drama.

Henry V by William Shakespeare

Henry V by William Shakespeare is a great example of a play that includes the Chorus as a character within the action. Within the play, the Chorus praises King Henry for his actions, provides commentary for the rest of the play, and sets the scene at the beginning of each act for what's to come

Romeo and Juliet Act I Prologue by William Shakespeare

The prologue of Romeo and Juliet is one of the best-known examples of a choral sonnet in any of Shakespeare's works. The Chorus enters the stage before the play's main characters and recites fourteen lines that set the scene and provide the audience with important information about what's about to happen. This includes foreshadowing as well as specific details.

6.Three Unities

The three literary unities are principles derived from classical Greek drama, particularly from Aristotle's "Poetics." They emphasize coherence and structural elements within a play:

Unity of Time: This refers to the idea that the events portrayed in a play or narrative should occur within a single day or a reasonable amount of time. It means the single revolution of the sun. The unity of time aims to create a sense of compactness and coherence in the storytelling.

Unity of Place: This suggests that the action of a play or story should develop in a single location or, at the most, in places that are nearby or connected. The unity of place helps focus the narrative and prevents unnecessary distractions by confining the action to a specific setting.

Unity of Action: This principle emphasizes that a play or story should have a single main plotline with no subplots unrelated to the main storyline. The unity of action encourages a tight structure by concentrating on a central conflict or theme without unnecessary diversions.

These unities were formalized by Aristotle and were considered guidelines for classical playwrights, particularly in Greek tragedies and later in neoclassical drama. However, their strict adherence has become less common in modern literature, allowing for more diverse and expansive storytelling techniques

7.Melodrama

Melodrama, in Western theatre, sentimental drama with an improbable plot that concerns the vicissitudes suffered by the virtuous at the hands of the villainous but ends happily with virtue triumphant. Featuring stock characters such as the noble hero, the long-suffering heroine, and the cold-blooded villain, the melodrama focusses not on character development but on sensational incidents and spectacular staging. In music, melodrama signifies lines spoken to a musical accompaniment.

The melodramatic stage play is generally regarded as having developed in France as a result of the impact of Jean-Jacques Rousseau's Pygmalion (1762; first performed 1770) on a society torn by violent political and social upheaval and exposed to the influences of the English Gothic novel and of Sturm und Drang (Storm and Stress) and Romanticism from Germany. The pioneer and prime exponent of the 18th-century French melodrama with its music, singing, and spectacular effects was Guilbert de Pixérécourt. His Coelina, ou l'enfant de mystère (1800) was translated as A Tale of Mystery (1802) by Thomas Holcroft and established the new genre in England. It was not utterly new to England, however; the restrictions of the Licensing Act of 1737 had been habitually evaded by combining drama with music, singing, and dancing.

Another prominent dramatist whose melodrama influenced other countries was the German August von Kotzebue. His Menschenhass und Reue (1789) became tremendously popular in England as The Stranger (1798); he also provided the original of Richard Brinsley Sheridan's Pizarro (1799). In the early 19th century, melodrama spread throughout the European theatre; in Russia the authorities welcomed it as diverting attention from more serious issues.

During the 19ᵗʰ century, music and singing were gradually eliminated. As technical developments in the theatre made greater realism possible, more emphasis was given to the spectacular—e.g., snowstorms, shipwrecks, battles, train wrecks, conflagrations, earthquakes, and horse races. Among the best known and most representative of the melodramas popular in England and the United States are The Octoroon (1859) and The Colleen Bawn (1860), both by Dion Boucicault. More sensational were The Poor of New York (1857), London by Night (1844), and Under the Gaslight (1867). The realistic staging and the social evils touched upon, however perfunctorily and sentimentally, anticipated the later theatre of the Naturalists.

With the growing sophistication of the theatre in the early 20ᵗʰ century, the theatrical melodrama declined in popularity. It was a vigorous form, though, in motion picture adventure serials until the advent of sound. The exaggerated gestures, dramatic chases, emotional scenes, simple flat characters, and impossible situations were later revived and parodied. Melodrama makes up a good part of contemporary television drama.

8.Conflict

Conflict is a key element in drama, the main catalyst that drives the story forward. It takes various forms, from external struggles between characters to internal dilemmas within an individual's mind. Conflict can be a simple plot device or a complex tool that enriches the narrative, aids character development, deepens themes, and engages the audience.

At its core, conflict starts and maintains the momentum of the dramatic work. It sets off the events that make up the plot, from the initial exposition through rising action to the climax, falling action, and, ultimately, resolution. Conflict isn't limited to external clashes; it also encompasses the characters' inner struggles, adding complexity to the drama.

Dramatists use various techniques to portray conflict, including dialogue, action, symbolism, and auditory and visual elements like sound and lighting. Each technique has advantages in highlighting the different aspects of conflict, whether to show subtle dynamics in relationships, emphasize a theme, or build emotional intensity

Types of Conflict in Drama

Traditionally, there are five types of conflict in drama: internal conflict, external conflict, interpersonal conflict, social and cultural conflict, and cosmic or fate-driven conflict.

1. Internal Conflict

Definition

Internal conflict refers to the psychological struggle or moral dilemma within a character's mind. It is often portrayed through monologues, soliloquies, or reflective dialogues.

Example

In William Shakespeare's tragedy "Hamlet," the protagonist, Prince Hamlet, faces a complex internal conflict regarding the moral implications of avenging his father's murder. Hamlet's soliloquies, most notably the "To be, or not to be" speech, reveal his moral and existential struggles. Torn between his sense of duty to his deceased father and his intellectual and ethical reservations about revenge, Hamlet's internal conflict serves as the psychological backbone of the drama. This internal tug-of-war complicates his relationships with other characters and delves into broad themes of morality, justice, and the human psyche.

2. External Conflict

Definition

External conflict denotes a struggle between a character and an external entity, whether it be another character, nature, society, or an abstract concept like fate.

Example

In Henrik Ibsen's "A Doll's House," Nora Helmer grapples with an external conflict against the stifling societal norms of 19th-century Norway. Nora's decision to forge her father's signature to save her husband, Torvald, imposes upon her a life within the constrained gender roles and expectations of her society. The external conflict reaches its zenith when Nora decides to leave her family, a radical act that defies the conventional social structures of her time. Nora's conflict, therefore, is not just with her husband but with the societal norms that prescribe her roles as a wife and mother.

CHAPTER TWO

Doctor Faustus : Text

THE TRAGICAL HISTORY

OF

DOCTOR FAUSTUS

By Christopher Marlowe

From The Quarto of 1604

DRAMATIS PERSONAE.

THE POPE.
  CARDINAL OF LORRAIN.
  THE EMPEROR OF GERMANY.
  DUKE OF VANHOLT.
  FAUSTUS.
  VALDES,] friends to FAUSTUS.
  CORNELIUS,]
  WAGNER, servant to FAUSTUS.
  Clown.

ROBIN.
RALPH.
Vintner.
Horse-courser.
A Knight.
An Old Man.
Scholars, Friars, and Attendants.
DUCHESS OF VANHOLT
LUCIFER.
BELZEBUB.
MEPHISTOPHILIS.
Good Angel.
Evil Angel.
The Seven Deadly Sins.
Devils.
Spirits in the shapes of ALEXANDER THE GREAT, of his Paramour
and of HELEN.
Chorus.

THE TRAGICAL HISTORY OF DOCTOR FAUSTUS

FROM THE QUARTO OF 1604.
Enter CHORUS.
CHORUS. Not marching now in fields of Thrasymene,
Where Mars did mate the Carthaginians;
Nor sporting in the dalliance of love,
In courts of kings where state is overturn'd;
Nor in the pomp of proud audacious deeds,
Intends our Muse to vaunt her heavenly verse:
Only this, gentlemen,—we must perform
The form of Faustus' fortunes, good or bad:
To patient judgments we appeal our plaud,
And speak for Faustus in his infancy.

Now is he born, his parents base of stock,
In Germany, within a town call'd Rhodes:
Of riper years, to Wertenberg he went,
Whereas his kinsmen chiefly brought him up.
So soon he profits in divinity,
The fruitful plot of scholarism grac'd,
That shortly he was grac'd with doctor's name,
Excelling all whose sweet delight disputes
In heavenly matters of theology;
Till swoln with cunning, of a self-conceit,
His waxen wings did mount above his reach,
And, melting, heavens conspir'd his overthrow;
For, falling to a devilish exercise,
And glutted now with learning's golden gifts,
He surfeits upon cursed necromancy;
Nothing so sweet as magic is to him,
Which he prefers before his chiefest bliss:
And this the man that in his study sits.
[Exit.]
FAUSTUS discovered in his study.
FAUSTUS. Settle thy studies, Faustus, and begin
To sound the depth of that thou wilt profess:
Having commenc'd, be a divine in shew,
Yet level at the end of every art,
And live and die in Aristotle's works.
Sweet Analytics, 'tis thou hast ravish'd me!
Bene disserere est finis logices.
Is, to dispute well, logic's chiefest end?
Affords this art no greater miracle?
Then read no more; thou hast attain'd that end:
A greater subject fitteth Faustus' wit:
Bid Economy farewell, and Galen come,
Seeing, Ubi desinit philosophus, ibi incipit medicus:
Be a physician, Faustus; heap up gold,
And be eterniz'd for some wondrous cure:

Summum bonum medicinae sanitas,
The end of physic is our body's health.
Why, Faustus, hast thou not attain'd that end?
Is not thy common talk found aphorisms?
Are not thy bills hung up as monuments,
Whereby whole cities have escap'd the plague,
And thousand desperate maladies been eas'd?
Yet art thou still but Faustus, and a man.
Couldst thou make men to live eternally,
Or, being dead, raise them to life again,
Then this profession were to be esteem'd.
Physic, farewell! Where is Justinian?
[Reads.]
Si una eademque res legatur duobus, alter rem,
alter valorem rei, &c.
A pretty case of paltry legacies!
[Reads.]
Exhoereditare filium non potest pater, nisi, &c.
Such is the subject of the institute,
And universal body of the law:
This study fits a mercenary drudge,
Who aims at nothing but external trash;
Too servile and illiberal for me.
When all is done, divinity is best:
Jerome's Bible, Faustus; view it well.
[Reads.]
Stipendium peccati mors est.
Ha!
Stipendium, &c.
The reward of sin is death: that's hard.
[Reads.]
Si peccasse negamus, fallimur, et nulla est in nobis veritas;
If we say that we have no sin, we deceive ourselves, and
there's no truth in us. Why, then, belike we must sin, and so
consequently die:

Ay, we must die an everlasting death.
What doctrine call you this, Che sera, sera,
What will be, shall be? Divinity, adieu!
These metaphysics of magicians,
And necromantic books are heavenly;
Lines, circles, scenes, letters, and characters;
Ay, these are those that Faustus most desires.
O, what a world of profit and delight,
Of power, of honour, of omnipotence,
Is promis'd to the studious artizan!
All things that move between the quiet poles
Shall be at my command: emperors and kings
Are but obeyed in their several provinces,
Nor can they raise the wind, or rend the clouds;
But his dominion that exceeds in this,
Stretcheth as far as doth the mind of man;
A sound magician is a mighty god:
Here, Faustus, tire thy brains to gain a deity.
Enter WAGNER.
Wagner, commend me to my dearest friends,
The German Valdes and Cornelius;
Request them earnestly to visit me.
WAGNER. I will, sir.
[Exit.]
FAUSTUS. Their conference will be a greater help to me
Than all my labours, plod I ne'er so fast.
Enter GOOD ANGEL and EVIL ANGEL.
GOOD ANGEL. O, Faustus, lay that damned book aside,
And gaze not on it, lest it tempt thy soul,
And heap God's heavy wrath upon thy head!
Read, read the Scriptures:—that is blasphemy.
EVIL ANGEL. Go forward, Faustus, in that famous art
Wherein all Nature's treasure is contain'd:
Be thou on earth as Jove is in the sky,
Lord and commander of these elements.

[Exeunt Angels.]
FAUSTUS. How am I glutted with conceit of this!
Shall I make spirits fetch me what I please,
Resolve me of all ambiguities,
Perform what desperate enterprise I will?
I'll have them fly to India for gold,
Ransack the ocean for orient pearl,
And search all corners of the new-found world
For pleasant fruits and princely delicates;
I'll have them read me strange philosophy,
And tell the secrets of all foreign kings;
I'll have them wall all Germany with brass,
And make swift Rhine circle fair Wertenberg;
I'll have them fill the public schools with silk,
Wherewith the students shall be bravely clad;
I'll levy soldiers with the coin they bring,
And chase the Prince of Parma from our land,
And reign sole king of all the provinces;
Yea, stranger engines for the brunt of war,
Than was the fiery keel at Antwerp's bridge,
I'll make my servile spirits to invent.
Enter VALDES and CORNELIUS.
Come, German Valdes, and Cornelius,
And make me blest with your sage conference.
Valdes, sweet Valdes, and Cornelius,
Know that your words have won me at the last
To practice magic and concealed arts:
Yet not your words only, but mine own fantasy,
That will receive no object; for my head
But ruminates on necromantic skill.
Philosophy is odious and obscure;
Both law and physic are for petty wits;
Divinity is basest of the three,
Unpleasant, harsh, contemptible, and vile:
'Tis magic, magic, that hath ravish'd me.

Then, gentle friends, aid me in this attempt;
And I, that have with concise syllogisms
Gravell'd the pastors of the German church,
And made the flowering pride of Wertenberg
Swarm to my problems, as the infernal spirits
On sweet Musaeus when he came to hell,
Will be as cunning as Agrippa was,
Whose shadow made all Europe honour him.
VALDES. Faustus, these books, thy wit, and our experience,
Shall make all nations to canonize us.
As Indian Moors obey their Spanish lords,
So shall the spiritsbof every element
Be always serviceable to us three;
Like lions shall they guard us when we please;
Like Almain rutters with their horsemen's staves,
Or Lapland giants, trotting by our sides;
Sometimes like women, or unwedded maids,
Shadowing more beauty in their airy brows
Than have thewhite breasts of the queen of love:
From Venice shall they drag huge argosies,
And from America the golden fleece
That yearly stuffs old Philip's treasury;
If learned Faustus will be resolute.
FAUSTUS. Valdes, as resolute am I in this
As thou to live: therefore object it not.
CORNELIUS. The miracles that magic will perform
Will make thee vow to study nothing else.
He that is grounded in astrology,
Enrich'd with tongues, well seen in minerals,
Hath all the principles magic doth require:
Then doubt not, Faustus, but to be renowm'd,
And more frequented for this mystery
Than heretofore the Delphian oracle.
The spirits tell me they can dry the sea,
And fetch the treasure of all foreign wrecks,

Ay, all the wealth that our forefathers hid
Within the massy entrails of the earth:
Then tell me, Faustus, what shall we three want?
FAUSTUS. Nothing, Cornelius. O, this cheers my soul!
Come, shew me some demonstrations magical,
That I may conjure in some lusty grove,
And have these joys in full possession.
VALDES. Then haste thee to some solitary grove,
And bear wise Bacon's and Albertus'works,
The Hebrew Psalter, and New Testament;
And whatsoever else is requisite
We will inform thee ere our conference cease.
CORNELIUS. Valdes, first let him know the words of art;
And then, all other ceremonies learn'd,
Faustus may try his cunning by himself.
VALDES. First I'll instruct thee in the rudiments,
And then wilt thou be perfecter than I.
FAUSTUS. Then come and dine with me, and, after meat,
We'll canvass every quiddity thereof;
For, ere I sleep, I'll try what I can do:
This night I'll conjure, though I die therefore.
[Exeunt.]
Enter two SCHOLARS.
FIRST SCHOLAR. I wonder what's become of Faustus, that was wont
to make our schools ring with sic probo.
SECOND SCHOLAR. That shall we know, for see, here comes his boy.
Enter WAGNER.
FIRST SCHOLAR. How now, sirrah! where's thy master?
WAGNER. God in heaven knows.
SECOND SCHOLAR. Why, dost not thou know?
WAGNER. Yes, I know; but that follows not.
FIRST SCHOLAR. Go to, sirrah! leave your jesting, and tell us where he is.

WAGNER. That follows not necessary by force of argument, that you,
    being licentiates, should stand upon: therefore acknowledge
    your error, and be attentive.
    SECOND SCHOLAR. Why, didst thou not say thou knewest?
    WAGNER. Have you any witness on't?
    FIRST SCHOLAR. Yes, sirrah, I heard you.
    WAGNER. Ask my fellow if I be a thief.
    SECOND SCHOLAR. Well, you will not tell us?
    WAGNER. Yes, sir, I will tell you: yet, if you were not dunces,
    you would never ask me such a question; for is not he corpus
    naturale? and is not that mobile? then wherefore should you
    ask me such a question? But that I am by nature phlegmatic,
    slow to wrath, and prone to lechery (to love, I would say),
    it were not for you to come within forty foot of the place
    of execution, although I do not doubt to see you both hanged
    the next sessions. Thus having triumphed over you, I will set
    my countenance like a precisian, and begin to speak thus:—
    Truly, my dear brethren, my master is within at dinner,
    with Valdes and Cornelius, as this wine, if it could speak,
    would inform your worships: and so, the Lord bless you,
    preserve you, and keep you, my dear brethren, my dear
brethren!
    [Exit.]
    FIRST SCHOLAR. Nay, then, I fear he is fallen into that damned art
    for which they two are infamous through the world.
    SECOND SCHOLAR. Were he a stranger, and not allied to me,
yet should
    I grieve for him. But, come, let us go and inform the Rector,
    and see if he by his grave counsel can reclaim him.
    FIRST SCHOLAR. O, but I fear me nothing can reclaim him!
    SECOND SCHOLAR. Yet let us try what we can do.
    [Exeunt.]
    Enter FAUSTUS to conjure.

FAUSTUS. Now that the gloomy shadow of the earth,
Longing to view Orion's drizzling look,
Leaps from th' antartic world unto the sky,
And dims the welkin with her pitchy breath,
Faustus, begin thine incantations,
And try if devils will obey thy hest,
Seeing thou hast pray'd and sacrific'd to them.
Within this circle is Jehovah's name,
Forward and backward anagrammatiz'd,
Th' abbreviated names of holy saints,
Figures of every adjunct to the heavens,
And characters of signs and erring stars,
By which the spirits are enforc'd to rise:
Then fear not, Faustus, but be resolute,
And try the uttermost magic can perform.—
Sint mihi dei Acherontis propitii! Valeat numen triplex Jehovoe!
Ignei, aerii, aquatani spiritus, salvete! Orientis princeps
Belzebub, inferni ardentis monarcha, et Demogorgon,
propitiamus
vos, ut appareat et surgat Mephistophilis, quod tumeraris:
per Jehovam, Gehennam, et consecratam aquam quam nunc
spargo,
signumque crucis quod nunc facio, et per vota nostra, ipse nunc
surgat nobis dicatus Mephistophilis!
Enter MEPHISTOPHILIS.
I charge thee to return, and change thy shape;
Thou art too ugly to attend on me:
Go, and return an old Franciscan friar;
That holy shape becomes a devil best.
[Exit MEPHISTOPHILIS.]
I see there's virtue in my heavenly words:
Who would not be proficient in this art?
How pliant is this Mephistophilis,
Full of obedience and humility!
Such is the force of magic and my spells:

No, Faustus, thou art conjuror laureat,
That canst command great Mephistophilis:
Quin regis Mephistophilis fratris imagine.
Re-enter MEPHISTOPHILIS like a Franciscan friar.
MEPHIST. Now, Faustus, what wouldst thou have me do?
FAUSTUS. I charge thee wait upon me whilst I live,
To do whatever Faustus shall command,
Be it to make the moon drop from her sphere,
Or the ocean to overwhelm the world.
MEPHIST. I am a servant to great Lucifer,
And may not follow thee without his leave:
No more than he commands must we perform.
FAUSTUS. Did not he charge thee to appear to me?
MEPHIST. No, I came hither of mine own accord.
FAUSTUS. Did not my conjuring speeches raise thee? speak.
MEPHIST. That was the cause, but yet per accidens;
For, when we hear one rack the name of God,
Abjure the Scriptures and his Saviour Christ,
We fly, in hope to get his glorious soul;
Nor will we come, unless he use such means
Whereby he is in danger to be damn'd.
Therefore the shortest cut for conjuring
Is stoutly to abjure the Trinity,
And pray devoutly to the prince of hell.
FAUSTUS. So Faustus hath
Already done; and holds this principle,
There is no chief but only Belzebub;
To whom Faustus doth dedicate himself.
This word "damnation" terrifies not him,
For he confounds hell in Elysium:
His ghost be with the old philosophers!
But, leaving these vain trifles of men's souls,
Tell me what is that Lucifer thy lord?
MEPHIST. Arch-regent and commander of all spirits.
FAUSTUS. Was not that Lucifer an angel once?

MEPHIST. Yes, Faustus, and most dearly lov'd of God.
FAUSTUS. How comes it, then, that he is prince of devils?
MEPHIST. O, by aspiring pride and insolence;
For which God threw him from the face of heaven.
FAUSTUS. And what are you that live with Lucifer?
MEPHIST. Unhappy spirits that fell with Lucifer,
Conspir'd against our God with Lucifer,
And are for ever damn'd with Lucifer.
FAUSTUS. Where are you damn'd?
MEPHIST. In hell.
FAUSTUS. How comes it, then, that thou art out of hell?
MEPHIST. Why, this is hell, nor am I out of it:
Think'st thou that I, who saw the face of God,
And tasted the eternal joys of heaven,
Am not tormented with ten thousand hells,
In being depriv'd of everlasting bliss?
O, Faustus, leave these frivolous demands,
Which strike a terror to my fainting soul!
FAUSTUS. What, is great Mephistophilis so passionate
For being deprived of the joys of heaven?
Learn thou of Faustus manly fortitude,
And scorn those joys thou never shalt possess.
Go bear these tidings to great Lucifer:
Seeing Faustus hath incurr'd eternal death
By desperate thoughts against Jove's deity,
Say, he surrenders up to him his soul,
So he will spare him four and twenty years,
Letting him live in all voluptuousness;
Having thee ever to attend on me,
To give me whatsoever I shall ask,
To tell me whatsoever I demand,
To slay mine enemies, and aid my friends,
And always be obedient to my will.
Go and return to mighty Lucifer,
And meet me in my study at midnight,

And then resolve me of thy master's mind.
MEPHIST. I will, Faustus.
[Exit.]
FAUSTUS. Had I as many souls as there be stars,
I'd give them all for Mephistophilis.
By him I'll be great emperor of the world,
And make a bridge thorough the moving air,
To pass the ocean with a band of men;
I'll join the hills that bind the Afric shore,
And make that country continent to Spain,
And both contributory to my crown:
The Emperor shall not live but by my leave,
Nor any potentate of Germany.
Now that I have obtain'd what I desir'd,
I'll live in speculation of this art,
Till Mcphistophilis rcturn again.
[Exit.]
Enter WAGNER and CLOWN.
WAGNER. Sirrah boy, come hither.
CLOWN. How, boy! swowns, boy! I hope you have seen many
boys
    with such pickadevaunts as I have: boy, quotha!
WAGNER. Tell me, sirrah, hast thou any comings in?
CLOWN. Ay, and goings out too; you may see else.
WAGNER. Alas, poor slave! see how poverty jesteth in his
nakedness!
    the villain is bare and out of service, and so hungry, that I know
    he would give his soul to the devil for a shoulder of mutton,
    though it were blood-raw.
CLOWN. How! my soul to the devil for a shoulder of mutton,
though
    'twere blood-raw! not so, good friend: by'r lady, I had need
    have it well roasted, and good sauce to it, if I pay so dear.
WAGNER. Well, wilt thou serve me, and I'll make thee go like
    Qui mihi discipulus?

CLOWN. How, in verse?

WAGNER. No, sirrah; in beaten silk and staves-acre.

CLOWN. How, how, knaves-acre! ay, I thought that was all the land

his father left him. Do you hear? I would be sorry to rob you of your living.

WAGNER. Sirrah, I say in staves-acre.

CLOWN. Oho, oho, staves-acre! why, then, belike, if I were your man, I should be full of vermin.

WAGNER. So thou shalt, whether thou beest with me or no. But, sirrah, leave your jesting, and bind yourself presently unto me for seven years, or I'll turn all the lice about thee into familiars, and they shall tear thee in pieces.

CLOWN. Do you hear, sir? you may save that labour; they are too

familiar with me already: swowns, they are as bold with my flesh as if they had paid for their meat and drink.

WAGNER. Well, do you hear, sirrah? hold, take these guilders. [Gives money.]

CLOWN. Gridirons! what be they?

WAGNER. Why, French crowns.

CLOWN. Mass, but for the name of French crowns, a man were as good

have as many English counters. And what should I do with these?

WAGNER. Why, now, sirrah, thou art at an hour's warning, whensoever

or wheresoever the devil shall fetch thee.

CLOWN. No, no; here, take your gridirons again.

WAGNER. Truly, I'll none of them.

CLOWN. Truly, but you shall.

WAGNER. Bear witness I gave them him.

CLOWN. Bear witness I give them you again.

WAGNER. Well, I will cause two devils presently to fetch thee away.—Baliol and Belcher!

CLOWN. Let your Baliol and your Belcher come here, and I'll
knock them, they were never so knocked since they were devils:
say I should kill one of them, what would folks say? "Do ye see
yonder tall fellow in the round slop? he has killed the devil."
So I should be called Kill-devil all the parish over.
Enter two DEVILS; and the CLOWN runs up and down crying.
WAGNER. Baliol and Belcher,—spirits, away!
[Exeunt DEVILS.]
CLOWN. What, are they gone? a vengeance on them! they have
vile
long nails. There was a he-devil and a she-devil: I'll tell you
how you shall know them; all he-devils has horns, and all
she-devils has clifts and cloven feet.
WAGNER. Well, sirrah, follow me.
CLOWN. But, do you hear? if I should serve you, would you
teach
me to raise up Banios and Belcheos?
WAGNER. I will teach thee to turn thyself to any thing, to a dog,
or a cat, or a mouse, or a rat, or any thing.
CLOWN. How! a Christian fellow to a dog, or a cat, a mouse,
or a rat! no, no, sir; if you turn me into any thing, let it be
in the likeness of a little pretty frisking flea, that I may be
here and there and every where: O, I'll tickle the pretty wenches'
plackets! I'll be amongst them, i'faith.
WAGNER. Well, sirrah, come.
CLOWN. But, do you hear, Wagner?
WAGNER. How!—Baliol and Belcher!
CLOWN. O Lord! I pray, sir, let Banio and Belcher go sleep.
WAGNER. Villain, call me Master Wagner, and let thy left eye be
diametarily fixed upon my right heel, with quasi vestigiis
nostris insistere.
[Exit.]
CLOWN. God forgive me, he speaks Dutch fustian. Well, I'll
follow
him; I'll serve him, that's flat.

[Exit.]

FAUSTUS discovered in his study.

FAUSTUS. Now, Faustus, must

Thou needs be damn'd, and canst thou not be sav'd:

What boots it, then, to think of God or heaven?

Away with such vain fancies, and despair;

Despair in God, and trust in Belzebub:

Now go not backward; no, Faustus, be resolute:

Why waver'st thou? O, something soundeth in mine ears,

"Abjure this magic, turn to God again!"

Ay, and Faustus will turn to God again.

To God? he loves thee not;

The god thou serv'st is thine own appetite,

Wherein is fix'd the love of Belzebub:

To him I'll build an altar and a church,

And offer lukewarm blood of new-born babes.

Enter GOOD ANGEL and EVIL ANGEL.

GOOD ANGEL. Sweet Faustus, leave that execrable art.

FAUSTUS. Contrition, prayer, repentance—what of them?

GOOD ANGEL. O, they are means to bring thee unto heaven!

EVIL ANGEL. Rather illusions, fruits of lunacy,

That make men foolish that do trust them most.

GOOD ANGEL. Sweet Faustus, think of heaven and heavenly things.

EVIL ANGEL. No, Faustus; think of honour and of wealth.

[Exeunt ANGELS.]

FAUSTUS. Of wealth!

Why, the signiory of Embden shall be mine.

When Mephistophilis shall stand by me,

What god can hurt thee, Faustus? thou art safe

Cast no more doubts.—Come, Mephistophilis,

And bring glad tidings from great Lucifer;—

Is't not midnight?—come, Mephistophilis,

Veni, veni, Mephistophile!

Enter MEPHISTOPHILIS.

Now tell me what says Lucifer, thy lord?
MEPHIST. That I shall wait on Faustus whilst he lives,
So he will buy my service with his soul.
FAUSTUS. Already Faustus hath hazarded that for thee.
MEPHIST. But, Faustus, thou must bequeath it solemnly,
And write a deed of gift with thine own blood;
For that security craves great Lucifer.
If thou deny it, I will back to hell.
FAUSTUS. Stay, Mephistophilis, and tell me, what good will my soul
do thy lord?
MEPHIST. Enlarge his kingdom.
FAUSTUS. Is that the reason why he tempts us thus?
MEPHIST. Solamen miseris socios habuisse doloris.
FAUSTUS. Why, have you any pain that torture others!
MEPHIST. As great as have the human souls of men.
But, tell me, Faustus, shall I have thy soul?
And I will be thy slave, and wait on thee,
And give thee more than thou hast wit to ask.
FAUSTUS. Ay, Mephistophilis, I give it thee.
MEPHIST. Then, Faustus, stab thine arm courageously,
And bind thy soul, that at some certain day
Great Lucifer may claim it as his own;
And then be thou as great as Lucifer.
FAUSTUS. [Stabbing his arm] Lo, Mephistophilis, for love of thee,
I cut mine arm, and with my proper blood
Assure my soul to be great Lucifer's,
Chief lord and regent of perpetual night!
View here the blood that trickles from mine arm,
And let it be propitious for my wish.
MEPHIST. But, Faustus, thou must
Write it in manner of a deed of gift.
FAUSTUS. Ay, so I will [Writes]. But, Mephistophilis,
My blood congeals, and I can write no more.

MEPHIST. I'll fetch thee fire to dissolve it straight.
[Exit.]
FAUSTUS. What might the staying of my blood portend?
Is it unwilling I should write this bill?
Why streams it not, that I may write afresh?
FAUSTUS GIVES TO THEE HIS SOUL: ah, there it stay'd!
Why shouldst thou not? is not thy soul shine own?
Then write again, FAUSTUS GIVES TO THEE HIS SOUL.
Re-enter MEPHISTOPHILIS with a chafer of coals.
MEPHIST. Here's fire; come, Faustus, set it on.
FAUSTUS. So, now the blood begins to clear again;
Now will I make an end immediately.
[Writes.]
MEPHIST. O, what will not I do to obtain his soul?
[Aside.]
FAUSTUS. Consummatum est; this bill is ended,
And Faustus hath bequeath'd his soul to Lucifer.
But what is this inscription on mine arm?
Homo, fuge: whither should I fly?
If unto God, he'll throw me down to hell.
My senses are deceiv'd; here's nothing writ:—
I see it plain; here in this place is writ,
Homo, fuge: yet shall not Faustus fly.
MEPHIST. I'll fetch him somewhat to delight his mind.
[Aside, and then exit.]
Re-enter MEPHISTOPHILIS with DEVILS, who give crowns
and rich apparel to FAUSTUS, dance, and then depart.
FAUSTUS. Speak, Mephistophilis, what means this show?
MEPHIST. Nothing, Faustus, but to delight thy mind withal,
And to shew thee what magic can perform.
FAUSTUS. But may I raise up spirits when I please?
MEPHIST. Ay, Faustus, and do greater things than these.
FAUSTUS. Then there's enough for a thousand souls.
Here, Mephistophilis, receive this scroll,
A deed of gift of body and of soul:

But yet conditionally that thou perform
All articles prescrib'd between us both.
MEPHIST. Faustus, I swear by hell and Lucifer
To effect all promises between us made!
FAUSTUS. Then hear me read them. [Reads] ON THESE CONDITIONS
FOLLOWING. FIRST, THAT FAUSTUS MAY BE A SPIRIT IN FORM AND
SUBSTANCE. SECONDLY, THAT MEPHISTOPHILIS SHALL BE HIS SERVANT,
AND AT HIS COMMAND. THIRDLY, THAT MEPHISTOPHILIS SHALL DO FOR HIM,
AND BRING HIM WHATSOEVER HE DESIRES. FOURTHLY, THAT HE SHALL
BE IN HIS CHAMBER OR HOUSE INVISIBLE. LASTLY, THAT HE SHALL APPEAR
TO THE SAID JOHN FAUSTUS, AT ALL TIMES, IN WHAT FORM OR SHAPE
SOEVER HE PLEASE. I, JOHN FAUSTUS, OF WERTENBERG, DOCTOR, BY
THESE PRESENTS, DO GIVE BOTH BODY AND SOUL TO LUCIFER PRINCE OF
THE EAST, AND HIS MINISTER MEPHISTOPHILIS; AND FURTHERMORE GRANT
UNTO THEM, THAT, TWENTY-FOUR YEARS BEING EXPIRED, THE ARTICLES
ABOVE-WRITTEN INVIOLATE, FULL POWER TO FETCH OR CARRY THE SAID
JOHN FAUSTUS, BODY AND SOUL, FLESH, BLOOD, OR GOODS, INTO THEIR
HABITATION WHERESOEVER. BY ME, JOHN FAUSTUS.
MEPHIST. Speak, Faustus, do you deliver this as your deed?
FAUSTUS. Ay, take it, and the devil give thee good on't!
MEPHIST. Now, Faustus, ask what thou wilt.
FAUSTUS. First will I question with thee about hell.

Tell me, where is the place that men call hell?

MEPHIST. Under the heavens.

FAUSTUS. Ay, but whereabout?

MEPHIST. Within the bowels of these elements,
Where we are tortur'd and remain for ever:
Hell hath no limits, nor is circumscrib'd
In one self place; for where we are is hell,
And where hell is, there must we ever be:
And, to conclude, when all the world dissolves,
And every creature shall be purified,
All places shall be hell that are not heaven.

FAUSTUS. Come, I think hell's a fable.

MEPHIST. Ay, think so still, till experience change thy mind.

FAUSTUS. Why, think'st thou, then, that Faustus shall be damn'd?

MEPHIST. Ay, of necessity, for here's the scroll
Wherein thou hast given thy soul to Lucifer.

FAUSTUS. Ay, and body too: but what of that?
Think'st thou that Faustus is so fond to imagine
That, after this life, there is any pain?
Tush, these are trifles and mere old wives' tales.

MEPHIST. But, Faustus, I am an instance to prove the contrary,
For I am damn'd, and am now in hell.

FAUSTUS. How! now in hell!
Nay, an this be hell, I'll willingly be damn'd here:
What! walking, disputing, &c.
But, leaving off this, let me have a wife,
The fairest maid in Germany;
For I am wanton and lascivious,
And cannot live without a wife.

MEPHIST. How! a wife!
I prithee, Faustus, talk not of a wife.

FAUSTUS. Nay, sweet Mephistophilis, fetch me one, for I will have
one.

MEPHIST. Well, thou wilt have one? Sit there till I come: I'll
fetch thee a wife in the devil's name.
[Exit.]
Re-enter MEPHISTOPHILIS with a DEVIL drest like a WOMAN,
with fire-works.
MEPHIST. Tell me, Faustus, how dost thou like thy wife?
FAUSTUS. A plague on her for a hot whore!
MEPHIST. Tut, Faustus,
Marriage is but a ceremonial toy;
If thou lovest me, think no more of it.
I'll cull thee out the fairest courtezans,
And bring them every morning to thy bed:
She whom thine eye shall like, thy heart shall have,
Be she as chaste as was Penelope,
As wise as Saba, or as beautiful
As was bright Lucifer before his fall.
Hold, take this book, peruse it thoroughly:
[Gives book.]
The iterating of these lines brings gold;
The framing of this circle on the ground
Brings whirlwinds, tempests, thunder, and lightning;
Pronounce this thrice devoutly to thyself,
And men in armour shall appear to thee,
Ready to execute what thou desir'st.
FAUSTUS. Thanks, Mephistophilis: yet fain would I have a book
wherein I might behold all spells and incantations, that I
might raise up spirits when I please.
MEPHIST. Here they are in this book.
[Turns to them.]
FAUSTUS. Now would I have a book where I might see all
characters
and planets of the heavens, that I might know their motions and
dispositions.
MEPHIST. Here they are too.
[Turns to them.]

FAUSTUS. Nay, let me have one book more,—and then I have done,—

wherein I might see all plants, herbs, and trees, that grow upon the earth.

MEPHIST. Here they be.

FAUSTUS. O, thou art deceived.

MEPHIST. Tut, I warrant thee.

[Turns to them.]

FAUSTUS. When I behold the heavens, then I repent,

And curse thee, wicked Mephistophilis,

Because thou hast depriv'd me of those joys.

MEPHIST. Why, Faustus,

Thinkest thou heaven is such a glorious thing?

I tell thee, 'tis not half so fair as thou,

Or any man that breathes on earth.

FAUSTUS. How prov'st thou that?

MEPHIST. 'Twas made for man, therefore is man more excellent.

FAUSTUS. If it were made for man, 'twas made for me:

I will renounce this magic and repent.

Enter GOOD ANGEL and EVIL ANGEL.

GOOD ANGEL. Faustus, repent; yet God will pity thee.

EVIL ANGEL. Thou art a spirit; God cannot pity thee.

FAUSTUS. Who buzzeth in mine ears I am a spirit?

Be I a devil, yet God may pity me;

Ay, God will pity me, if I repent.

EVIL ANGEL. Ay, but Faustus never shall repent.

[Exeunt ANGELS.]

FAUSTUS. My heart's so harden'd, I cannot repent:

Scarce can I name salvation, faith, or heaven,

But fearful echoes thunder in mine ears,

"Faustus, thou art damn'd!" then swords, and knives,

Poison, guns, halters, and envenom'd steel

Are laid before me to despatch myself;

And long ere this I should have slain myself,

Had not sweet pleasure conquer'd deep despair.
Have not I made blind Homer sing to me
Of Alexander's love and Oenon's death?
And hath not he, that built the walls of Thebes
With ravishing sound of his melodious harp,
Made music with my Mephistophilis?
Why should I die, then, or basely despair?
I am resolv'd; Faustus shall ne'er repent.—
Come, Mephistophilis, let us dispute again,
And argue of divine astrology.
Tell me, are there many heavens above the moon
Are all celestial bodies but one globe,
As is the substance of this centric earth?
MEPHIST. As are the elements, such are the spheres,
Mutually folded in each other's orb,
And, Faustus,
All jointly move upon one axletree,
Whose terminine is term'd the world's wide pole;
Nor are the names of Saturn, Mars, or Jupiter
Feign'd, but are erring stars.
FAUSTUS. But, tell me, have they all one motion, both situ et
tempore?
MEPHIST. All jointly move from east to west in twenty-four
hours
upon the poles of the world; but differ in their motion upon
the poles of the zodiac.
FAUSTUS. Tush,
These slender trifles Wagner can decide:
Hath Mephistophilis no greater skill?
Who knows not the double motion of the planets?
The first is finish'd in a natural day;
The second thus; as Saturn in thirty years; Jupiter in twelve;
Mars in four; the Sun, Venus, and Mercury in a year; the Moon
in
twenty-eight days. Tush, these are freshmen's suppositions.

But, tell me, hath every sphere a dominion or intelligentia?

MEPHIST. Ay.

FAUSTUS. How many heavens or spheres are there?

MEPHIST. Nine; the seven planets, the firmament, and the empyreal

heaven.

FAUSTUS. Well, resolve me in this question; why have we not

conjunctions, oppositions, aspects, eclipses, all at one time,

but in some years we have more, in some less?

MEPHIST. Per inoequalem motum respectu totius.

FAUSTUS. Well, I am answered. Tell me who made the world?

MEPHIST. I will not.

FAUSTUS. Sweet Mephistophilis, tell me.

MEPHIST. Move me not, for I will not tell thee.

FAUSTUS. Villain, have I not bound thee to tell me any thing?

MEPHIST. Ay, that is not against our kingdom; but this is. Think

thou on hell, Faustus, for thou art damned.

FAUSTUS. Think, Faustus, upon God that made the world.

MEPHIST. Remember this.

[Exit.]

FAUSTUS. Ay, go, accursed spirit, to ugly hell!

'Tis thou hast damn'd distressed Faustus' soul.

Is't not too late?

Re-enter GOOD ANGEL and EVIL ANGEL.

EVIL ANGEL. Too late.

GOOD ANGEL. Never too late, if Faustus can repent.

EVIL ANGEL. If thou repent, devils shall tear thee in pieces.

GOOD ANGEL. Repent, and they shall never raze thy skin.

[Exeunt ANGELS.]

FAUSTUS. Ah, Christ, my Saviour,

Seek to save distressed Faustus' soul!

Enter LUCIFER, BELZEBUB, and MEPHISTOPHILIS.

LUCIFER. Christ cannot save thy soul, for he is just:

There's none but I have interest in the same.

FAUSTUS. O, who art thou that look'st so terrible?

LUCIFER. I am Lucifer,
And this is my companion-prince in hell.
FAUSTUS. O, Faustus, they are come to fetch away thy soul!
LUCIFER. We come to tell thee thou dost injure us;
Thou talk'st of Christ, contrary to thy promise:
Thou shouldst not think of God: think of the devil,
And of his dam too.
FAUSTUS. Nor will I henceforth: pardon me in this,
And Faustus vows never to look to heaven,
Never to name God, or to pray to him,
To burn his Scriptures, slay his ministers,
And make my spirits pull his churches down.
LUCIFER. Do so, and we will highly gratify thee. Faustus, we are
come from hell to shew thee some pastime: sit down, and thou
shalt see all the Seven Deadly Sins appear in their proper shapes.
FAUSTUS. That sight will be as pleasing unto me,
As Paradise was to Adam, the first day
Of his creation.
LUCIFER. Talk not of Paradise nor creation; but mark this show:
talk of the devil, and nothing else.—Come away!
Enter the SEVEN DEADLY SINS.
Now, Faustus, examine them of their several names and
dispositions.
FAUSTUS. What art thou, the first?
PRIDE. I am Pride. I disdain to have any parents. I am like to
Ovid's flea; I can creep into every corner of a wench; sometimes,
like a perriwig, I sit upon her brow; or, like a fan of feathers,
I kiss her lips; indeed, I do—what do I not? But, fie, what a
scent is here! I'll not speak another word, except the ground
were perfumed, and covered with cloth of arras.
FAUSTUS. What art thou, the second?
COVETOUSNESS. I am Covetousness, begotten of an old churl,
in an
old leathern bag: and, might I have my wish, I would desire that
this house and all the people in it were turned to gold, that I

might lock you up in my good chest: O, my sweet gold!

FAUSTUS. What art thou, the third?

WRATH. I am Wrath. I had neither father nor mother: I leapt out

of a lion's mouth when I was scarce half-an-hour old; and ever
since I have run up and down the world with this case
of rapiers, wounding myself when I had nobody to fight withal.
I was born in hell; and look to it, for some of you shall be
my father.

FAUSTUS. What art thou, the fourth?

ENVY. I am Envy, begotten of a chimney-sweeper and an oyster-wife.

I cannot read, and therefore wish all books were burnt. I am lean
with seeing others eat. O, that there would come a famine through
all the world, that all might die, and I live alone! then thou
shouldst see how fat I would be. But must thou sit, and I stand?
come down, with a vengeance!

FAUSTUS. Away, envious rascal!—What art thou, the fifth?

GLUTTONY. Who I, sir? I am Gluttony. My parents are all dead,
and the devil a penny they have left me, but a bare pension, and
that is thirty meals a-day and ten bevers,—a small trifle
to suffice nature. O, I come of a royal parentage! my grandfather
was a Gammon of Bacon, my grandmother a Hogshead of Claret-wine;

my godfathers were these, Peter Pickle-herring and Martin
Martlemas-beef; O, but my godmother, she was a jolly gentlewoman,
and well-beloved in every good town and city; her name was Mistress
Margery March-beer. Now, Faustus, thou hast heard all my progeny;
wilt thou bid me to supper?

FAUSTUS. No, I'll see thee hanged: thou wilt eat up all my victuals.

GLUTTONY. Then the devil choke thee!

FAUSTUS. Choke thyself, glutton!—What art thou, the sixth?

SLOTH. I am Sloth. I was begotten on a sunny bank, where I have

lain ever since; and you have done me great injury to bring me
from thence: let me be carried thither again by Gluttony and
Lechery. I'll not speak another word for a king's ransom.

FAUSTUS. What are you, Mistress Minx, the seventh and last?

LECHERY. Who I, sir? I am one that loves an inch of raw mutton
better than an ell of fried stock-fish; and the first letter
of my name begins with L.

FAUSTUS. Away, to hell, to hell!

[Exeunt the SINS.]

LUCIFER. Now, Faustus, how dost thou like this?

FAUSTUS. O, this feeds my soul!

LUCIFER. Tut, Faustus, in hell is all manner of delight.

FAUSTUS. O, might I see hell, and return again,
How happy were I then!

LUCIFER. Thou shalt; I will send for thee at midnight.
In meantime take this book; peruse it throughly,
And thou shalt turn thyself into what shape thou wilt.

FAUSTUS. Great thanks, mighty Lucifer!
This will I keep as chary as my life.

LUCIFER. Farewell, Faustus, and think on the devil.

FAUSTUS. Farewell, great Lucifer.

[Exeunt LUCIFER and BELZEBUB.]

Come, Mephistophilis.

[Exeunt.]

Enter CHORUS.

CHORUS. Learned Faustus,
To know the secrets of astronomy
Graven in the book of Jove's high firmament,
Did mount himself to scale Olympus' top,
Being seated in a chariot burning bright,
Drawn by the strength of yoky dragons' necks.

He now is gone to prove cosmography,
And, as I guess, will first arrive at Rome,
To see the Pope and manner of his court,
And take some part of holy Peter's feast,
That to this day is highly solemniz'd.
[Exit.]
Enter FAUSTUS and MEPHISTOPHILIS.
FAUSTUS. Having now, my good Mephistophilis,
Pass'd with delight the stately town of Trier,
Environ'd round with airy mountain-tops,
With walls of flint, and deep-entrenched lakes,
Not to be won by any conquering prince;
From Paris next, coasting the realm of France,
We saw the river Maine fall into Rhine,
Whose banks are set with groves of fruitful vines;
Then up to Naples, rich Campania,
Whose buildings fair and gorgeous to the eye,
The streets straight forth, and pav'd with finest brick,
Quarter the town in four equivalents:
There saw we learned Maro's golden tomb,
The way he cut,an English mile in length,
Thorough a rock of stone, in one night's space;
From thence to Venice, Padua, and the rest,
In one of which a sumptuous temple stands,
That threats the stars with her aspiring top.
Thus hitherto hath Faustus spent his time:
But tell me now what resting-place is this?
Hast thou, as erst I did command,
Conducted me within the walls of Rome?
MEPHIST. Faustus, I have; and, because we will not be unprovided,
I have taken up his Holiness' privy-chamber for our use.
FAUSTUS. I hope his Holiness will bid us welcome.
MEPHIST.
Tut, 'tis no matter; man; we'll be bold with his good cheer.

And now, my Faustus, that thou mayst perceive
What Rome containeth to delight thee with,
Know that this city stands upon seven hills
That underprop the groundwork of the same:
Just through the midst runs flowing Tiber's stream
With winding banks that cut it in two parts;
Over the which four stately bridges lean,
That make safe passage to each part of Rome:
Upon the bridge call'd Ponte Angelo
Erected is a castle passing strong,
Within whose walls such store of ordnance are,
And double cannons fram'd of carved brass,
As match the days within one complete year;
Besides the gates, and high pyramides,
Which Julius Caesar brought from Africa.
FAUSTUS. Now, by the kingdoms of infernal rule,
Of Styx, of Acheron, and the fiery lake
Of ever-burning Phlegethon, I swear
That I do long to see the monuments
And situation of bright-splendent Rome:
Come, therefore, let's away.
MEPHIST. Nay, Faustus, stay: I know you'd fain see the Pope,
And take some part of holy Peter's feast,
Where thou shalt see a troop of bald-pate friars,
Whose summum bonum is in belly-cheer.
FAUSTUS. Well, I'm content to compass then some sport,
And by their folly make us merriment.
Then charm me, that I
May be invisible, to do what I please,
Unseen of any whilst I stay in Rome.
[Mephistophilis charms him.]
MEPHIST. So, Faustus; now
Do what thou wilt, thou shalt not be discern'd.
Sound a Sonnet. Enter the POPE and the CARDINAL OF
LORRAIN to the banquet, with FRIARS attending.

POPE. My Lord of Lorrain, will't please you draw near?
FAUSTUS. Fall to, and the devil choke you, an you spare!
POPE. How now! who's that which spake?—Friars, look about.
FIRST FRIAR. Here's nobody, if it like your Holiness.
POPE. My lord, here is a dainty dish was sent me from the Bishop
of Milan.
FAUSTUS. I thank you, sir.
[Snatches the dish.]
POPE. How now! who's that which snatched the meat from me? will
no man look?—My lord, this dish was sent me from the Cardinal
of Florence.
FAUSTUS. You say true; I'll ha't.
[Snatches the dish.]
POPE. What, again!—My lord, I'll drink to your grace.
FAUSTUS. I'll pledge your grace.
[Snatches the cup.]
C. OF LOR. My lord, it may be some ghost, newly crept out of
Purgatory, come to beg a pardon of your Holiness.
POPE. It may be so.—Friars, prepare a dirge to lay the fury
of this ghost.—Once again, my lord, fall to.
[The POPE crosses himself.]
FAUSTUS. What, are you crossing of yourself?
Well, use that trick no more, I would advise you.
[The POPE crosses himself again.]
Well, there's the second time. Aware the third;
I give you fair warning.
[The POPE crosses himself again, and FAUSTUS hits him a box
of the ear; and they all run away.]
Come on, Mephistophilis; what shall we do?
MEPHIST. Nay, I know not: we shall be cursed with bell, book,
and candle.
FAUSTUS. How! bell, book, and candle,—candle, book, and
bell,—

Forward and backward, to curse Faustus to hell!
Anon you shall hear a hog grunt, a calf bleat, and an ass bray,
Because it is Saint Peter's holiday.
Re-enter all the FRIARS to sing the Dirge.
FIRST FRIAR.
Come, brethren, let's about our business with good devotion.
They sing.
CURSED BE HE THAT STOLE AWAY HIS HOLINESS' MEAT FROM THE
TABLE! maledicat Dominus!
CURSED BE HE THAT STRUCK HIS HOLINESS A BLOW ON THE FACE!
maledicat Dominus!
CURSED BE HE THAT TOOK FRIAR SANDELO A BLOW ON THE PATE!
maledicat Dominus!
CURSED BE HE THAT DISTURBETH OUR HOLY DIRGE! maledicat
Dominus!
CURSED BE HE THAT TOOK AWAY HIS HOLINESS' WINE! maledicat
Dominus? ['?' sic]
Et omnes Sancti! Amen!
[MEPHISTOPHILIS and FAUSTUS beat the FRIARS, and fling
fire-works among them; and so exeunt.]
Enter CHORUS.
CHORUS. When Faustus had with pleasure ta'en the view
Of rarest things, and royal courts of kings,
He stay'd his course, and so returned home;
Where such as bear his absence but with grief,
I mean his friends and near'st companions,
Did gratulate his safety with kind words,
And in their conference of what befell,
Touching his journey through the world and air,
They put forth questions of astrology,

Which Faustus answer'd with such learned skill
As they admir'd and wonder'd at his wit.
Now is his fame spread forth in every land:
Amongst the rest the Emperor is one,
Carolus the Fifth, at whose palace now
Faustus is feasted 'mongst his noblemen.
What there he did, in trial of his art,
I leave untold; your eyes shall see['t] perform'd.
[Exit.]
Enter ROBIN the Ostler, with a book in his hand.
ROBIN. O, this is admirable! here I ha' stolen one of Doctor
Faustus' conjuring-books, and, i'faith, I mean to search some
circles for my own use. Now will I make all the maidens in our
parish dance at my pleasure, stark naked, before me; and so
by that means I shall see more than e'er I felt or saw yet.
Enter RALPH, calling ROBIN.
RALPH. Robin, prithee, come away; there's a gentleman tarries
to have his horse, and he would have his things rubbed and made
clean: he keeps such a chafing with my mistress about it; and
she has sent me to look thee out; prithee, come away.
ROBIN. Keep out, keep out, or else you are blown up, you are
dismembered, Ralph: keep out, for I am about a roaring piece
of work.
RALPH. Come, what doest thou with that same book? thou canst
not read?
ROBIN. Yes, my master and mistress shall find that I can read,
he for his forehead, she for her private study; she's born to
bear with me, or else my art fails.
RALPH. Why, Robin, what book is that?
ROBIN. What book! why, the most intolerable book for
conjuring
that e'er was invented by any brimstone devil.
RALPH. Canst thou conjure with it?
ROBIN. I can do all these things easily with it; first, I can
make thee drunk with ippocras at any tabern in Europe

for nothing; that's one of my conjuring works.

RALPH. Our Master Parson says that's nothing.

ROBIN. True, Ralph: and more, Ralph, if thou hast any mind to

Nan Spit, our kitchen-maid, then turn her and wind her to thy

own

use, as often as thou wilt, and at midnight.

RALPH. O, brave, Robin! shall I have Nan Spit, and to mine own

use? On that condition I'll feed thy devil with horse-bread as

long as he lives, of free cost.

ROBIN. No more, sweet Ralph: let's go and make clean our boots,

which lie foul upon our hands, and then to our conjuring in the

devil's name.

[Exeunt.]

Enter ROBIN and RALPHwith a silver goblet.

ROBIN. Come, Ralph: did not I tell thee, we were for ever made

by this Doctor Faustus' book? ecce, signum! here's a simple

purchase for horse-keepers: our horses shall eat no hay as

long as this lasts.

RALPH. But, Robin, here comes the Vintner.

ROBIN. Hush! I'll gull him supernaturally.

Enter VINTNER.

Drawer, I hope all is paid; God be with you!—Come, Ralph.

VINTNER. Soft, sir; a word with you. I must yet have a goblet

paid

from you, ere you go.

ROBIN. I a goblet, Ralph, I a goblet!—I scorn you; and you are

but a, &c. I a goblet! search me.

VINTNER. I mean so, sir, with your favour.

[Searches ROBIN.]

ROBIN. How say you now?

VINTNER. I must say somewhat to your fellow.—You, sir!

RALPH. Me, sir! me, sir! search your fill. [VINTNER searches

him.]

Now, sir, you may be ashamed to burden honest men with a

matter

of truth.

VINTNER. Well, tone of you hath this goblet about you.

ROBIN. You lie, drawer, 'tis afore me [Aside].—Sirrah you, I'll teach you to impeach honest men;—stand by;—I'll scour you for a goblet;—stand aside you had best, I charge you in the name of Belzebub.—Look to the goblet, Ralph [Aside to RALPH].

VINTNER. What mean you, sirrah?

ROBIN. I'll tell you what I mean. [Reads from a book] Sanctobulorum

Periphrasticon—nay, I'll tickle you, Vintner.—Look to the goblet, Ralph [Aside to RALPH].—[Reads] Polypragmos Belseborams framanto

pacostiphos tostu, Mephistophilis, &c.

Enter MEPHISTOPHILIS, sets squibs at their backs, and then exit. They run about.

VINTNER. O, nomine Domini! what meanest thou, Robin? thou hast no

goblet.

RALPH. Peccatum peccatorum!—Here's thy goblet, good Vintner.

[Gives the goblet to VINTNER, who exit.]

ROBIN. Misericordia pro nobis! what shall I do? Good devil, forgive

me now, and I'll never rob thy library more.

Re-enter MEPHISTOPHILIS.

MEPHIST. Monarch of Hell, under whose black survey

Great potentates do kneel with awful fear,

Upon whose altars thousand souls do lie,

How am I vexed with these villains' charms?

From Constantinople am I hither come,

Only for pleasure of these damned slaves.

ROBIN. How, from Constantinople! you have had a great journey:

will you take sixpence in your purse to pay for your supper, and be gone?

MEPHIST. Well, villains, for your presumption, I transform thee
into an ape, and thee into a dog; and so be gone!
[Exit.]
ROBIN. How, into an ape! that's brave: I'll have fine sport with
the boys; I'll get nuts and apples enow.
RALPH. And I must be a dog.
ROBIN. I'faith, thy head will never be out of the pottage-pot.
[Exeunt.]
Enter   EMPEROR,   FAUSTUS,   and   a   KNIGHT,   with
ATTENDANTS.
EMPEROR. Master Doctor Faustus, I have heard strange report
of thy knowledge in the black art, how that none in my empire
nor in the whole world can compare with thee for the rare
effects
of magic: they say thou hast a familiar spirit, by whom thou canst
accomplish what thou list. This, therefore, is my request, that
thou let me see some proof of thy skill, that mine eyes may be
witnesses to confirm what mine ears have heard reported: and
here
I swear to thee, by the honour of mine imperial crown, that,
whatever thou doest, thou shalt be no ways prejudiced or
endamaged.
KNIGHT. I'faith, he looks much like a conjurer.
[Aside.]
FAUSTUS. My gracious sovereign, though I must confess myself
far
inferior to the report men have published, and nothing
answerable
to the honour of your imperial majesty, yet, for that love and
duty
binds me thereunto, I am content to do whatsoever your majesty
shall command me.
EMPEROR. Then, Doctor Faustus, mark what I shall say.
As I was sometime solitary set
Within my closet, sundry thoughts arose

About the honour of mine ancestors,
How they had won by prowess such exploits,
Got such riches, subdu'd so many kingdoms,
As we that do succeed, or they that shall
Hereafter possess our throne, shall
(I fear me) ne'er attain to that degree
Of high renown and great authority:
Amongst which kings is Alexander the Great,
Chief spectacle of the world's pre-eminence,
The bright shining of whose glorious acts
Lightens the world with his reflecting beams,
As when I hear but motion made of him,
It grieves my soul I never saw the man:
If, therefore, thou, by cunning of thine art,
Canst raise this man from hollow vaults below,
Where lies entomb'd this famous conqueror,
And bring with him his beauteous paramour,
Both in their right shapes, gesture, and attire
They us'd to wear during their time of life,
Thou shalt both satisfy my just desire,
And give me cause to praise thee whilst I live.
FAUSTUS. My gracious lord, I am ready to accomplish your request,
so far forth as by art and power of my spirit I am able to perform.
KNIGHT. I'faith, that's just nothing at all.
[Aside.]
FAUSTUS. But, if it like your grace, it is not in my ability
to present before your eyes the true substantial bodies of those
two deceased princes, which long since are consumed to dust.
KNIGHT. Ay, marry, Master Doctor, now there's a sign of grace in
you, when you will confess the truth.
[Aside.]
FAUSTUS. But such spirits as can lively resemble Alexander and
his paramour shall appear before your grace, in that manner that

they both lived in, in their most flourishing estate; which
I doubt not shall sufficiently content your imperial majesty.
EMPEROR. Go to, Master Doctor; let me see them presently.
KNIGHT. Do you hear, Master Doctor? you bring Alexander and his
paramour before the Emperor!
FAUSTUS. How then, sir?
KNIGHT. I'faith, that's as true as Diana turned me to a stag.
FAUSTUS. No, sir; but, when Actaeon died, he left the horns for
you.—Mephistophilis, be gone.
[Exit MEPHISTOPHILIS.]
KNIGHT. Nay, an you go to conjuring, I'll be gone.
[Exit.]
FAUSTUS. I'll meet with you anon for interrupting me so.
—Here they are, my gracious lord.
Re-enter MEPHISTOPHILIS with SPIRITS in the shapes of ALEXANDER
and his PARAMOUR.
EMPEROR. Master Doctor, I heard this lady, while she lived, had a
wart or mole in her neck: how shall I know whether it be so or no?
FAUSTUS. Your highness may boldly go and see.
EMPEROR. Sure, these are no spirits, but the true substantial
bodies of those two deceased princes.
[Exeunt Spirits.]
FAUSTUS. Wilt please your highness now to send for the knight
that was so pleasant with me here of late?
EMPEROR. One of you call him forth.
[Exit ATTENDANT.]
Re-enter the KNIGHT with a pair of horns on his head.
How now, sir knight! why, I had thought thou hadst been a
bachelor,
but now I see thou hast a wife, that not only gives thee horns,
but makes thee wear them. Feel on thy head.

KNIGHT. Thou damned wretch and execrable dog,
Bred in the concave of some monstrous rock,
How dar'st thou thus abuse a gentleman?
Villain, I say, undo what thou hast done!
FAUSTUS. O, not so fast, sir! there's no haste: but, good, are
you remembered how you crossed me in my conference with the
Emperor? I think I have met with you for it.
EMPEROR. Good Master Doctor, at my entreaty release him: he hath
done penance sufficient.
FAUSTUS. My gracious lord, not so much for the injury he offered
me here in your presence, as to delight you with some mirth, hath
Faustus worthily requited this injurious knight; which being all
I desire, I am content to release him of his horns:—and,
sir knight, hereafter speak well of scholars.—Mephistophilis,
transform him straight. [MEPHISTOPHILIS removes the horns.]
—Now, my good lord, having done my duty, I humbly take my leave.
EMPEROR. Farewell, Master Doctor: yet, ere you go,
Expect from me a bounteous reward.
[Exeunt EMPEROR, KNIGHT, and ATTENDANTS.]
FAUSTUS. Now, Mephistophilis, the restless course
That time doth run with calm and silent foot,
Shortening my days and thread of vital life,
Calls for the payment of my latest years:
Therefore, sweet Mephistophilis, let us
Make haste to Wertenberg.
MEPHIST. What, will you go on horse-back or on foot[?]
FAUSTUS. Nay, till I'm past this fair and pleasant green,
I'll walk on foot.
Enter a HORSE-COURSER.
HORSE-COURSER. I have been all this day seeking one Master
Fustian:

mass, see where he is!—God save you, Master Doctor!

FAUSTUS. What, horse-courser! you are well met.

HORSE-COURSER. Do you hear, sir? I have brought you forty dollars

for your horse.

FAUSTUS. I cannot sell him so: if thou likest him for fifty, take him.

HORSE-COURSER. Alas, sir, I have no more!—I pray you, speak for

me.

MEPHIST. I pray you, let him have him: he is an honest fellow, and he has a great charge, neither wife nor child.

FAUSTUS. Well, come, give me your money [HORSE-COURSER gives

FAUSTUS the money]: my boy will deliver him to you. But I must

tell you one thing before you have him; ride him not into the water, at any hand.

HORSE-COURSER. Why, sir, will he not drink of all waters?

FAUSTUS. O, yes, he will drink of all waters; but ride him not into the water: ride him over hedge or ditch, or where thou wilt, but not into the water.

HORSE-COURSER. Well, sir.—Now am I made man for ever: I'll not

leave my horse for forty: if he had but the quality of hey-ding-ding, hey-ding-ding, I'd make a brave living on him: he has a buttock as slick as an eel [Aside].—Well, God b'wi'ye, sir: your boy will deliver him me: but, hark you, sir; if my horse be sick or ill at ease, if I bring his water to you, you'll tell me what it is?

FAUSTUS. Away, you villain! what, dost think I am a horse-doctor?

[Exit HORSE-COURSER.]

What art thou, Faustus, but a man condemn'd to die?

Thy fatal time doth draw to final end;

Despair doth drive distrust into my thoughts:
Confound these passions with a quiet sleep:
Tush, Christ did call the thief upon the Cross;
Then rest thee, Faustus, quiet in conceit.
[Sleeps in his chair.]
Re-enter HORSE-COURSER, all wet, crying.
HORSE-COURSER. Alas, alas! Doctor Fustian, quoth a? mass, Doctor
Lopus was never such a doctor: has given me a purgation, has
purged me of forty dollars; I shall never see them more. But yet,
like an ass as I was, I would not be ruled by him, for he bade me
I should ride him into no water: now I, thinking my horse had had
some rare quality that he would not have had me know of,I,
like a venturous youth, rid him into the deep pond at the town's
end. I was no sooner in the middle of the pond, but my horse
vanished away, and I sat upon a bottle of hay, never so near
drowning in my life. But I'll seek out my doctor, and have my
forty dollars again, or I'll make it the dearest horse!—O,
yonder is his snipper-snapper.—Do you hear? you, hey-pass,
where's your master?
MEPHIST. Why, sir, what would you? you cannot speak with him.
HORSE-COURSER. But I will speak with him.
MEPHIST. Why, he's fast asleep: come some other time.
HORSE-COURSER. I'll speak with him now, or I'll break his
glass-windows about his ears.
MEPHIST. I tell thee, he has not slept this eight nights.
HORSE-COURSER. An he have not slept this eight weeks, I'll
speak with him.
MEPHIST. See, where he is, fast asleep.
HORSE-COURSER. Ay, this is he.—God save you, Master Doctor,
Master Doctor, Master Doctor Fustian! forty dollars, forty dollars
for a bottle of hay!

MEPHIST. Why, thou seest he hears thee not.
HORSE-COURSER. So-ho, ho! so-ho, ho! [Hollows in his ear.] No,
will you not wake? I'll make you wake ere I go. [Pulls FAUSTUS
by the leg, and pulls it away.] Alas, I am undone! what shall
I do?
FAUSTUS. O, my leg, my leg!—Help, Mephistophilis! call the
officers.—My leg, my leg!
MEPHIST. Come, villain, to the constable.
HORSE-COURSER. O Lord, sir, let me go, and I'll give you forty
dollars more!
MEPHIST. Where be they?
HORSE-COURSER. I have none about me: come to my ostry,
and I'll give them you.
MEPHIST. Be gone quickly.
[HORSE-COURSER runs away.]
FAUSTUS. What, is he gone? farewell he! Faustus has his leg
again,
and the Horse-courser, I take it, a bottle of hay for his labour:
well, this trick shall cost him forty dollars more.
Enter WAGNER.
How now, Wagner! what's the news with thee?
WAGNER. Sir, the Duke of Vanholt doth earnestly entreat your
company.
FAUSTUS. The Duke of Vanholt! an honourable gentleman, to
whom
I must be no niggard of my cunning.—Come, Mephistophilis,
let's away to him.
[Exeunt.]
Enter the DUKE OF VANHOLT, the DUCHESS, and FAUSTUS.
DUKE. Believe me, Master Doctor, this merriment hath much
pleased
me.
FAUSTUS. My gracious lord, I am glad it contents you so well.
—But it may be, madam, you take no delight in this. I have heard

that great-bellied women do long for some dainties or other: what

is it, madam? tell me, and you shall have it.

DUCHESS. Thanks, good Master Doctor: and, for I see your courteous

intent to pleasure me, I will not hide from you the thing my heart
desires; and, were it now summer, as it is January and the dead
time of the winter, I would desire no better meat than a dish
of ripe grapes.

FAUSTUS. Alas, madam, that's nothing!—Mephistophilis, be gone.

[Exit MEPHISTOPHILIS.] Were it a greater thing than this, so it
would content you, you should have it.

Re-enter MEPHISTOPHILIS with grapes.

Here they be, madam: wilt please you taste on them?

DUKE. Believe me, Master Doctor, this makes me wonder above the

rest, that being in the dead time of winter and in the month of
January, how you should come by these grapes.

FAUSTUS. If it like your grace, the year is divided into two
circles over the whole world, that, when it is here winter with
us, in the contrary circle it is summer with them, as in India,
Saba, and farther countries in the east; and by means of a
swift spirit that I have, I had them brought hither, as you see.
—How do you like them, madam? be they good?

DUCHESS. Believe me, Master Doctor, they be the best grapes that

e'er I tasted in my life before.

FAUSTUS. I am glad they content you so, madam.

DUKE. Come, madam, let us in, where you must well reward this
learned man for the great kindness he hath shewed to you.

DUCHESS. And so I will, my lord; and, whilst I live, rest
beholding for this courtesy.

FAUSTUS. I humbly thank your grace.

DUKE. Come, Master Doctor, follow us, and receive your reward.

[Exeunt.]

Enter WAGNER.

WAGNER. I think my master means to die shortly,

For he hath given to me all his goods:

And yet, methinks, if that death were near,

He would not banquet, and carouse, and swill

Amongst the students, as even now he doth,

Who are at supper with such belly-cheer

As Wagner ne'er beheld in all his life.

See, where they come! belike the feast is ended.

[Exit.]

Enter FAUSTUS with two or three SCHOLARS, and MEPHISTOPHILIS.

FIRST SCHOLAR. Master Doctor Faustus, since our conference about

fair ladies, which was the beautifulest in all the world, we have

determined with ourselves that Helen of Greece was the admirablest

lady that ever lived: therefore, Master Doctor, if you will do us

that favour, as to let us see that peerless dame of Greece, whom

all the world admires for majesty, we should think ourselves much

beholding unto you.

FAUSTUS. Gentlemen,

For that I know your friendship is unfeign'd,

And Faustus' custom is not to deny

The just requests of those that wish him well,

You shall behold that peerless dame of Greece,

No otherways for pomp and majesty

Than when Sir Paris cross'd the seas with her,

And brought the spoils to rich Dardania.

Be silent, then, for danger is in words.

[Music sounds, and HELEN passeth over the stage.]

SECOND SCHOLAR. Too simple is my wit to tell her praise,
Whom all the world admires for majesty.
THIRD SCHOLAR. No marvel though the angry Greeks pursu'd
With ten years' war the rape of such a queen,
Whose heavenly beauty passeth all compare.
FIRST SCHOLAR. Since we have seen the pride of Nature's works,
And only paragon of excellence,
Let us depart; and for this glorious deed
Happy and blest be Faustus evermore!
FAUSTUS. Gentlemen, farewell: the same I wish to you.
[Exeunt SCHOLARS.]
Enter an OLD MAN.
OLD MAN. Ah, Doctor Faustus, that I might prevail
To guide thy steps unto the way of life,
By which sweet path thou mayst attain the goal
That shall conduct thee to celestial rest!
Break heart, drop blood, and mingle it with tears,
Tears falling from repentant heaviness
Of thy most vile and loathsome filthiness,
The stench whereof corrupts the inward soul
With such flagitious crimes of heinous sin
As no commiseration may expel,
But mercy, Faustus, of thy Saviour sweet,
Whose blood alone must wash away thy guilt.
FAUSTUS. Where art thou, Faustus? wretch, what hast thou done?
Damn'd art thou, Faustus, damn'd; despair and die!
Hell calls for right, and with a roaring voice
Says, "Faustus, come; thine hour is almost come;"
And Faustus now will come to do thee right.
[MEPHISTOPHILIS gives him a dagger.]
OLD MAN. Ah, stay, good Faustus, stay thy desperate steps!
I see an angel hovers o'er thy head,
And, with a vial full of precious grace,

Offers to pour the same into thy soul:
Then call for mercy, and avoid despair.
FAUSTUS. Ah, my sweet friend, I feel
Thy words to comfort my distressed soul!
Leave me a while to ponder on my sins.
OLD MAN. I go, sweet Faustus; but with heavy cheer,
Fearing the ruin of thy hopeless soul.
[Exit.]
FAUSTUS. Accursed Faustus, where is mercy now?
I do repent; and yet I do despair:
Hell strives with grace for conquest in my breast:
What shall I do to shun the snares of death?
MEPHIST. Thou traitor, Faustus, I arrest thy soul
For disobedience to my sovereign lord:
Revolt, or I'll in piece-meal tear thy flesh.
FAUSTUS. Sweet Mephistophilis, entreat thy lord
To pardon my unjust presumption,
And with my blood again I will confirm
My former vow I made to Lucifer.
MEPHIST. Do it, then, quickly, with unfeigned heart,
Lest greater danger do attend thy drift.
FAUSTUS. Torment, sweet friend, that base and crooked age,
That durst dissuade me from thy Lucifer,
With greatest torments that our hell affords.
MEPHIST. His faith is great; I cannot touch his soul;
But what I may afflict his body with
I will attempt, which is but little worth.
FAUSTUS. One thing, good servant, let me crave of thee,
To glut the longing of my heart's desire,—
That I might have unto my paramour
That heavenly Helen which I saw of late,
Whose sweet embracings may extinguish clean
Those thoughts that do dissuade me from my vow,
And keep mine oath I made to Lucifer.
MEPHIST. Faustus, this, or what else thou shalt desire,

Shall be perform'd in twinkling of an eye.
Re-enter HELEN.
FAUSTUS. Was this the face that launch'd a thousand ships,
And burnt the topless towers of Ilium—
Sweet Helen, make me immortal with a kiss.—
[Kisses her.]
Her lips suck forth my soul: see, where it flies!—
Come, Helen, come, give me my soul again.
Here will I dwell, for heaven is in these lips,
And all is dross that is not Helena.
I will be Paris, and for love of thee,
Instead of Troy, shall Wertenberg be sack'd;
And I will combat with weak Menelaus,
And wear thy colours on my plumed crest;
Yea, I will wound Achilles in the heel,
And then return to Helen for a kiss.
O, thou art fairer than the evening air
Clad in the beauty of a thousand stars;
Brighter art thou than flaming Jupiter
When he appear'd to hapless Semele;
More lovely than the monarch of the sky
In wanton Arethusa's azur'd arms;
And none but thou shalt be my paramour!
[Exeunt.]
Enter the OLD MAN.
OLD MAN. Accursed Faustus, miserable man,
That from thy soul exclud'st the grace of heaven,
And fly'st the throne of his tribunal-seat!
Enter DEVILS.
Satan begins to sift me with his pride:
As in this furnace God shall try my faith,
My faith, vile hell, shall triumph over thee.
Ambitious fiends, see how the heavens smile
At your repulse, and laugh your state to scorn!
Hence, hell! for hence I fly unto my God.

[Exeunt,—on one side, DEVILS, on the other, OLD MAN.]
Enter FAUSTUS, with SCHOLARS.
FAUSTUS. Ah, gentlemen!
FIRST SCHOLAR. What ails Faustus?
FAUSTUS. Ah, my sweet chamber-fellow, had I lived with thee,
then had I lived still! but now I die eternally. Look, comes
he not? comes he not?
SECOND SCHOLAR. What means Faustus?
THIRD SCHOLAR. Belike he is grown into some sickness by
being
over-solitary.
FIRST SCHOLAR. If it be so, we'll have physicians to cure him.
—'Tis but a surfeit; never fear, man.
FAUSTUS. A surfeit of deadly sin, that hath damned both body
and soul.
SECOND SCHOLAR. Yet, Faustus, look up to heaven; remember
God's
mercies are infinite.
FAUSTUS. But Faustus' offence can ne'er be pardoned: the
serpent
that tempted Eve may be saved, but not Faustus. Ah, gentlemen,
hear me with patience, and tremble not at my speeches! Though
my heart pants and quivers to remember that I have been a
student
here these thirty years, O, would I had never seen Wertenberg,
never read book! and what wonders I have done, all Germany
can
witness, yea, all the world; for which Faustus hath lost both
Germany and the world, yea, heaven itself, heaven, the seat of
God, the throne of the blessed, the kingdom of joy; and must
remain in hell for ever, hell, ah, hell, for ever! Sweet friends,
what shall become of Faustus, being in hell for ever?
THIRD SCHOLAR. Yet, Faustus, call on God.
FAUSTUS. On God, whom Faustus hath abjured! on God, whom
Faustus

hath blasphemed! Ah, my God, I would weep! but the devil draws in
my tears. Gush forth blood, instead of tears! yea, life and soul!
O, he stays my tongue! I would lift up my hands; but see, they
hold them, they hold them!

ALL. Who, Faustus?

FAUSTUS. Lucifer and Mephistophilis. Ah, gentlemen, I gave them
my soul for my cunning!

ALL. God forbid!

FAUSTUS. God forbade it, indeed; but Faustus hath done it: for
vain pleasure of twenty-four years hath Faustus lost eternal joy
and felicity. I writ them a bill with mine own blood: the date
is expired; the time will come, and he will fetch me.

FIRST SCHOLAR. Why did not Faustus tell us of this before,
that divines might have prayed for thee?

FAUSTUS. Oft have I thought to have done so; but the devil
threatened to tear me in pieces, if I named God, to fetch both
body and soul, if I once gave ear to divinity: and now 'tis too
late. Gentlemen, away, lest you perish with me.

SECOND SCHOLAR. O, what shall we do to save Faustus?

FAUSTUS. Talk not of me, but save yourselves, and depart.

THIRD SCHOLAR. God will strengthen me; I will stay with Faustus.

FIRST SCHOLAR. Tempt not God, sweet friend; but let us into the
next room, and there pray for him.

FAUSTUS. Ay, pray for me, pray for me; and what noise soever
ye hear, come not unto me, for nothing can rescue me.

SECOND SCHOLAR. Pray thou, and we will pray that God may have
mercy upon thee.

FAUSTUS. Gentlemen, farewell: if I live till morning, I'll visit
you; if not, Faustus is gone to hell.

ALL. Faustus, farewell.

[Exeunt SCHOLARS.—The clock strikes eleven.]
FAUSTUS. Ah, Faustus,
Now hast thou but one bare hour to live,
And then thou must be damn'd perpetually!
Stand still, you ever-moving spheres of heaven,
That time may cease, and midnight never come;
Fair Nature's eye, rise, rise again, and make
Perpetual day; or let this hour be but
A year, a month, a week, a natural day,
That Faustus may repent and save his soul!
O lente, lente currite, noctis equi!
The stars move still, time runs, the clock will strike,
The devil will come, and Faustus must be damn'd.
O, I'll leap up to my God!—Who pulls me down?—
See, see, where Christ's blood streams in the firmament!
One drop would save my soul, half a drop: ah, my Christ!—
Ah, rend not my heart for naming of my Christ!
Yet will I call on him: O, spare me, Lucifer!—
Where is it now? 'tis gone: and see, where God
Stretcheth out his arm, and bends his ireful brows!
Mountains and hills, come, come, and fall on me,
And hide me from the heavy wrath of God!
No, no!
Then will I headlong run into the earth:
Earth, gape! O, no, it will not harbour me!
You stars that reign'd at my nativity,
Whose influence hath allotted death and hell,
Now draw up Faustus, like a foggy mist.
Into the entrails of yon labouring cloud[s],
That, when you vomit forth into the air,
My limbs may issue from your smoky mouths,
So that my soul may but ascend to heaven!
[The clock strikes the half-hour.]
Ah, half the hour is past! 'twill all be past anon
O God,

If thou wilt not have mercy on my soul,
Yet for Christ's sake, whose blood hath ransom'd me,
Impose some end to my incessant pain;
Let Faustus live in hell a thousand years,
A hundred thousand, and at last be sav'd!
O, no end is limited to damned souls!
Why wert thou not a creature wanting soul?
Or why is this immortal that thou hast?
Ah, Pythagoras' metempsychosis, were that true,
This soul should fly from me, and I be chang'd
Unto some brutish beast! all beasts are happy,
For, when they die,
Their souls are soon dissolv'd in elements;
But mine must live still to be plagu'd in hell.
Curs'd be the parents that engender'd me!
No, Faustus, curse thyself, curse Lucifer
That hath depriv'd thee of the joys of heaven.
[The clock strikes twelve.]
O, it strikes, it strikes! Now, body, turn to air,
Or Lucifer will bear thee quick to hell!
[Thunder and lightning.]
O soul, be chang'd into little water-drops,
And fall into the ocean, ne'er be found!
Enter DEVILS.
My God, my god, look not so fierce on me!
Adders and serpents, let me breathe a while!
Ugly hell, gape not! come not, Lucifer!
I'll burn my books!—Ah, Mephistophilis!
[Exeunt DEVILS with FAUSTUS.]
Enter CHORUS.
CHORUS. Cut is the branch that might have grown full straight,
And burned is Apollo's laurel-bough,
That sometime grew within this learned man.
Faustus is gone: regard his hellish fall,
Whose fiendful fortune may exhort the wise,

Only to wonder at unlawful things,
Whose deepness doth entice such forward wits
To practice more than heavenly power permits.
[Exit.]
Terminat hora diem; terminat auctor opus.

CHAPTER THREE

Doctor Faustus: Analysis

Critical Analysis of Christopher Marlowe's DR FAUSTUS

ABOUT THE PLAYWRIGHT

Christopher Marlowe was an English playwright born in the year 1564, the same year **William Shakespeare** was born. During his lifetime, he was a translator, poet and one of the foremost tragedians of Elizabethan era. Tamburlaine (1590) was his first play performed on a regular stage in London and also was the first English play written in blank verse. He wrote several other plays apart from Tamburlaine. These plays include Hero and the Leander (1598), The Passionate Shepherd (1598), Dr Faustus (1604), Edward II (1594).

His play, **The Tragic History of the Life and Death of Doctor Faustus**, was one of the most controversial tragedies of the Elizabethan era apart from Shakespeare's plays. In fact, it is considered important as it is Christopher Marlowe's greatest play and masterpiece.

Marlowe was murdered by **Igram Frizer**, who stabbed him in the forehead, in the year 1593.

BACKGROUND OF THE PLAY

The play, **The Tragic History of Doctor Faustus** by Christopher Marlowe, was published in the year 1604 in the 17th century. Before its publication, it was premiered in 1592 and was first staged in

1593.

The thirteen scene play has Doctor Faustus as its protagonist hero. This fact makes the play an eponymous play. The author is known for writing on characters whose ambitions/behaviours led to their fall. As at the time the play was written, magic was held in high reverence which Christianity frowns at.

The play is all about a German scholar named Faustus who after the fame he had through his traditional forms of knowledge became dissatisfied and decided to practice magic. He got what he craved for from Lucifer by trading his soul with the devil.

The play was written at the time when the use of magic and the possession of magical powers were considered very important as those who possessed these powers were regarded as "gods" in the society and behaved as such. They were always held in high esteem.

From the standpoint of religion, Christianity frowned at the use of magic. This is properly justified in how the "Old Man" advised Dr. Faustus to abstain from magic:

"*OLD MAN. Ah, Doctor Faustus, that I might*
prevail
To guide thy steps unto the way of life,
By which sweet path thou mayst attain the goal
That shall conduct thee to celestial rest!
Break heart, drop blood, and mingle it with
tears,
Tears falling from repentant heaviness
Of thy most vile and loathsome filthiness,
The stench whereof corrupts the inward soul
With such flagitious crimes of heinous sin
As no commiseration may expel,
But mercy, Faustus, of thy Saviour sweet,
Whose blood alone must wash away thy guilt."
(Act V, Scene 1)

Another such instance that reflects disapproval of magical arts is the constant persuasion placed on Dr. Faustus by the two Scholars in order to dissuade him from his practice of magic. While magic was treated with reverence as seen in the Palace of the Emperor of Germany and several other instances, it was considered a sin from the religion angle.

SETTING

Places mentioned in this play include: Rhode, where Faustus was born; Wittenberg where he was raised and educated; the Papal Palace where he played magical tricks on the Pope and his subordinates; the Palace of German Emperor where he raised Alexander the Great and his Paramour to satisfy the curiosity of the Emperor of Germany; and Vanholt where he met the duke and his duchess. Also mentioned in the play are Paris, Padua, and Venice.

It is right to say the setting of the play is in Europe, specifically in Germany and Italy around the Elizabethan era in the 16th century.

THE PLOT

(I) The Exposition: We are introduced to Doctor FAUSTUS, a German scholar of high intelligence and vast knowledge and understanding in the field of medicine, law, logic and theology. He is dissatisfied with the secular knowledge he has and craves for magical power. His crave for magic is so strong that he forsakes his scholarly studies and concludes they are impotent.

(II) The Rising Action: The rising action begins when Faustus instructs Wagner to call to his presence, Valdes and Cornelius. Thus, he consults his two friends who urged him on. Faustus begins his experiment with magical chant and incantations which subsequently summons Mephistopheles to his presence. Mephistopheles, we learn, is one of devil's chief ministers. At first Mephistophilis appeared in an awful way, Faustus sends him away for him to reappear in the form of a friar. He then discovers that it is not his conjuration or incantation that has brought Mephistopheles to him, rather when one curses divinity or speaks ill of God, devil's agents will appear.

(III) The Climax: This begins when Faustus enters into a blood contract with Lucifer through Mephistopheles. Faustus trades his soul to the devil in exchange for Mephistopheles's service for a period of twenty four years. Here, Faustus asks Mephistopheles questions about existence of hell and who created the world. Mephistopheles snubs his question on who created the Universe, and confirms the existence of hell. Doubts and confusion starts to set in within Faustus mind. Faustus finds himself in a state of dilemma on what to do and what not to do. He later succumbs to his crave for magic, and binds himself to Lucifer through a second oath.

(IV) The Falling Action: Faustus travels all over the world and performs magical wonders at several places of prominence. He went to the inner chamber of the Pope, the palace of the Emperor of Germany, Duke of Vanholt. We can easily deduce that he travelled to several other places from his soliloquy.

(V) Resolution/Denouement: Faustus after a whole number of years, discovers that his allotted time of twenty four years was almost over and it dawns on him the reality of hell and damnation. He realizes that he only sold his soul to devil for nothing, and has wasted his magical powers on frivolities. He thinks it was too late for him to change and believes he had sinned beyond redemption that he considered the gravity of his sin as more than that of Adam and Eve.

So, when his hour of damnation clocked, he was dragged into hell by Lucifer and his agents.

THEMES

(A) Thirst for Magic: Faustus has a thirst for magical knowledge, but he is unable to acquire wisdom in the process. His knowledge is subsequently overshadowed by his complete inability to understand certain truths. Because of this weakness, FAUSTUS could not use his knowledge to better himself or his world. He ends his life with a head full of facts, and vital understanding gained too late to save him.

(B) Dilemma: This theme elicits the divided nature of man. Dr. FAUSTUS is constantly undecided about whether to repent or continue to follow his pact with Lucifer. This internal struggle goes on throughout the play as a part of him wants to serve God while the other part of him (perhaps the dominant part) lusts after the power Mephistophilis promises. The good and bad angels, who appear in order to urge him in different directions, symbolise this struggle. While these angels may be intended as an actual pair of supernatural beings, they clearly represent Faustus's divided will which compels Faustus to commit to Mephistopheles but also to question this commitment continually.

(C) Freewill and Fate: The action and damnation of Dr Faustus lingers between freewill and fate. From the standpoint of freewill, Dr Faustus evidently has power over his decisions, and that is properly justified in how he weighs the arguments from both Good Angel and Bad Angel before choosing what his heart binds on him. When we look at this from the viewpoint of fate, Dr Faustus is destined to be sentenced damnation or so it seems. Despite persuasions from various angles [right from Good Angel, the two Scholars to the Old Man], he still ends up doing what he is urged to desist from, which subsequently leads to his downfall.

(D) Pride and Sin: Within the Christian framework, pride is a lethal motivation because it makes the sinner forget his fallen state. Faustus' first great sin is pride. He does not stop there. Reflecting the Christian view, pride gives rise to all of the other sins and ends ironically with the proud man's abasement. Faustus is over-pompous and full of hubris in the play. Looking at Faustus' possession of magic from the Christian perspective, his act is considered a sin.

(E) Blasphemy and Damnation: At the beginning of the play, it is evident that Dr FAUSTUS is blasphemous in his utterances. He speaks ill of God and divinity and places Lucifer above God even when he is conscious of God's existence and indoctrination of Christianity. His choice of actions later results to his inevitable damnation. In other words, he is condemned to eternal punishment in Hell.

(F) Self-Condemnation: Even before he was finally condemned to eternal damnation, Dr Faustus has already decided his fate. He believes enormity of his sin makes him unredeemable. He even believed that his sin is thus the greatest sin ever committed by humankind.

(G) Wasted Skills: Early in the play before he goes into pact with Lucifer, Faustus is full of ideas for how to use the power he seeks. He aspires to discover the mysteries of Universe and pile a fortune for himself. These ambitions lend a grandeur to Faustus schemes and make his quest for personal power seem almost heroic, a sense that is reinforced by the eloquence of his early soliloquies. When he gains the practically limitless power, however, his horizons seem to narrow. He seems to be contented with performing tricks for the kings and noblemen and transforms his boundless ambition into a meaningless delight in petty celebrity.

LANGUAGE

The play is written in blank verse in Elizabethan English, which is identified linguistically as Early Modern English and is a Germanic language structured from a composition of Anglo, Saxon, Latin, Celtic and Norman influences that reflect the history of England. Many literary devices employed include allusion, digression, simile and metaphor.

THE MOST DRAMATIC SCENE

The most dramatic scene in the play is arguably set at the banquet meeting of the Pope, cardinals, and friars where Dr FAUSTUS and MEPHISTOPHILIS played tricks and teased the former.

COMIC RELIEF

There is no gainsaying that, despite its tragical quality, the play admixes comedy with tragedy. The clown is portrayed as an archetype for comic relief in the play. Digressions made by Dr Faustus at Pope's banquet and with the House courser reflect comic relief.

Christopher Marlowe – Doctor Faustus – Summary

The legend of Faust became a frequently related myth from the times of medieval period itself in Europe and the tragic story of Faust has spread across continents since then. There are a lot of contributors who made this feat possible and one of the earliest references to the story is believed to be the description of Simon

Magus, the magician in the Bible's New Testament. Christopher Marlowe, Johann Wolfgang von Goethe, Thomas Mann, etc. fuelled the thought of a practitioner of magical arts who goes by the name of Doctor Faustus.

However, it was Christopher Marlowe's version of "Doctor Faustus" that gained a huge impetus for it being written in blank verse and the style so complex yet understandable – seems as if it is actually reflecting the thoughts of the legendary magician himself.

<u>Prologue by Chorus:</u>

The chorus enters with clearly stating their intent of appearing on stage. They do not want to sing of the battles of Roman gods nor do they want to praise the great heroes of the past. Instead, it is of the mighty Faustus they want to talk about and introduce a bit about the man. Faustus was born in Rhodes, Germany to humble parents and left to Wertenberg, where his relatives took care of him. He had great curiosity for knowledge and mastered many fields of knowledge and was awarded with doctor of divinity for his Theological debates and comprehension of the divine material. After all the praise on Doctor Faustus, the chorus sobs on the fact that he was absorbed by pride and went on to darker realms of knowledge which were forbidden. He took Necromancy or the art of summoning spirits as his subject which led to his demise. As the first scene is revealed, the chorus gives a clear notion of the man who is seen in his study room.

<u>Act – 1, Scene -1 (Reading room in the house):</u>

Faustus, alone in his reading room disputes with himself as to which field of knowledge he wants to pursue in the future. He thinks of logic, but then again stops as he reads about the ultimate achievement of logic is to speak well in debates of all kinds.

"Is, to dispute well logic's chiefest end?

Affords this art no greater miracle?"

He understands that he doesn't need logic as he's well-versed in the art of logical debates. Doctor Faustus goes on with different fields considering Medical science, divinity, law and at the end turns to the art of magic. His urge to become a god amongst men comes forth with learning the powerful art, hence decides to practice magic. He asks his servant Wagner to call his friends Cornelius and Valdes so that he can take advice in the matter.

As Wagner exits, good angel and evil angel enter, the former to ensure that Doctor Faustus doesn't end his life in damnation while the latter tries to influence him in pursuing the evil book of magic. He becomes obsessed with the idea of getting unlimited power while on Earth which would immortalize his name after death. Meanwhile, his friends visit and are delighted to know about the interests of Faustus and give plenty of reading suggestions. Valdes, Cornelius and Faustus decide to have a dinner and start with conjuring that night.

Act – 1, Scene – 2 (Before the house of Doctor Faustus):

Two scholars are looking for the whereabouts of their teacher Faustus and from their dialogues it is apparent that Faustus has not been teaching for quite some time. Wagner has his share of fun with the scholars when they enquire about his (Wagner) master. They eventually find out that Faustus is involved in studying Necromancy and is now involved with the necromancers Valdes and Cornelius. The First Scholar believes that Faustus is doomed, whereas the other hopes there is still hope and they decide to inform of the horrible matter to the Rector.

Act – 1, Scene – 3 (Grove):

Faustus has determined to offer his soul to the Devil and draws a blasphemous circle so to prove his willingness to join the dark side. He begins the incantations and after the invocation of the Devil is complete Mephistopheles, the servant of Lucifer appears. However, he finds Mephistopheles too repulsive and asks the dark angel to disperse and come back with a neat form. The devil returns in the form of a friar and asks Doctor Faustus of the purpose of incantation. However, the curious doctor asks a lot of questions and asks Mephistopheles to serve as his slave. The devil rejects the offer as it is Lucifer to whom the devil is obedient and without his permission he cannot take such liberal decisions like serving others.

Mephistopheles explains that all devils are eager to appear whenever there is a conjuring of the devil so that they can claim the soul of the conjuror. Faustus' curiosity makes him a willing individual to swear allegiance. Mephistopheles describes of the events that led to the downfall of Lucifer and the others and describes that being separated from God is Hell. But, Faustus doesn't take the words of the devil into consideration and asks him to forward a message to Lucifer about the willingness to offer his (Faustus) soul. In exchange of the soul, Doctor Faustus asks the obedience of Mephistopheles for 24-years and granting of limitless power. The devil exits and Faustus wishes that if he had more souls like the number of the stars he would give them for being the Emperor of the world and being treated as god amongst mortals.

Act – 1, Scene – 4 (Street):

(Christopher Marlowe, after revealing cosmic matters of Necromancy provides with a bit of comic relief with Wagner in this scene.)

The page of Doctor Faustus, Wagner is seen to lure a clown into becoming his servant. Initially, he offers mutton for which the clown refuses profoundly. He gives some money to the clown, but he tries to give them back. However, Wagner who has learnt a few conjuring tricks himself makes Baliol and Belcher (demons) appear. The clown terrified at the sight of demons accepts to serve Wagner. He further asks his new master to teach him magic. Wagner promises the clown to teach the art of changing oneself into animal. However, if there be any disobedience Wagner warns the clown to conjure the demons again, which makes the clown to follow Wagner in silence.

Act – 2, Scene – 1 (Faustus in reading room):

Faustus thinks of repenting and rethinks of his decision. He feels that it is too late to repent; moreover, he sees Lucifer as a trustworthy Devil and decides to be resolute about his decision. As he becomes resolute to build altars for the Devil; Good Angel and Bad Angel enter trying to persuade Doctor Faustus to join their own side. However, the Bad Angel wins and leaves Faustus to think of wealth, honour and position. He calls on Mephistopheles who comes with the news that Lucifer has accepted the offer of Faustus.

Thrilled to hear the news, Faustus cuts his arm to write a blood covenant but his blood thickens and Mephistopheles goes to obtain fire. Faustus thinks that the thickening of the blood is some sort of warning to get him away from all the misdeeds. After the devil brings fire and makes the blood to flow again, he completes signing the blood covenant. Suddenly, on his arm appears a two word inscription – "Homo fuge" (Man fly). Faustus has misgivings but he knows there is no turning back now. Mephistopheles in order to distract his new master arranges a dance of the spirits who offer great gifts to Faustus. He becomes happy again and turns over the agreement to Mephistopheles.

After enjoying the presence of the spirits, Faustus asks Mephistopheles to bring a wife, but the devil returns with a spirit dressed as a woman and explains the downsides of marriage. He falls for the false interpretation of the devil and asks for books on spells, heavenly bodies and flora, which Mephistopheles is quite happy to bring him.

Act – 2, Scene – 2 (Near an Inn):

The name of the Clown is revealed as Robin and he steals one of the magic books owned by Doctor Faustus. The Clown though is in possession of the book cannot read but boasts of doing magic. He gets into banter with a servant named Dick and later on they decide to head to a tavern.

Act – 2, Scene – 3 (Home of Faustus):

Faustus' misgivings increase and he curses Mephistopheles for pursuing him to write the agreement. However, Mephistopheles reiterates that it was Faustus who wanted to exchange his soul. Faustus decides to repent when the Good Angel enters and encourages him. But, the Bad Angel intervenes and tilts the interest of Faustus towards Hell again. He turns to Mephistopheles to discuss of the constellations, heavens and planets. The devil gives out what all he could but denies to reveal about the Creator of the world for which Faustus gets frustrated. He thinks of salvation again, but this time Mephistopheles comes with Lucifer and Beelzebub.

They offer all kind of offerings to Doctor Faustus and Beelzebub summons "The Seven Deadly Sins" to appease the man. Faustus expresses his desire to see Hell and Lucifer shows willingness to take him to Hell that midnight. Before their departure, Beelzebub gives Faustus a book that contains secret knowledge on how to transform oneself into any shape and the doctor is very pleased.

Act – 3, Chorus:

The Chorus sings of the great deeds achieved by Doctor Faustus with the powers he got from the exchange. It's mentioned that Faustus has visited Mount Olympus, flew with dragons riding the chariot and even dealt with Cosmography. Now, he longs to visit Rome and involve himself in the feast of St. Peter's Day.

Act – 3, Scene – 1 (Rome):

After reaching Rome, Faustus and Mephistopheles wait for the arrival of Pope at his chamber. The devil narrates of the wonders of the Rome and Doctor Faustus expresses his wish to tour them; but Mephistopheles holds him back by reminding Faustus about their purpose to visit Rome i.e. to take part in the St. Peter's Day feast. As they are uninvited Faustus asks Mephistopheles to perform a charm of invisibility so that no one can see them and the devil gladly does so.

As the Pope enters the chamber along with King of Hungary (Raymond), Cardinals and Bishops, it is seen that he also has a man bound in chains. The man, Bruno, was selected as the worthy man to become the Pope by German Emperor. The Pope chides him and uses abusive language. Faustus desires to restore the liberty of Bruno and expresses the same to Mephistopheles and they achieve the feat quite easily.

Act – 3, Scene – 2 (Pope's chamber):

The Pope is shown as the sufferer due to the hilarious tricks generated by the invisible Doctor Faustus. He abuses the Pope, takes away the food and creates a lot of confusion in the chamber. As a Bishop recognizes the presence of a ghost the Friars hurry to prepare for the rites so they can drive the ghost away. Meanwhile, the Pope is hit by Faustus and he exits with all the companions. The Friars come back to perform the rites and Faustus along with Mephistopheles hammer them and set fireworks to the place before leaving.

The chorus re-enters at this point, to describe of the returning of home of Doctor Faustus. He becomes very famous due to his magical abilities and expansive Astronomical knowledge. As a result, Faustus becomes the best-loved individual to the German Emperor Carolus the Fifth and is due to present his feats at the court shortly.

Act – 3, Scene – 3 (Tavern):

The Clown, Robin is shown taking care of horses (ostler) who boasts a great deal in front of Rafe about performing magic to attain pleasure. Robin and his friend end up stealing a silver cup from Vintner. As the Vintner recognizes that his silver cup is stolen by the two, he follows them. As he catches up on them, Robin to escape from his hands conjures Mephistopheles. The devil gets furious with the summoning as the two fools are not worthy enough to call upon someone like Mephistopheles. So, the devil puts fireworks on Robin and his friend, who run around scared. Rafe unable to continue takes the silver cup and gives it back to Vintner. However, the Vintner couldn't see Mephistopheles and returns with his cup. Whereas, Mephistopheles warns the two about transforming one to an ape (Robin) and the other to a dog (Rafe) and the devil disappears. They love the fact that they can get transformed into animals and think of all the deeds they could perform by being an ape and a dog.

Act – 4, Scene – 1 (The Emperor's Palace at Innsbruck):

As the scene opens two nobles serving Carolus the Fifth, Frederick and Martino are seen conversing. They talk of Bruno and how he came back riding on a demon. Both the men are eager to look at Doctor Faustus and help themselves with amusement as Faustus pleasures the Emperor. They share their excitement with their friend and Knight Benvolio who shows disinterest and states to watch Faustus from a window.

Act – 4, Scene – 2 (The Emperor's Palace at Innsbruck):

The Emperor Carolus the Fifth enters the court along with Doctor Faustus, Bruno and other attendants. The Knight Benvolio is seen near the window watching over the proceedings. Carolus declares gratitude for saving Bruno and Faustus promises to show the court many wonders. On hearing the claims of Faustus Benvolio mocks him for which Faustus takes revenge afterwards. Based on the wish of the Emperor to see Darius, Alexander and his Paramour, Faustus with the help of Mephistopheles conjures their spirits. Faustus agrees that he cannot summon them in flesh and they are only spirits; nonetheless the Emperor is mighty pleased to see the shapes of the great names. Meanwhile, Faustus uses his powers to grow antlers on Benvolio's head as he mocked his capabilities. With Emperor's involvement Faustus restores the natural shape of Benvolio.

Act – 4, Scene – 3 (The Same):

Benvolio longs to take revenge and reveals his plot to Frederick and Martino. They both agree to the plan and wait to ambush on Doctor Faustus. As Faustus is seen coming on the same path, they all attack him at once and Benvolio cuts the head of Faustus. He longs to place horns on the head of the doctor with the help on nails. However, Faustus' head unites with the body again as he cannot die until the agreed 24-years of life are complete. Furious at the imbecile efforts of the three, he commands his devils to drag each man to various places of wilderness. The trio arise to see that there are horns on each man and they decide to live the rest of their lives (or as long as the horns are present) concealing themselves in the castle of Benvolio.

Faustus, with all his mighty ambitions is shown to have turned into a court jester appeasing the wills of the Emperor. He declines further by playing pranks and summoning demons to punish three foolish men. Christopher Marlowe through the actions of Faustus provides a message that with the unlimited power gained through forbidden means man tends to sway off the natural course and forgets the initial ambitions and turn up only to amuse others rather than making use of the powers they acquired.

Act – 4, Scene – 4 (A Green):

Doctor Faustus is seen with Mephistopheles, talking about the end of days as promised by the Devil. So, he wishes to return to his place of birth. Meanwhile, a horse-courser interesting at the horse of Faustus asks to sell the horse. He does so, but warns not to ride the horse in water and sends him off. But the horse courser doesn't heed the advice of Faustus and runs the horse into water and the horse become hay. He comes back to Faustus wailing, complaining and tugging at the leg of Faustus. The doctor plays a prank again and the leg comes off which leaves the horse courser terrified. Mephistopheles threatens to complain the matter and the horse courser offers some money and leaves them. Meanwhile, Wagner enters to inform that the Duke is expecting Faustus to perform at his court but Faustus shows no disinterest.

Act -4, Scene – 5 (Tavern):

A comic relief scene, where the people cheated by Doctor Faustus such as the Horse-courser, Carter, etc. talk of the misbehaviour of Faustus and decides to find him to deal with their problems appropriately.

Act – 4, Scene – 6 (The court of the Duke of Vanholt):

Faustus with all his power and magical abilities pleases the Duke and asks the Duchess to wish for anything. She politely requests to have ripe grapes and everyone wonders how this feat is possible as it is the month of January, the most unlikely season to have grapes. However, with the help of Mephistopheles Faustus presents the grapes to the Duchess and explains about the difference of seasons in different hemispheres. As the Duke shows interest and asks to give lecture, the fellows cheated by Faustus bang at the gates. As they are allowed in, they question about the injustice they've faced and Faustus turns each one into a mute and they all exit. This feat amuses the Duke and the Duchess and Faustus takes leave.

Act – 5, Scene – 1 (The study room of Doctor Faustus):

[Faustus stoops further and further, only to entertain the crowd and through the 24-years of time he couldn't achieve what he sought for initially.]

With great lightning and thunder Mephistopheles and other devils are seen on the stage with Mephistopheles showing the way to reach Doctor Faustus.

Wagner expresses to the audience that the end is near for his master and he is ready for the final journey. So, Faustus gives everything he has to Wagner by writing a will claiming that Wagner is the sole possessor of all his properties. On his final day, Faustus is seen dining and making merry with the three scholars. It is at this moment and at his last day of time he summons the Helen of Troy. As the scholars exit, an Old Man comes in to warn the doctor. He asks the doctor to repent and states that God will always do well for those who think of Him. However, the thoughts of Faustus are fixed towards damnation and thinks it is too late.

The Old Man exits and Faustus contemplates on the sins he has done. Mephistopheles warns Faustus to not vary with the pact or else he will tear the body of the doctor. Threatened by Mephistopheles, Faustus asks the devil to torment the Old Man who created a delusion of happiness in his mind. However, Mephistopheles clearly states that the Old Man is pure of heart and soul, and such individuals cannot be harmed by devils. Unable to get his first request, Doctor Faustus asks to summon Helen of Troy so that he can forget all that has happened and live in bliss for the remainder of his time. Mephistopheles is happy to conjure the spirit of Helen of Troy and Faustus is seen to be amused and filled with pleasure by the sight of her.

<u>Act – 5, Scene – 2 (The study room of Doctor Faustus):</u>

Lucifer, Mephistopheles and Beelzebub seem to be waiting for the clock to strike midnight so that thcy can have the most valuable soul of Faustus.

Faustus and Wagner talk of the will written and Wagner expresses his joy and gratitude towards hi master. Meanwhile, the three scholars enter and the pact with the Devil is revealed. The first scholar is confused as to why this was not revealed earlier? Faustus exclaims that the devils would have tormented him physically. The third scholar doesn't want to leave Faustus, but as it is too dangerous the rest of the two convince him to not to stay. They tell Faustus that they will in the next room praying for his welfare. Mephistopheles is blamed by Faustus by luring him into damnation and the devil loves the fact that he could offer Lucifer such a soul as of Faustus' to the Devil.

"Fools that laugh on Earth, must weep in Hell." (Mephistopheles)

A final effort is made by the Good Angel by lamenting of the fact that Faustus can never have the gates of Heaven open to him. She bids Faustus goodbye as there is no place in Hell for virtues and Faustus is doomed to Hell. The Evil Angel terrifies Faustus by opening the gates of Hell.

As the clock strikes Eleven, Doctor Faustus has only an hour of life left and he starts to show signs of remorse. He thinks of God and how even a half drop of Christ's blood is enough to save his soul. He envisions God being angry with him and he is rushed with a lot of horrible aspects which won't stop from terrifying his mind. He is angry with his parents, angry with himself and Lucifer also but he is a helpless soul lost in the wilderness. He swam so deep into darkness that he cannot come back to light again.

The time comes and with great lightning and thunder the devils enter. Doctor Faustus pleads to dissolve his soul in air or water so that there is no chance for the devils to torment him. However, in the late hour there is no help for Faustus and he is dragged away by the devils to eternal damnation.

Act – 5, Scene – 3 (The study room of Doctor Faustus):

The Three Scholars disturbed the devilish noises in the room where Faustus was left alone come to see what has happened. Their prayers go in vain and they find the body of Doctor Faustus torn from limb to limb in many pieces.

Epilogue by Chorus:

The chorus lament that a great potential like that of Doctor Faustus was cut short due to his longing for unlawful knowledge. A man who was acclaimed to be an equal to Apollo himself brought himself down to a mere conjuror who with ill knowledge couldn't become wise and brought his own destruction. The chorus emphasizes that the tragic end of Faustus should be a lesson to anyone who dwell in understanding the forbidden fruits of knowledge.

Dr. Faustus Major Characters

Faustus, **John (Doctor):** The main character of the story, Faustus is a professor of divinity at Wittenberg, as well as a renowned physician and scholar. Not satisfied with the limitations of human knowledge and power, he begins to practice necromancy. He eventually makes a deal with Lucifer (commonly referred to as the "Faustian bargain"), whereby he exchanges his soul for twenty-four years of the devil's service to him. In the next twenty-four years, Faustus obtains all kinds of knowledge and power through his devil-servant, Mephistophilis. They travel all over the world, playing practical jokes on peasants and even the Pope, displaying magical powers to the emperor and the nobility; Faustus wishes and whims are played out in his various adventures. At times Faustus experiences doubt and despair over having sold his soul to the devil. He comes close to repenting at several crucial points in the story, but never follows through. Even to the end, Faustus refuses to fully repent, and he is eventually taken by the devils to hell. The character of Faustus comes from a well-known legend of a German physician who reported sold his soul to the devil in exchange for magical powers. In Marlowe's rendition, he is portrayed as a tragic hero in that his unbridled ambitions lead him to an unfortunate end. But at a deeper level, the tragedy is twofold. First, there is a clear devolvement of his character, from a confident, ambitious scholar, to a self-satisfied, low-level practical joker. Although he makes a name for himself as an expert magician, Faustus never accomplishes the lofty goals he initially sets for himself. Second, there are times when Faustus despairs over his decision and comes close to repenting, only to back away at the last moment. On the other hand, Faustus can be seen as a hero in that he rejects God's authority and determines his own course of life. Faustus is the paragon of the Renaissance Man—turning away from the religious strictures of the Medieval Age (God-centeredness) in favor of the enlightened age of reason and human achievement (man-centeredness).

Wagner: Faustus' servant and eventual heir of his fortunes, Wagner is a pale reflection of Faustus; he displays a nature similar to his master, even trying to obtain his own servant through the practice of magic. Wagner's background is not known, but it is clear from his language and demeanor that he is a young servant who looks up to Faustus. Wagner tries to imitate Faustus in many ways, in the way he talks and even in his taking up of magic. Wagner is Faustus' image-bearing progeny. That he inherits Faustus' fortunes suggests he might even be of physical progeny. At several points, Wagner acts as a narrator, filling in gaps in the story.

Good Angel: An agent of God who appears in pair with the Evil Angel, the Good Angel tries to make Faustus think about God and of heavenly things. The Good Angel represents the good side in the good/evil dichotomy. In a literary sense, the Good Angel reflects the good side of Faustus' conscience, for Marlowe tries to show that Faustus, like every human being, has two natures, both good and bad. What the Good Angel says mirrors what Faustus' good nature is thinking. Thus, the interchanges between the Good Angel and the Evil Angel reveal Faustus' inner struggles with himself. The Good Angel's main message to Faustus is that it is never too late to turn to God.

Evil Angel: An agent of Lucifer who appears in pair with the Good Angel, the Evil Angel tries to keep Faustus focused on power, wealth, and worldly pleasures. In direct contrast to the Good Angel, the Evil Angel represents the evil side in the good/evil dichotomy. In a literary sense, the Evil Angel reflects the evil side of Faustus' conscience, for Marlowe tries to show that Faustus, like every human being, has two natures, both good and bad. What the Evil Angel says mirrors what Faustus' evil nature is thinking. Thus, the interchanges between the Good Angel and the Evil Angel reveal Faustus' inner struggles with himself. The Evil Angel main message to Faustus is that God will not accept his repentance.

Mephistophilis: The devil that appears before Faustus, Mephistophilis makes the deal where he is to serve Faustus for twenty-four years in exchange for Faustus' soul. Mephistophilis is the main antagonist in the story, but he is also a conflicted character in his own right. As part of the rebellion of heaven, Mephistophilis was cast out with the other angels and sent to hell. When Faustus inquires about hell, Mephistophilis admits that he regrets forgoing the joys of heaven for the torment of hell. Mephistophilis tries to talk Faustus out of making a pact with Lucifer. But when Faustus makes the deal, Mephistophilis dutifully fulfills Faustus' wishes, whims, and desires for the next twenty-four years. Although Mephistophilis warns Faustus about the torments of hell, once the deal is made, Mephistophilis uses his power and cunning to prevent Faustus from repenting.

Lucifer: The Prince of the devils, Lucifer was once an angel of God who was cast out of heaven with other rebel angels because of their pride and insolence. Lucifer authorizes the deal between Faustus and Mephistophilis. If Mephistophilis is a conflicted devil, Lucifer shows no such weaknesses or signs of remorse for having been cast out of heaven. When Faustus cries upon the name of Christ, Lucifer comes, as though Mephistophilis is not crafty enough in such urgent cases. Lucifer masterly prevents Faustus from turning back to God at key points in the story.

Minor Characters

Chorus: A stage and literary device associated with Greek tragedy, the Chorus narrates and fills in parts of the story.

Valdes and Cornelius: Friends of Faustus, they are reputed to be practitioners of magic. Faustus calls on them to teach him the black arts. Valdes and Cornelius tell Faustus that with his wit, he will be powerful, and together they will be famous all over the world.

Two scholars: Faustus' fellow colleagues at the university, they are concerned that he has not been around. They ask Wagner about Faustus' whereabouts. When they find out Faustus has been with Valdes and Cornelius, they decide to tell the Rector of the university.

Belzebub: A companion prince of Lucifer, Faustus refers to Belzebub when he denounces God.

Clown: A poor, beggar-like character, the Clown is threatened by Wagner to be his servant. When the clown refuses, Wagner conjures up some spirits to scare him. The Clown follows Wagner, but asks Wagner to teach him magic.

Baliol and Belcher: Two spirits that Wagner conjures up to scare the Clown into serving him, Baliol and Belcher is a he-devil and a she-devil respectively.

Seven Deadly Sins: At the behest of Lucifer, Pride, Covetousness, Wrath, Envy, Gluttony, Sloth, and Lechery appear before Faustus. Faustus is delighted by their presence.

Pope: Faustus intrudes upon the Pope's privy-chamber and creates havoc, even hitting the Pope on the head.

Cardinal of Lorrain: The Pope's guest when Faustus enters the privy-chamber, the Cardinal thinks the invisible Faustus is a ghost from purgatory.

Emperor Carolus the Fifth: Faustus visits the German Emperor, Carolus the Fifth, who makes a request to see Alexander the Great and his paramour in person.

Robin the Ostler: An employee of an inn, Robin steals one of Faustus' magic books and makes Mephistophilis appear. He is turned into an ape by Mephistophilis.

Ralph: A fellow employee with Robin at the inn, Robin is turned into a dog by Mephistophilis.

Vintner: The Vintner, a wine merchant, comes to collect from Robin a silver goblet that is owed him. Robin tries to elude the Vintner by conjuring up a spirit, but it backfires.

Knight: The Knight, who serves in the court of Emperor Carolus the Fifth, is skeptical about Faustus' magical powers. In spite, Faustus makes horns grow on his head.

Alexander the Great: Alexander the Great, the famous Macedonian conqueror, and his Paramour are the two figures of the past that the Emperor Carolus the Fifth wants Faustus to produce.

Paramour: Emperor Carolus the Fifth is curious to know if Alexander the Great's lover, the Paramour, has a mole or a wart on her neck.

Horse-Courser: The Horse-Courser purchases a horse from Faustus. He is warned by Faustus not to ride the horse through water, but does not listen. When the Horse-Courser rides into water, the horse turns into a bottle of hay. The Horse-Courser tries to get Faustus' attention by pulling on his leg while he is sleeping. But Faustus plays a joke on him by making his leg fall off, scaring the Horse-Courser away.

Duke of Vanholt: Faustus visits the court of the Duke of Vanholt. The Duke is impressed with Faustus' magical powers.

Duchess of Vanholt: The Duchess of Vanholt, who is pregnant, desires ripe grapes in the dead of winter. Faustus is able to get her the best grapes she has ever had. The Duke and Duchess agree to reward Faustus handsomely.

Helen of Troy: The figure over which the Trojan War was fought, Helen of Troy is deemed to be the most admirable beauty in history. Faustus makes her appear before his colleagues. Faustus' last request to Mephistophilis is to have Helen of Troy as his lover.

Old Man: The Old Man appears to Faustus in order to convince him to repent and turn to God. A contrast to Faustus, the Old Man keeps his faith even through persecution from devils.

Doctor FaustusFamous Quotes Explained

1.*The reward of sin is death? That's hard.*

Si peccasse negamus, fallimur, et nulla est in nobis veritas.

If we say that we have no sin,

We deceive ourselves, and there's no truth in us.

Why then belike we must sin,

And so consequently die.
Ay, we must die an everlasting death.
What doctrine call you this? Che sarà, sarà:
What will be, shall be! Divinity, adieu!
These metaphysics of magicians,
And necromantic books are heavenly!
(1.40–50)

Faustus speaks these lines near the end of his opening soliloquy. In this speech, he considers various fields of study one by one, beginning with logic and proceeding through medicine and law. Seeking the highest form of knowledge, he arrives at theology and opens the Bible to the New Testament, where he quotes from Romans and the first book of John. He reads that "[t]he reward of sin is death," and that "[i]f we say we that we have no sin, / We deceive ourselves, and there's no truth in us." The logic of these quotations—everyone sins, and sin leads to death—makes it seem as though Christianity can promise only death, which leads Faustus to give in to the fatalistic "What will be, shall be! Divinity, adieu!" However, Faustus neglects to read the very next line in John, which states, "If we confess our sins, [God] is faithful and just to forgive us our sins, and to cleanse us from all unrighteousness" (1 John 1:9). By ignoring this passage, Faustus ignores the possibility of redemption, just as he ignores it throughout the play. Faustus has blind spots; he sees what he wants to see rather than what is really there. This blindness is apparent in the very next line of his speech: having turned his back on heaven, he pretends that "[t]hese metaphysics of magicians, / And necromantic books are heavenly." He thus inverts the cosmos, making black magic "heavenly" and religion the source of "everlasting death."

2.MEPHASTOPHILIS: Why this is hell, nor am I out of it.
Think'st thou that I, who saw the face of God,
And tasted the eternal joys of heaven,
Am not tormented with ten thousand hells
In being deprived of everlasting bliss?
O Faustus, leave these frivolous demands,

Which strike a terror to my fainting soul.
FAUSTUS: What, is great Mephastophilis so passionate
For being deprivèd of the joys of heaven?
Learn thou of Faustus manly fortitude,
And scorn those joys thou never shalt possess.
(3.76–86)

This exchange shows Faustus at his most willfully blind, as he listens to Mephastophilis describe how awful hell is for him even as a devil, and as he then proceeds to dismiss Mephastophilis's words blithely, urging him to have "manly fortitude." But the dialogue also shows Mephastophilis in a peculiar light. We know that he is committed to Faustus's damnation—he has appeared to Faustus because of his hope that Faustus will renounce God and swear allegiance to Lucifer. Yet here Mephastophilis seems to be urging Faustus against selling his soul, telling him to "leave these frivolous demands, / Which strike a terror to my fainting soul." There is a parallel between the experience of Mephastophilis and that of Faustus. Just as Faustus now is, Mephastophilis was once prideful and rebelled against God; like Faustus, he is damned forever for his sin. Perhaps because of this connection, Mephastophilis cannot accept Faustus's cheerful dismissal of hell in the name of "manly fortitude." He knows all too well the terrible reality, and this knowledge drives him, in spite of himself, to warn Faustus away from his t-errible course.

3.MEPHASTOPHILIS.: Hell hath no limits, nor is circumscribed
In one self-place; for where we are is hell,
And where hell is, there must we ever be.

. . .

All places shall be hell that is not heaven.
FAUSTUS: Come, I think hell's a fable.
MEPHASTOPHILISs.: Ay, think so still, till experience change
thy mind.

. . .

FAUSTUS: Think'st thou that Faustus is so fond to imagine
That after this life there is any pain?

Tush, these are trifles and mere old wives' tales.
(5.120–135)

This exchange again shows Mephastophilis warning Faustus about the horrors of hell. This time, though, their exchange is less significant for what Mephastophilis says about hell than for Faustus's response to him. Why anyone would make a pact with the devil is one of the most vexing questions surrounding Doctor Faustus, and here we see part of Marlowe's explanation. We are constantly given indications that Faustus doesn't really understand what he is doing. He is a secular Renaissance man, so disdainful of traditional religion that he believes hell to be a "fable" even when he is conversing with a devil. Of course, such a belief is difficult to maintain when one is trafficking in the supernatural, but Faustus has a fallback position. Faustus takes Mephastophilis's assertion that hell will be "[a]ll places ... that is not heaven" to mean that hell will just be a continuation of life on earth. He fails to understand the difference between him and Mephastophilis: unlike Mephastophilis, who has lost heaven permanently, Faustus, despite his pact with Lucifer, is not yet damned and still has the possibility of repentance. He cannot yet understand the torture against which Mephastophilis warns him, and imagines, fatally, that he already knows the worst of what hell will be.

4.*Was this the face that launched a thousand ships,*
And burnt the topless towers of Ilium?
Sweet Helen, make me immortal with a kiss:
Her lips sucks forth my soul, see where it flies!
Come Helen, come, give me my soul again.
Here will I dwell, for heaven be in these lips,
And all is dross that is not Helena!
(12.81–87)

These lines come from a speech that Faustus makes as he nears the end of his life and begins to realize the terrible nature of the bargain he has made. Despite his sense of foreboding, Faustus enjoys his powers, as the delight he takes in conjuring up Helen makes clear. While the speech marks a return to the eloquence that he shows early in the play, Faustus continues to display the same blind spots and wishful thinking that characterize his behavior throughout the drama. At the beginning of the play, he dismisses religious transcendence in favor of magic; now, after squandering his powers in petty, self-indulgent behavior, he looks for transcendence in a woman, one who may be an illusion and not even real flesh and blood. He seeks heavenly grace in Helen's lips, which can, at best, offer only earthly pleasure. "[M]ake me immortal with a kiss," he cries, even as he continues to keep his back turned to his only hope for escaping damnation—namely, repentance.

5.*Now hast thou but one bare hour to live,*
And then thou must be damned perpetually.

. . .

The stars move still, time runs, the clock will strike,
The devil will come, and Faustus must be damned.
O I'll leap up to my God! Who pulls me down?
See, see where Christ's blood streams in the firmament!
One drop would save my soul, half a drop: ah my Christ—
Ah, rend not my heart for naming of my Christ;
Yet will I call on him—O spare me, Lucifer!

. . .

Earth, gape! O no, it will not harbor me.
You stars that reigned at my nativity,
Whose influence hath allotted death and hell,
Now draw up Faustus like a foggy mist
Into the entrails of yon laboring cloud,
That when you vomit forth into the air
My limbs may issue from your smoky mouths,
So that my soul may but ascend to heaven.

. . .

O God, if thou wilt not have mercy on my soul,

. . .

Let Faustus live in hell a thousand years,
A hundred thousand, and at last be saved.

. . .

Cursed be the parents that engendered me:
No, Faustus, curse thy self, curse Lucifer,
That hath deprived thee of the joys of heaven.

. . .

My God, my God, look not so fierce on me!

. . .

Ugly hell gape not! Come not, Lucifer!
I'll burn my books—ah, Mephastophilis!
(13.57–113)

These lines come from Faustus's final speech, just before the devils take him down to hell. It is easily the most dramatic moment in the play, and Marlowe uses some of his finest rhetoric to create an unforgettable portrait of the mind of a man about to carried off to a horrific doom. Faustus goes from one idea to another, desperately seeking a way out. But no escape is available, and he ends by reaching an understanding of his own guilt: "No, Faustus, curse thy self, curse Lucifer, / That hath deprived thee of the joys of heaven." This final speech raises the question of why Faustus does not repent earlier and, more importantly, why his desperate cries to Christ for mercy are not heard. In a truly Christian framework, Faustus would be allowed a chance at redemption even at the very end. But Marlowe's play ultimately proves more tragic than Christian, and so there comes a point beyond which Faustus can no longer be saved. He is damned, in other words, while he is still alive.

Faustus's last line aptly expresses the play's representation of a clash between Renaissance and medieval values. "I'll burn my books," Faustus cries as the devils come for him, suggesting, for the first time since scene 2, when his slide into mediocrity begins, that his pact with Lucifer is about gaining limitless knowledge, an ambition that the Renaissance spirit celebrated but that medieval Christianity denounced as an expression of sinful human pride. As he is carried off to hell, Faustus seems to give in to the Christian worldview, denouncing, in a desperate attempt to save himself, the quest for knowledge that has defined most of his life.

6.Faustus, thou art damned! No creature loves thee!

The quote by Dr. Faustus, "Faustus, thou art damned! No creature loves thee!" encapsulates the tragic realization of his own fate and the depth of his despair. This agonizing exclamation reflects his profound regret at having sold his soul to the devil in exchange for worldly knowledge and power. Dr. Faustus acknowledges his damnation, recognizing that he is completely detached from any form of affection or love. This serves as a poignant reminder of the dire consequences of his pride, arrogance, and pursuit of forbidden knowledge. As the weight of his decision settles upon him, he is left to face a lonely and tormented existence, devoid of any compassion or affection from both humans and supernatural beings alike.

7.By aspiring pride and insolence, for which God threw him from the face of heaven.

The quote by Dr. Faustus, "By aspiring pride and insolence, for which God threw him from the face of heaven," emphasizes the consequences of excessive pride and arrogance. It alludes to the biblical story of Lucifer, who was cast out of heaven for rebelling against God. Dr. Faustus highlights the idea that an individual's hubris and disrespect for higher powers can lead to their downfall. This quote serves as a cautionary reminder that there are consequences for those who defy the natural order of things and seek to elevate themselves above their rightful place.

Doctor faustus short questions and answers

1. Who are the university wits?

Ans: The 'University wits' refer to a group of pre-Shakespearean playwrights associated with the University of Cambridge or Oxford. They are: Thomas Kyd, John Lyly, George Peele, Robert Greene, Thomas Lodge, Thomas Nash and Christopher Marlowe.

2. Who was the greatest of the dramatists of Shakespeare's predecessors?

Ans: Christopher Marlowe was the greatest of the dramatists of

Shakespeare's predecessors.

3. Who was the greatest of the university wits?

Ans: Christopher Marlowe was the greatest of the university wits.

4.Who is Faustus?

Ans: Faustus is the hero of the play, Doctor Faustus. His original is supposed to be Johann Faust, a rich burgher of Mainz, associated with Gutenberg. Historically, he is a reputed professor of the black art, a native of Germany, who flourished at the end of the 15th century and the beginning of the 16th century.

5. Who are Good Angel and Evil Angel?

Ans: The Good Angel and the Evil Angel are the personifications of Faustus' inner turmoil. The Evil Angel encourages Faustus to take the path of damnation, while the Good Angel tries to save him. Their characters reflect Christian belief that humans are assigned guardian angels, and that devils can influence human thoughts.

6. Who is Lucifer?

Ans: Lucifer is sometimes thought to be another name of Satan. In Doctor Faustus, Marlowe uses "Lucifer" as Satan's proper name.

7. Who is Belzebub?

Ans: Belzebub is one of Lucifer's officers. He is a powerful demon. Faustus identifies him as God.

8. Who is Robin?

Ans: Robin is an ostler, that is, a horse-keeper. He is in charge of the stable and has therefore to look after the horses.

9. Who is Ralph?

Ans: Ralph is the assistant of Robin.

10. Who is Horse-Courser?

Ans: He is the man who buys Faustus' horse. Faustus swindles him.

11. What is Chorus?

Ans: Chorus is a group of characters who takes part with the actors in the dialogue of a drama and expresses their sentiments in song at intervals when there is no character on the stage.

12.Who is Mars?

Ans: Mars is the Roman god of war. He allied himself with the Carthaginians to defeat the Romans.

13. What was Carthage?

Ans: Carthage was an ancient city situated to the north of Africa. It was founded by the Phoenicians and destroyed by the Romans 146 BC.

14. Why is Carthage famous?

Ans: Carthage is famous for trade and strong force.

15. Where was Dr Faustus born?

Ans: Dr Faustus was born in Germany in town called Rhodes.

16. What do you know about the learning of Dr. Faustus?

Ans: Faustus acquired extensive knowledge in the field's divinity and theology and was honoured with the Doctor's title.

17. What is necromancy?

Ans: Necromancy is the vicious art of calling up the spirits of dead.

18. Who was Mephistopheles?

Ans: Mephistopheles is the servant or deputy of Lucifer.

19. Why does Faustus decide to practice necromancy?

Ans: Faustus decides to practice necromancy because it offers unlimited profit, power, honour and authority to him.

20. "A sound magician is a mighty god." – From where is the line quoted?

Ans: The line is quoted from Marlowe's tragic play Doctor Faustus.

21.Who is Valdes?

Ans: Valdes is a person of uncertain identification considered to be a friend of Faustus.

22. How did Faustus bring Mephistopheles before him?

Ans: Faustus brought Mephistopheles before him by reciting spells.

23. What do Faustus and Lucifer have in common?

Ans: Both Faustus and Lucifer have excessive pride and insolence.

24. What is the Trinity?

Ans: The Trinity, in the Christian religion, means the union of Father, Son and Holy Spirit in one God.

25. What is Mephistopheles's idea of hell?

Ans: According to Mephistopheles hell does not mean any particular place to which Lucifer and his followers have been confined. To him, hell means the loss of heaven.

26. For what period of time does Faustus sells his soul in exchange for the service from the devil?

Ans: Faustus sells his soul in exchange for the service of the devil for twenty-four years. "So he will spare him four and twenty years".

27. What does Faustus identify as his God?

Ans: Faustus identifies Belzebub or Devil as his God.

28. What hinders the signing of the contract?

Ans: The coagulation of Faustus's blood hinders the signing of the contract.

29. What does Mephistopheles do when Faustus's blood congeals?

Ans: Mephistopheles fetches him a chafer of fire to loosen the blood and Faustus continues on to finish the contract.

30. Why does Faustus's blood congeal when he approaches to sign the bond?

Ans: When Faustus approaches to sign the bond his blood congeals. It signifies that his blood or soul is unwilling to sign the unduly contract.

Some long Questions and Answers

1.Doctor Faustus' as a Morality Play

The morality play is really a fusion of allegory and the religious drama of the miracle plays. In this play the characters were personified abstractions of vice or virtues such as Good deeds, Faith, Mercy, Anger, Truth, Pride etc. The theme of the moralities was the struggle between the good and evil powers for capturing the man's soul and good always won. The morality play often ended with a solemn moral. In the light of these points we may call Marlowe's "Dr. Faustus" a belated morality play in spite of its tragic ending.

In morality plays the characters were personified abstractions of vice or virtues. In "Dr. Faustus" also we find the Good and Evil angels, the former stand for the path of virtue and the latter for sin and damnation, one for conscience and the other for desires. He symbolizes the forces of righteousness and morality. The seven deadly sins are also there in a grand spectacle to cheer up the despairing soul of Faustus. If the, general theme of morality plays was theological dealing with the struggle of forces of good and evil for man's soul, then "Dr. Faustus" may be called a religious or morality play to a very great extent.

We find Marlowe's hero, Faustus, abjuring the scriptures, the Trinity and Christ. He surrenders his soul to the Devil out of his inordinate ambition to gain: "-----a world of profit and delight' Of power, of honour, of omnipotence." Through knowledge by mastering the unholy art of magic. About the books of magic, he declares:

"These metaphysics of magicians, And necromantic books are heavenly."

By selling his soul to the Devil he lives a blasphemous life full of vain and sensual pleasures just for only twenty-four years. There is struggle between his overwhelming ambition and conscience which are externalized by good angel and evil angel. But Faustus has already accepted the opinion of Evil Angel, who says: "Be thou on earth as Jove in the sky." Faustus is also fascinated by the thought: "A sound magician is a mighty god, Here, Faustus, tire thy brains to gain a deity." When the final hours approaches, Faustus find himself at the edge of eternal damnation and cries with deep sorrow: "My God, my God, look not so fierce to me!"

Through this story Marlowe gives the lesson that the man, who desires to be God, is doomed to eternal damnation. The chief aim of morality play was didactic. It was a dramatized guide to Christian living and Christian dying. Whosoever discards the path of virtue and faith in God and Christ is destined to despair and eternal damnation--- this is also the message of Marlowe's Dr. Faustus.

The tradition of chorus is also maintained. We find the chorus introducing the story just before the beginning of the first scene and subsequently filling in the gaps in the narrative and announcing the end of the play with a very solemn moral. The appearance of seven deadly sins shows that Marlowe in "Dr. Faustus" adopted some of the conventions of the old Morality plays.

We may conclude in the words of a critic: "Dr. Faustus" is both the consummation of the English Morality, tradition and the last and the finest of Marlowe's heroic plays.

2.Doctor Faustus as a Tragic Hero

Doctor Faustus is the most famous play of Christopher Marlowe he was of high skilled as a playwright and he could write very good drama. It is a tragedy of Doctor Faustus that is the main point of this story. Before moving on further, we should discuss about the definition of a tragic hero. A tragic hero is obviously a hero of a tragedy drama. However, a hero of the tragedy should not be an ordinary man but should be some higher and extra ordinary. He is exceptional to other people.

Furthermore, tragedy proves to overcome the higher and extra ordinary, even hero can be brought to ruin. Usually based on valor and ethical choices made for better or worst. Doctor Faustus is a good example of a tragic hero who loses focus and makes tragic choices that take him to alow beyond the worst of fates. Being that hero should have a socially elevated status and suffer a reversal of fortune in which he experience great suffering. This is all certainly true of Faustus, who is highly regarded as both a lecturer at the University of Wittenberg, and an accomplished scholar.

During his life, he performs extraordinary feats, which were unlike anything experienced by lesser mortals he uses his powers for amazing adventures like learning the secrets of astronomy upon the summit of mount Olympus, which, again, are befitting of the tragic hero. Doctor Faustus, scholar and lover of beauty, unsettled with human limitation. In his finest moments, Faustus speaks of the desire for freedom in us, and to have an interest in greatness to the extent that his actions undercut the fine speeches.

He gives voice to the Greek desire to defy Necessity, and live as master of one's own fate, even for a short time, even if it means disaster. Though he fancies himself to be a seeker of Greek greatness, he seeks to achieve to be like a God himself, and so he leaves behind the Christian conceptions of human limitation. His actions go on to show he has no common understanding of valor, blinded by his own pride. If we look at the opening scene then we will notice that he was unhappy because he grew tired of life. He was a scholar and he wanted new knowledge.

He got all the knowledge but except black magic. He realized that he did not have all that was knowledge and there was something missing. As Europe emerged from the Middle Ages, contact with previously lost Greek learning had a revelatory effect on man's conception of himself. While the Christian worldview places man below God, and requires obedience to him, the Greek worldview places man at the center of the universe. For the Greeks, man defies the gods at his own peril, for man has nobility. Faustus is a "renaissance man who had to pay the medieval price for being one. But the play itself would suggest that Faustus is not a true Renaissance man. He is someone incapable of living up to the standards of the medieval era, and he is equally incapable of living up the Greek-influenced standards of the Renaissance. He rejects the submissive morality of Christianity, cutting himself off from goodness, but he cannot live up to Renaissance greatness. Faustus fails to live up the standards of a tragic hero. He has amathia (an opposite of wisdom) a plenty, a necessary ingredient in the constitution of a tragic hero.

Amathia is a Greek word, meaning a man's failure to recognize his own nature. But Faustus lacks nobleness, and from the start his interest in selling his soul seems to come from boredom and restlessness. In Act One, he makes long-winded boasts about the uses to which he'll put his power. What we learn subsequently is that Faustus' amathia is a bit of a letdown. He fails to recognize that he's a lazy slob. He is all talk, and no action. So, he sought the new knowledge like Prometheus(who was the Titan god of forethought and crafty counsel who was entrusted with the task of molding mankind out of clay.

His attempts to better the lives of his creation brought him into direct conflict with Zeus. Firstly he tricked the gods out of the best portion of the sacrificial feast, acquiring the meat for the feasting of man.)he accepts eternal torture as the price for a prized goal. But Prometheus sacrifices himself for the benefit of the human race. Faustus is fearless as he closes the deal with lucifer for his eternal soul. Once Faustus has omnipotence, but a definite end to it, he has no incentive to grow as a human being, and he seems too lazy to look beyond his lifetime.

Leaving behind an empire, or an improved world, just don't hold any interest for him, just as being a doctor, in his pre-Faustian bargain days held no interest for him. Magnified powers haven't magnified Faustus' capacity for care, or his love of humanity, and he spends his twenty-four years as a lascivious and pathetic loser a tragedy in which a human being makes a clear choice for good or bad, with some knowledge of the possible outcome. When you think Faustus can't go any lower, lower he goes, Faustus' opponents become more pathetic as the story goes. Even when wielded by an ass, presents some kind of target.

Knights at a court, when they threaten his life, seem like sport. But Faustus now has degenerated to swindling peasants out of money. These are the uses to which he puts his vast power. Faustus reversal of fortune is also typically tragic. During the final scene of the play, in which we witness Faustus' finally before being taken off to hell, he is, like all heroes of classical tragedy, completely isolated. There is a contrast in Faustus' degeneration from the successful, revered conjurer of the previous scenes, to the disillusioned scholar we see here. In despair, he tries to conjure and command the elements of universe.

Faustus only reflects on his own diminishing time: "What are thou, Faustus, but a man condemned to die? " (4. 5. 41). Knowledge of a final end paralyzes him, and Faustus seems what modern people would call depressed. But his rhetorical question shows how poor his understanding is of the Christian God, and God's plan for mankind. He is more than a man condemned to die. He is a child of God, ransomed by Christ's blood, and invited to take part in eternal life. He has amathia aplenty, a necessary ingredient in the constitution of a tragic hero. Amathia is a Greek word, meaning a man's failure to recognize his own nature.

But Faustus lacks nobleness, and from the start his interest in selling his soul seems to come from boredom and restlessness. In Act One, he makes long-winded boasts about the uses to which he'll put his power. What we learn subsequently is that Faustus' amathia is a bit of a letdown. He fails to recognize that he's a lazy slob. He is all talk, and no action. A tragedy without a doubt, however it is plain to see that a hero he is not although Faustus had the makings to be a hero he chose to wonder at unlawful things. Who's deepness doth entice such forward wits. To practice more than heavenly power permits.

3.Function of Chorus in Doctor Faustus

In Doctor Faustus by Marlowe the chorus appears four times. it makes its first appearance at the very outset of the play and serves the purpose of the prologue. The chorus speaks directly to the audience and tells the basic background history of Faustus and explains that the play is to concern his downfall. Thus, the opening speech of the chorus functions as a prologue to define the scope of the play. The chorus makes its second appearance at the beginning of the third Act to bridge the gap between Act II and Act III. Here the chorus narrates the unstated events to the audience to enable them to follow the career of Dr. Faustus without feeling any void in the story. The chorus delivers its third speech in the fourth Act. Here chorus narrate the return of Faustus to his home after he it tells us that Faustus's fame has speared far and wide. Here again, the chorus bridges the time gap and also hints at the further course of action. The chorus appears for the last time at the end of the play and serves the purpose of the epilogue. The chorus here moralizes that man should not hanker after limitless power and pelf at the cost of human soul.

4 Significance of the Good and the Evil Angel

The Good Angel and the Evil Angel create inner conflict in the mind of Faustus when the Good Angel urges him to shun black art of magic, and the Evil Angel tempts hi with infinite power which magic will provide for him. The Good and the Evil Angels gives the touch of Morality play to Doctor Faustus. The characters of the Morality play are allegorical. They ae personified as abstractions of vice or virtues. The Good and the Evil Angels represent the path of virtue, and sin and damnation respectively. Their characters also reflect Christian belief that humans are assigned guardian angels, and that devils can influence human thoughts.

The Good and Evil Angels personify the two aspects of Faustus's character. The former stands for order, virtue or goodness and the latter represents the baser spirit of Faustus, his indomitable passions and desires. One stands for his conscience and the other, his curiosity for 'unlawful things.

5.Why does Faustus sell his soul?

Dr. Faustus has spent years establishing his lauded reputation as a scholar, where his knowledge of logic, medicine, science, and law has brought him great regard. However, such acclaim has not brought him personal satisfaction. Growing restless with the limits of what can be accomplished in the world of academia, Dr. Faustus considers that magic could make him a god himself. After discussing his vision to Valdes and Cornelius, they teach him the ways of dark magic, promising him that he will absorb great powers if he does. Once he begins to practice, Dr. Faustus summons Mephastophilis, demands his service, and is all too willing to sell his soul in exchange for further knowledge.

6.Why does Faustus request twenty-four years of service?

Though the text never explicitly provides an explanation from Faustus as to why he asks for only twenty-four years of unlimited power, one interpretation of the number's narrative significance draws a parallel to the twenty-four hours in a day, emphasizing a ticking time on Faustus's own fate and the idea that unlimited power does have its limits; indeed, once Faustus gets everything he's ever wanted, he becomes listless. The novelty of what he has achieved is gone, and only the looming knowledge of his fate remains.

7.Is Faustus to blame for his own downfall?

Like so many tragic figures before him, Faustus's own hubris is the cause of his downfall. His quest for knowledge causes him to seek out a deal with the devil, and his arrogance prevents him from fully understanding the consequences of what has agreed to. Despite Mephastophilis's insistence that hell is ceaseless and torturous, and despite the Good Angel's attempts at persuasion, Faustus sets aside any hesitation he might be experiencing and indulges his own desires.

8.What are the terms of Faustus's agreement with Lucifer?

Faustus agrees to constant service from Mephastophilis if, in twenty-four years, Faustus gives his body and soul to Lucifer, who is looking to expand his own kingdom of suffering souls. While employed, Mephastophilis grants Faustus secret knowledge of the world and a book of magic to learn from. From here, Faustus travels the world, expanding the reach of his magical abilities.

9.What is the significance of the inscription on Faustus's arm?

To sign his contract in blood, Faustus stabs himself in the arm. However, his blood congeals, rendering him unable to sign. Though this brings him a moment of pause, as he wonders if this is an ominous sign, he ultimately goes through with the agreement. After signing the deed, he receives another warning: the Latin inscription "Homo fuge" (meaning "O man, fly") appears etched on his arm, likely a warning to escape that Faustus instead interprets as a prompt to continue, wondreing where he should fly first.

10.Description of Hell in the play Dr. Faustus

In Christopher Marlowe's play "Doctor Faustus," hell is depicted as a terrifying and gruesome place, where the souls of the damned are tormented for all eternity. The play provides a vivid description of hell, which serves to underscore the consequences of Faustus's sinful actions and the price he pays for his ambition.

The depiction of hell in the play is heavily influenced by Christian theology, and the punishments suffered by the souls in hell are drawn from the Bible. Hell is described as a place of fire and brimstone, where the souls of the damned are subjected to endless agony and suffering.

One of the most prominent descriptions of hell in the play comes from Faustus himself, who is visited by a group of devils towards the end of the play. The devils take Faustus on a tour of hell, where he witnesses the horrors that await him in the afterlife.

Hell creatures

As they descend into the depths of hell, Faustus is confronted with a series of horrific sights. He sees the souls of the damned writhing in agony, tortured by a variety of instruments of torture. He sees men and women being boiled in cauldrons of oil, devoured by serpents, and torn apart by demons. The screams of the damned fill the air, adding to the sense of horror and dread.

Faustus is also confronted with the sight of Satan himself, who is depicted as a fearsome and terrifying figure. Satan is described as having enormous wings and a hideous face, and his presence fills Faustus with a sense of terror and dread.

The depiction of hell in the play is also notable for its emphasis on the psychological torment suffered by the souls of the damned. The play suggests that the greatest punishment of hell is not physical pain, but the sense of isolation and despair that comes from being separated from God.

Throughout the play, Faustus is haunted by the fear of damnation and the thought of spending eternity in hell. This fear is reinforced by the constant presence of the devils, who serve as a reminder of the consequences of Faustus's actions.

In many ways, the depiction of hell in the play serves as a warning to the audience about the dangers of sin and the importance of leading a virtuous life. The play suggests that the pursuit of knowledge and power can be a dangerous path, and that the price of ambition can be high.

In conclusion, the depiction of hell in "Doctor Faustus" is a vivid and terrifying portrait of the consequences of sin. The play emphasizes the physical and psychological torment suffered by the souls of the damned and underscores the importance of leading a virtuous life. The play serves as a warning to the audience about the dangers of ambition and the high price that can come with the pursuit of knowledge and power.

CHAPTER FOUR

Every Man in His Humour: Text & Analysis

EVERY MAN IN HIS HUMOUR

TO THE MOST LEARNED, AND MY HONOURED FRIEND
MASTER CAMDEN CLARENCIEUX

SIR,—There are, no doubt, a supercilious race in the world, who will esteem all office, done you in this kind, an injury; so solemn a vice it is with them to use the authority of their ignorance, to the crying down of Poetry, or the professors: but my gratitude must not leave to correct their error; since I am none of those that can suffer the benefits conferred upon my youth to perish with my age. It is a frail memory that remember s but present things: and, had the favour of the times so conspired with my disposition, as it could have brought forth other, or better, you had had the same proportion, and number of the fruits, the first. Now I pray you to accept this; such wherein neither the confession of my manners shall make you blush; nor of my studies, repent you to have been the instructor: and for the profession of my thankfulness, I am sure it will, with good men, find either praise or excuse. Your true lover,

BEN JONSON.

DRAMATIS PERSONAE

KNOWELL, an old Gentleman: OLIVER COB, a Water-bearer.

EDWARD KNOWELL, his Son. JUSTICE CLEMENT, an old merry

BRAINWORM, the Father's Man Magistrate.
GEORGE DOWNRIGHT, a plain Squire. ROGER FORMAL, his Clerk.
WELLBRED, his Half-Brother. Wellbred's Servant
KITELY, a merchant. DAME KITELY, KITELY'S Wife.
CAPTAIN BOBADILL, a Paul's Man. MRS. BRIDGET his Sister.
MASTER STEPHEN, a Country Gull. TIB Cob's Wife
MASTER MATHEW, the Town Gull.
THOMAS CASH, KITELY'S Cashier. Servants, etc.
SCENE,—-LONDON
PROLOGUE.
Though need make many poets, and some such
As art and nature have not better'd much;
Yet ours for want hath not so loved the stage,
As he dare serve the ill customs of the age,
Or purchase your delight at such a rate,
As, for it, he himself must justly hate:
To make a child now swaddled, to proceed
Man, and then shoot up, in one beard and weed,
Past threescore years; or, with three rusty swords,
And help of some few foot and half-foot words,
Fight over York and Lancaster's king jars,
And in the tyring-house bring wounds to scars.
He rather prays you will be pleas'd to see
One such to-day, as other plays should be;
Where neither chorus wafts you o'er the seas,
Nor creaking throne comes down the boys to please;
Nor nimble squib is seen to make afeard
The gentlewomen; nor roll'd bullet heard
To say, it thunders; nor tempestuous drum
Rumbles, to tell you when the storm doth come;
But deeds, and language, such as men do use,
And persons, such as comedy would choose,
When she would shew an image of the times,
And sport with human follies, not with crimes.

Except we make them such, by loving still
Our popular errors, when we know they're ill.
I mean such errors as you'll all confess,
By laughing at them, they deserve no less:
Which when you heartily do, there's hope left then,
You, that have so grac'd monsters, may like men.

ACT I

SCENE I.—-A Street.

Enter KNOWELL, at the door of his house.

Know. A goodly day toward, and a fresh morning.—Brainworm!
Enter Brainworm.
Call up your young master: bid him rise, sir.
Tell him, I have some business to employ him.
Brai. I will, sir, presently.
Know. But hear you, sirrah,
If he be at his book, disturb him not.
Brai. Very good, sir.
Know. How happy yet should I esteem myself,
Could I, by any practice, wean the boy
From one vain course of study he affects.
He is a scholar, if a man may trust
The liberal voice of fame in her report,
Of good account in both our Universities,
Either of which hath favoured him with graces:
But their indulgence must not spring in me
A fond opinion that he cannot err.
Myself was once a student, and indeed,
Fed with the self-same humour he is now,
Dreaming on nought but idle poetry,
That fruitless and unprofitable art,
Good unto none, but least to the professors;
Which then I thought the mistress of all knowledge:
But since, time and the truth have waked my judgment.
And reason taught me better to distinguish T
he vain from the useful learnings.

Enter Master STEPHEN.

Cousin Stephen, What news with you, that you are here so early?

Step. Nothing, but e'en come to see how you do, unclo.

Know. That's kindly done; you are welcome, coz.

Step. Ay, I know that, sir; I would not have come else.

How does my cousin Edward, uncle?

Know. O, well, coz; go in and see; I doubt he be scarce stirring yet.

Step. Uncle, afore I go in, can you tell me, an he have e'er a book of the science of hawking and hunting; I would fain borrow it.

Know. Why, I hope you will not a hawking now, will you?

Step. No, wusse; but I'll practise against next year, uncle. I have bought me a hawk, and a hood, and bells and all; I lack nothing but a book to keep it by.

Know. Oh, most ridiculous!

Step. Nay, look you now, you are angry, uncle:—Why, you know an a

man have not skill in the hawking and hunting languages now-a-days,

I'll not give a rush for him: they are more studied than the Greek, or the Latin. He is for no gallant's company without them; and by

gadslid I scorn it, I, so I do, to be a consort for every humdrum: hang them, scroyles! there's nothing in them i' the world. What do

you talk on it? Because I dwell at Hogsden, I shall keep company with none but the archers of Finsbury, or the citizens that come a

ducking to Islington ponds! A fine jest, i' faith! 'Slid, a gentleman mun shew himself like a gentleman. Uncle, I pray you be

not angry; I know what I have to do, I trow. I am no novice.

Know. You are a prodigal, absurd coxcomb, go to!

Nay, never look at me, 'tis I that speak;

Take't as you will, sir, I'll not flatter you.

Have you not yet found means enow to waste
That which your friends have left you, but you must
Go cast away your money on a buzzard,
And know not how to keep it, when you have done?
O, it is comely! this will make you a gentleman!
Well, cousin, well, I see you are e'en past hope
Of all reclaim:—-ay, so; now you are told on't,
You look another way.
Step. What would you ha' me do?
Know. What would I have you do? I'll tell you, kinsman;
Learn to be wise, and practise how to thrive;
That would I have you do: and not to spend
Your coin on every bauble that you fancy,
Or every foolish brain that humours you.
I would not have you to invade each place,
Nor thrust yourself on all societies,
Till men's affections, or your own desert,
Should worthily invite you to your rank.
He that is so respectless in his courses,
Oft sells his reputation at cheap market.
Nor would I, you should melt away yourself
In flashing bravery, lest, while you affect
To make a blaze of gentry to the world,
A little puff of scorn extinguish it;
And you be left like an unsavoury snuff,
Whose property is only to offend.
I'd have you sober, and contain yourself,
Not that your sail be bigger than your boat;
But moderate your expenses now, at first,
As you may keep the same proportion still:
Nor stand so much on your gentility,0
Which is an airy and mere borrow'd thing,
From dead men's dust and bones; and none of yours,
Except you make, or hold it.
Enter a Servant.

Who comes here?

Serv. Save you, gentlemen!

Step. Nay, we do not stand much on our gentility, friend; yet you are welcome: and I assure you mine uncle here is a man of a thousand a year, Middlesex land. He has but one son in all the world, I am his next heir, at the common law, master Stephen, as simple as I stand here, if my cousin die, as there's hope he will: I have a pretty living O' mine own too, beside, hard by here.

Serv. In good time, sir.

Step. In good time, sir! why, and in very good time, sir! You do not flout, friend, do you?

Servo. Not I, sir.

Step. Not you, sir! you were best not, sir; an you should; here be them can perceive it, and that quickly too; go to: and they can give it again soundly too, an need be.

Servo. Why, sir, let this satisfy you; good faith, I had no such intent.

Step. Sir, an I thought you had, I would talk with you, and that presently.

Serv. Good master Stephen, so you may, sir, at your pleasure.

Step. And so I would, sir, good my saucy companion! an you were out

O' mine uncle's ground, I can tell you; though I do not stand upon

my gentility neither, in't.

Know. Cousin, cousin, will this ne'er be left?

Step. Whoreson, basefellow! a mechanical serving-man! By this cudgel, an 'twere not for shame, I would—

Know. What would you do, you peremptory gull?

If you cannot be quiet, get you hence.

You see the honest man demeans himself

Modestly tow'rds you, giving no reply

To your unseason'd, quarrelling, rude fashion;

And still you huff it, with a kind of carriage

As void of wit, as of humanity.

Go, get you in; 'fore heaven, I am ashamed
Thou hast a kinsman's interest in me. *[Exit Stephen]*
Serv. I pray, sir, is this master Knowell's house?
Know. Yes, marry is it, sir.
Serv. I should inquire for a gentleman here, one master Edward
Knowell; do you know any such, sir, I pray you?
Know. I should forget myself else, sir.
Serv. Are you the gentleman? cry you mercy, sir: I was required
by
a gentleman in the city, as I rode out at this end O' the town, to
deliver you this letter, sir.
Know. To me, sir! What do you mean? pray you remember your
court'sy. *[Reads.]* To his most selected friend, master Edward
Knowell. What might the gentleman's name be, sir, that sent it?
Nay, pray you be covered.
Serv. One master Wellbred, sir.
Know. Master Wellbred! a young gentleman, is he not?
Serv. The same, sir; master Kitely married his sister; the rich
merchant in the Old Jewry.
Know. You say very true.—-Brainworm! [Enter Brainworm.
Brai. Sir.
Know. Make this honest friend drink here: pray you, go in.
[Exeunt Brainworm and Servant].
This letter is directed to my son;
Yet I am Edward Knowell too, and may,
With the safe conscience of good manners, use
The fellow's error to my satisfaction.
Well, I will break it ope (old men are curious),
Be it but for the style's sake and the phrase;
To see if both do answer my son's praises,
Who is almost grown the idolater
Of this young Wellbred. What have we here?
What's this? *[Reads]*
Why, Ned, I beseech thee, hast thou forsworn all thy friends in
the

Old Jewry? or dost thou think us all Jews that inhabit there? yet,
if thou dost, come over, and but see our frippery; change an old
shirt for a whole smock with us: do not conceive that antipathy
between us and Hogsden, as was between Jews and hogs-flesh.
Leave
thy vigilant father alone, to number over his green apricots,
evening and morning, on the north-west wall: an I had been his
son,
I had saved him the labour long since, if taking in all the young
wenches that pass by at the back-door, and codling every kernel
of
the fruit for them, would have served, But, pr'ythee, come over
to
me quickly this morning; I have such a present for thee!—our
Turkey company never sent the like to the Grand Signior.
One is a rhymer, sir, of your own batch, your own leaven;
but doth think himself poet-major of the town, willing to be
shewn,
and worthy to be seen. The other—I will not venture his
description with you, till you come, because I would have you
make
hither with an appetite. If the worst of 'em be not worth your
journey draw your bill of charges, as unconscionable as any
Guildhall verdict will give it you, and you shall be allowed your
viaticum. From the Windmill.
From the Bordello it might come as well,
The Spittle, or Pict-hatch. Is this the man
My son hath sung so, for the happiest wit,
The choicest brain, the times have sent us forth!
I know not what he may be in the arts,
Nor what in schools; but, surely, for his manners,
I judge him a profane and dissolute wretch;
Worse by possession of such great good gifts,
Being the master of so loose a spirit.
Why, what unhallowed ruffian would have writ

In such a scurrilous manner to a friend!
Why should he think I tell my apricots,
Or play the Hesperian dragon with my fruit,
To watch it? Well, my son, I had thought you
Had had more judgment to have made election
Of your companions, than t' have ta'en on trust
Such petulant, jeering gamesters, that can spare
No argument or subject from their jest.
But I perceive affection makes a fool
Of any man too much the father.—-Brainworm!
Enter BRAINWORM.
Brai. Sir.
Know. Is the fellow gone that brought this letter?
Brai. Yea, sir, a pretty while since.
Know. And where is your young master?
Brai. In his chamber, sir.
Know. He spake not with the fellow, did he?
Brai. No, sir, he saw him not.
Know. Take you this letter, and deliver it my son;
but with no notice that I have opened it, on your life.
Brai. O Lord, sir! that were a jest indeed. [Exit.
Know. I am resolved I will not stop his journey,
Nor practise any violent means to stay
The unbridled course of youth in him; for that
Restrain'd, grows more impatient; and in kind
Like to the eager, but the generous greyhound,
Who ne'er so little from his game withheld,
Turns head, and leaps up at his holder's throat.
There is a way of winning more by love,
And urging of tho modesty, than fear:
Force works on servile natures, not the free.
He that's compell'd to goodness may be good,
But 'tis but for that fit; where others, drawn
By softness and example, get a habit.
Then, if they stray, but warn them, and the same

They should for virtue have done, they'll do for shame. [Exit.]

SCENE II.-A Room in KNOWELL.'S House.

Enter E. KNOWELL, with a letter in his hand, followed by BRAINWORM.

E. Know. Did he open it, say'st thou?

Brai. Yes, O' my word, sir, and read the contents.

E. Know. That scarce contents me. What countenance, prithee, made

he in the reading of it? was he angry, or pleased?

Brai. Nay, sir, I saw him not read it, nor open it, I assure your Worship.

E. Know. No! how know'st thou then that he did either?

Brai. Marry, sir, because he charged me, on my life, to tell nobody

that he open'd it; which, unless he had done, he would never fear to have it revealed.

E. Know. That's true: well, I thank thee, Brainworm.

Enter STEPHEN.

Step. O, Brainworm, didst thou not see a fellow here in what-sha-call-him doublet? he brought mine uncle a letter e'en now.

Brai. Yes, master Stephen; what of him?

Step. O, I have such a mind to beat him—where is he, canst thou tell?

Brai. Faith, he is not of that mind: he is gone, master Stephen.

Step. Gone! which way? when went he? how long since?

Brai. He is rid hence; he took horse at the street-door.

Step. And I staid in the fields! Whoreson scanderbag rogue! O that

I had but a horse to fetch him back again!

Brai. Why, you may have my master's gelding, to save your longing, sir.

Step. But I have no boots, that's the spite on't.

Brai. Why, a fine wisp of hay, roll'd hard, master Stephen.

Step. No, faith, it's no boot to follow him now: let him e'en go and hang. Prithee, help to truss me a little: he does so vex me—

Brai. You'll be worse vexed when you are trussed, master Stephen.

Best keep unbraced, and walk yourself till you be cold; your choler

may founder you else.

Step. By my faith, and so I will, now thou tell'st me on't: how dost thou like my leg, Brainworm?

Brai. A very good leg, master Stephen; but the woollen stocking does not commend it so well.

Step. Foh! the stockings be good enough, now summer is coming on,

for the dust: I'll have a pair of silk against winter, that I go to dwell in the town. I think my leg would shew in a silk hose—

Brai. Believe me, master Stephen, rarely well.

Step. In sadness, I think it would: I have a reasonable good leg.

Brai. You have an excellent good leg, master Stephen; but I can not

stay to praise it longer now, and I am very sorry for it.
[Exit].

Step. Another time will serve, Brainworm. Gramercy for this.

E. Know. Ha, ha, ha.

Step. 'Slid, I hope he laughs not at me; an he do—

E. Know. Here was a letter indeed, to be intercepted by a man's father, and do him good with him! He cannot but think most virtuously, both of me, and the sender, sure, that make the careful

costermonger of him in our familiar epistles. Well, if he read this with patience I'll be gelt, and troll ballads for master John Trundle yonder, the rest of my mortality. It is true, and likely, my father may have as much patience as another man, for he takes

much physic; and oft taking physic makes a man very patient. But

would your packet, master Wellbred, had arrived at him in such
a
minute of his patience! then we had known the end of it, which
now
is doubtful, and threatens—[Sees Master Stephen.] What, my
wise
cousin! nay, then I'll furnish our feast with one gull more toward
the mess. He writes to me of a brace, and here's one, that's three:
oh, for a fourth, Fortune, if ever thou' It use thine eyes, I
entreat thee—
Step. Oh, now I see who he laughed at: he laughed at somebody
in
that letter. By this good light, an he had laughed at me—
E. Know. How now, cousin Stephen, melancholy?
Step. Yes, a little: I thought you had laughed at me, cousin.
E. Know. Why, what an I had, coz? what would you have done?
Step. By this light, I would have told mine uncle.
E. Know. Nay, if you would have told your uncle, I did laugh at
you, coz.
Step. Did you, indeed?
E. Know. Yes, indeed.
Step. Why then
E. Know. What then?
Step. I am satisfied; it is sufficient.
E. Know. Why, be so, gentle coz: and, I pray you, let me entreat
a
courtesy of you. I am sent for this morning by a friend in the Old
Jewry, to come to him; it is but crossing over the fields to
Moorgate: Will you bear me company? I protest it is not to draw
you
into bond or any plot against the state, coz.
Step. Sir, that's all one an it were; you shall command me twice
so
far as Moorgate, to do you good in such a matter. Do you think I
would leave you? I protest.

E. Know. No, no, you shall not protest, coz.

Step. By my fackings, but I will, by your leave:—I'll protest more to my friend, than I'll speak of at this time.

E. Know. You speak very well, coz.

Step. Nay, not so neither, you shall pardon me: but I speak to serve my turn.

E. Know. Your turn, coz! do you know what you say? A gentleman
of your sorts, parts, carriage, and estimation, to talk of your
turn in this company, and to me alone, like a tankard-bearer
at a conduit! fie! A wight that, hitherto, his every step
hath left the stamp of a great foot behind him, as every word
the savour of a strong spirit, and he! this man! so graced, gilded,
or, to use a more fit metaphor, so tenfold by nature, as not ten
housewives' pewter, again a good time, shews more bright to the
world than he! and he! (as I said last, so I say again, and still
shall say it) this man! to conceal such real ornaments as these,
and shadow their glory, as a milliner's wife does her wrought
stomacher, with a smoaky lawn, or a black cyprus! O, coz! it cannot
be answered; go not about it: Drake's old ship at Deptford may
sooner circle the world again. Come, wrong not the quality of your
desert, with looking downward, coz; but hold up your head, so: and
let the idea of what you are be portrayed in your face, that men
may read in your physnomy, here within this place is to be seen the
true, rare, and accomplished monster, or miracle of nature, which
is all one. What think you of this, coz?

Step. Why, I do think of it: and I will be more proud, and
melancholy, and gentlemanlike, than I have been, I'll insure you.

E. Know. Why, that's resolute, master Stephen!—Now, if I can but hold him up to his height, as it is happily begun, it will do well

for a suburb humour: we may hap have a match with the city,
and

play him for forty pound.—Come, coz.

Step. I'll follow you.

E. Know. Follow me! you must go before.

Step. Nay, an I must, I will. Pray you shew me, good cousin.

[Exeunt.]

SCENE III.-The Lane before Cob's House.

Enter Master MATHEW:

Mat. I think this be the house: what ho!

Enter COB.

Cob. Who's there? O, master Mathew! give your worship good

morrow.

Mat. What, Cob! how dost thou, good Cob? dost thou inhabit

here,

Cob?

Cob. Ay, sir, I and my lineage have kept a poor house here, in

Our

days.

Mat. Thy lineage, monsieur Cob! what lineage, what lineage?

Cob. Why, sir, an ancient lineage, and a princely. Mine ance'try

came from a king's belly, no worse man; and yet no man either,

by

your worship's leave, I did lie in that, but herring, the king of

fish (from his belly I proceed), one of the monarchs of the

world,

I assure you. The first red herring that was broiled in Adam and

Eve's kitchen, do I fetch my pedigree from, by the harrot's book.

His cob was my great, great, mighty great grandfather.

Mat. Why mighty, why mighty, I pray thee?

Cob. O, it was a mighty while ago, sir, and a mighty great cob.

Mat. How know'st thou that?

Cob. How know I! why, I smell his ghost ever and anon.

Mat. Smell a ghost! O unsavoury jest! and the ghost of a herring cob?

Cob. Ay, sir: With favour of your worship's nose, master Mathew,

why not the ghost of a herring cob, as well as the ghost of Rasher Bacon?

Mat. Roger Bacon, thou would'st say.

Cob. I say Rasher Bacon. They were both broiled on the coals; and a

man may smell broiled meat, I hope! you are a scholar, upsolve me

that now.

Mat. O raw ignorance!—Cob, canst thou shew me of a gentleman, one

captain Bobadill, where his lodging is?

Cob. O, my guest, sir, you mean.

Mat. Thy guest! alas, ha, ha, ha!

Cob. Why do you laugh, sir? do you not mean captain Bobadill?

Mat. Cob, pray thee advise thyself well; do not wrong the

gentleman, and thyself too. I dare be sworn, he scorns thy house;

he! he lodge in such a base obscure place as thy house! Tut, I know

his disposition so well, he would not lie in thy bed if thou'dst give it him.

Cob. I will not give it him though, sir. Mass, I thought somewhat was in it, we could not get him to bed all night: Well, sir, though he lie not on my bed, he lies on my bench: an't please you to go up, sir, you shall find him with two cushions under his head, and his cloak wrapped about him, as though he had neither won nor lost,

and yet, I warrant, he ne'er cast better in his life, than he has done to-night.

Mat. Why, was he drunk?

Cob. Drunk, sir! you hear not me say so: perhaps he swallowed a tavern-token, or some such device, sir, I have nothing to do withal. I deal with water and not with wine—Give me my tankard

there, ho!—God be wi' you, sir. It's six o'clock: I should have
carried two turns by this. What ho! my stopple! come.

Enter Tib with a water-tankard.

Mat. Lie in a water-bearer's house! a gentleman of his havings!
Well, I'll tell him my mind.

Cob. What, Tib; shew this gentleman up to the captain.[Exit Tib
with Master Mathew.] Oh, an my house were the Brazen-head

now!

faith it would e'en speak Moe fools yet. You should have some

now

would take this master Mathew to be a gentleman, at the least.

His

father's an honest man, a worshipful fishmonger, and so forth;

and

now does he creep and wriggle into acquaintance with all the

brave

gallants about the town, such as my guest is (O, my guest is a fine
man!), and they flout him invincibly. He useth every day to a
merchant's house where I serve water, one master Kitely's, in

the

Old Jewry; and here's the jest, he is in love with
my master's sister, Mrs. Bridget, and calls her mistress; and there
he will sit you a whole afternoon sometimes, reading of these

same

abominable, vile (a pox on 'em! I cannot abide them), rascally
verses, poetrie, poetrie, and speaking of interludes; 'twill make a
man burst to hear him. And the wenches, they do so jeer, and ti-

he

at him—Well, should they do so much to me, I'd forswear them

all,

by the foot of Pharaoh! There's an oath! How many water-

bearers

shall you hear swear such an oath? O, I have a guest—he teaches me-he does swear the legiblest of any man christened: By St.

George! the foot of Pharaoh! the body of me! as I am a gentleman

and a soldier! such dainty oaths! and withal he does take this same

filthy roguish tobacco, the finest and cleanliest! it would do a

man good to see the fumes come forth at's tonnels.—Well, he owes

me forty shillings, my wife lent him out of her purse, by sixpence

at a time, besides his lodging: I would I had it! I shall have it,

he says, the next action. Helterskelter, hang sorrow, care'll kill

a cat, up-tails all, and a louse for the hangman.

[Exit.]

SCENE IV.-A Room in COB'S House.

BOBADILL discovered lying on a bench.

Bob. Hostess, hostess!

Enter TIB.

Tib. What say you, sir?

Bob. A cup of thy small beer, sweet hostess.

Tib. Sir, there's a gentleman below would speak with you.

Bob. A gentleman! 'odso, I am not within.

Tib. My husband told him you were, sir.

Bob. What a plague-what meant he?

Mat. [below.] Captain Bobadill!

Bob. Who's there!-Take away the bason, good hostess;—Come up, sir.

Tib. He would desire you to come up, cleanly house, here!

Enter MATHEW.

Mat. Save you, sir; save you, captain!

Bob. Gentle master Mathew! Is it you, sir? down.

Mat. Thank you, good captain; you may see I am somewhat audacious.

Bob. Not so, sir. I was requested to supper last night by a sort of gallants, where you were wished for, and drunk to, I assure you.

Mat. Vouchsafe me, by whom, good captain?

Bob. Marry, by young Wellbred, and others.—Why, hostess, stool

here for this gentleman.

Mat. No haste, sir, 'tis very well.

Bob. Body O' me! it was so late ere we parted last night, I can
scarce open my eyes yet; I was but new risen, as you came; how
passes the day abroad, sir? you can tell.

Mat. Faith, some half hour to seven; Now, trust me, you have an
exceeding fine lodging here, very neat, and private.

Bob. Ay, sir: sit down, I pray you. Master Mathew, in any case
possess no gentlemen of our acquaintance with notice of my
lodging.

Mat. Who? I, sir; no.

Bob. Not that I need to care who know it, for the cabin is
convenient; but in regard I would not be too popular, and
generally
visited, as some are.

Mat. True, captain, I conceive you.

Bob. For, do you see, sir, by the heart of valour in me, except it
be to some peculiar and choice spirits, to whom I am
extraordinarily engaged, as yourself, or so, I could not extend
thus far.

Mat. O Lord, sir! I resolve so.

Bob. I confess I love a cleanly and quiet privacy, above all the
tumult and roar of fortune. What new book have you there?
What! Go
by, Hieronymo?

Mat. Ay: did you ever see it acted? Is't not well penned?

[While Master Mathew reads, Bobadill makes himself ready.

Bob. Well penned! I would fain see all the poets of these times
pen
such another play as that was: they'll prate and swagger, and
keep
a stir of art and devices, when, as I am a gentleman, read 'em,

they are the most shallow, pitiful, barren fellows, that live upon the: face of the earth again.

Mat. Indeed here are a number of fine speeches in this book. O eyes, no eyes, but fountains fraught with tears! there's a conceit! fountains fraught with tears! O life, no life, but lively form of death! another. O world, no world, but mass of public wrongs! a third. Confused and fill'd with murder and misdeeds! a fourth. O,

the muses! Is't not excellent? Is't not simply the best that ever you heard, captain? Ha! how do you like it?

Bob. 'Tis good.

Mat. To thee, the purest object to my sense,

The most refined essence heaven covers,

Send I these lines, wherein I do commence

The happy state of turtle-billing lovers.

If they prove rough, unpolish'd, harsh, and rude,

Haste made the waste: thus mildly I conclude.

Bob. Nay, proceed, proceed. Where's this?

Mat. This, sir! a toy of mine own, in my non-age; the infancy of my

muses. But when will you come and see my study? good faith, I can

shew you some very good things I have done of late.—That boot becomes your leg passing well, captain, methinks.

Bob. So, so; it's the fashion gentlemen now use.

Mat. Troth, captain, and now you speak of the fashion, master Wellbred's elder brother and I are fallen out exceedingly: This other day, I happened to enter into some discourse of a hanger, which, I assure you, both for fashion and workmanship, was most

peremptory beautiful and gentlemanlike: yet he condemned, and cried

it down for the most pied and ridiculous that ever he saw.

Bob. Squire Downright, the half brother, was't not?

Mat. Ay, sir, he.

Bob. Hang him, rook! he! why he-has no more judgment than a malt

horse: By St. George, I wonder you'd lose a thought upon such an

animal; the most peremptory absurd clown of Christendom, this day,

he is holden. I protest to you, as I am a gentleman and a soldier,

I ne'er changed with his like. By his discourse, he should eat

nothing but hay; he was born for the manger, pannier, or

pack-saddle. He has not so much as a good phrase in his belly, but

all old iron and rusty proverbs: a good commodity for some smith to

make hob-nails of.

Mat. Ay, and he thinks to carry it away with his manhood still,

where he comes: he brags he will give me the bastinado, as I hear.

Bob. How! he the bastinado! how came he by that word, trow?

Mat. Nay, indeed, he said cudgel me; I termed it so, for my more

grace.

Bob. That may be: for I was sure it was none of his word; but when,

when said he so?

Mat. Faith, yesterday, they say; a young gallant, a friend of mine,

told me so.

Bob. By the foot of Pharaoh, an 'twere my case now, I should send

him a chartel presently. The bastinado! a most proper and

sufficient dependence, warranted by the great Caranza. Come hither,

you shall chartel him; I'll shew you a trick or two you shall kill

him with at pleasure; the first stoccata, if you will, by this air.

Mat. Indeed, you have absolute knowledge in the mystery, I have

heard, sir.

Bob. Of whom, of whom, have you heard it, I beseech you?

Mat. Troth, I have heard it spoken of divers, that you have very rare, and un-in-one-breath-utterable skill, sir.

Bob. By heaven, no, not I; no skill in the earth; some small rudiments in the science, as to know my time, distance, or so. I have professed it more for noblemen and gentlemen's use, than mine own practice, I assure you.—Hostess, accommodate us with another bed-staff here quickly. Lend us another bed-staff—the woman does not understand the words of action.—Look you, sir: exalt not your point above this state, at any hand, and let your poniard maintain your defence, thus:—give it the gentleman, and leave us. [Exit Tib.] So, sir. Come on: O, twine your body more about, that you may fall to a more sweet, comely, gentlemanlike guard; so! indifferent: hollow your body more, sir, thus: now, stand fast O' your left leg, note your distance, keep your due proportion of time—oh, you disorder your point most i rregularly.

Mat. How is the bearing of it now, sir?

Bob. O, out of measure ill: a well-experienced hand would pass upon you at pleasure.

Mat. How mean you, sir, pass upon me?

Bob. Why, thus, sir,—make a thrust at me—[Master Mathew pushes at Bobadill] come in upon the answer, control your point, and make a full career at the body: The best-practised gallants of the time name it the passado; a most desperate thrust, believe it.

Mat. Well, come, sir.

Bob. Why, you do not manage your weapon with any facility or grace

to invite me. I have no spirit to play with you; your dearth of
judgment renders you tedious.

Mat. But one venue, sir.

Bob. Venue! fie; the most gross denomination as ever I heard: O,
the stoccata, while you live, sir; note that.—Come, put on your
cloke, and we'll go to some private place where you are
acquainted;
some tavern, or so—and have a bit. I'll send for one of these
fencers, and he shall breathe you, by my direction; and then I
will
teach you your trick: you shall kill him with it at the first, if
you please. Why, I will learn you, by the true judgment of the
eye,
hand, and foot, to control any enemy's point in the world.
Should
your adversary confront you with a pistol, 'twere nothing, by
this
hand! you should, by the same rule, control his bullet, in a line,
except it were hail shot, and spread. What money have you
about
you, master Mathew?

Mat. Faith, I have not past a two shilling or so.

Bob. 'Tis somewhat with the least; but come; we will have a
bunch
of radish and salt to taste our wine, and a pipe of tobacco to
close the orifice of the stomach: and then we'll call upon young
Wellbred: perhaps we shall meet the Corydon his brother there,
and
put him to the question.

Every Man in His Humour Summary and Analysis of Act I

Summary

Prologue

The speaker acknowledges that there are many poets, but the
poet whose work the audience is to see today is a singular one. He
has no Chorus; no "creaking throne comes down" (7); no bullets or

roiling drums disrupt the scene. Instead, he will use the language and write of the deeds of regular men, of the times they live in, of such errors "as you'll all confess / By laughing at them" (7). He reminds the audience to be wise, to be good with money, to not go where one is not wanted, and be temperate, moderate, and humble.

Scene 1

A servant enters. Master Stephen and <u>Knowell</u> are in the room, and Stephen introduces himself as the old man's next heir (if his cousin dies). Stephen is querulous and rude to the servant, and Knowell, his uncle, rebukes him and tells him to leave.

The servant asks if this is Master Knowell's house and Knowell says it is. The servant says he is here to deliver a letter from master <u>Wellbred</u>. Knowell is intrigued, and asks if Wellbred is a young man. The servant replies that he is, and master <u>Kitely</u> married his sister.

Knowell calls for his man, <u>Brainworm</u>, and has him take the servant out. When alone, Knowell comments that he knows the letter is for his son, Edward, but that he is also an "<u>Edward Knowell</u>" and he wants to see what Wellbred says about and to his son.

The letter calls for "Ned" to come join the fun, and says that Wellbred has presents for him, one being a rhymer and the other something he will not say any more about. Ned ought to leave his father alone and come visit him.

Knowell reads this and is offended that this "unhallow'd ruffian" should write "in such a scurrilous manner to a friend" (13). He rues that his son does not have better judgement and chose "petulant, jeering gamesters" (13) as his friends. He calls Brainworm again, and tells him to bring the letter to his son and not to say that Knowell already read it.

After Brainworm leaves, Knowell sighs that he will not get in his son's way, and he will let the "unbridled course of youth" (13) continue as it would. He can win more by love than by control, knowing that "force works on servile natures, not the free" (14).

Scene 2

Edward Knowell asks Brainworm if his father read the letter, and, if he did, what his face looked like. Brainworm says he did not see Knowell's face when he opened it.

Stephen enters and asks where the servant is who brought the letter. He is angry, and desirous of finding the man and trussing him up. Brainworm tells him to calm his choler.

Brainworm leaves and Edward Knowell laughs as he reads the letter. For a moment Stephen is worried that his cousin is laughing at *him*. Edward knows his father is a patient man but wishes this letter had come at a less patient time so he could just hear the end of it. He then sees his cousin and greets him.

Stephen is relieved he was not being laughed at. Edward teases him that he was, to Stephen's consternation. Edward then asks if he'd like to accompany him to a friend's place in the Old Jewry. Stephen is pleased and proclaims he'd accompany Edward twice as far as he asked.

Stephen asks if he can speak, and Edward theatrically says his face ought to speak for itself in its nobility and miraculous nature. Stephen is thrilled with this and states that he will be as melancholy, gentlemanly, and proud as he can be.

Scene 3

Mr. Matthew stands in the lane before Cob's house. Cob comes out and Matthew is surprised the water-bearer lives here, but Cob states that he has an ancient, princely lineage and can smell the ghosts of his ancestors. Matthew is impatient with him, and asks if there is a Captain Bobadil lodging nearby.

Cob replies that Bobadil is actually lodging here, which surprises Matthew. He thinks it a "base, obscure place" (19) for Bobadil. Cob shrugs and says nonetheless he is here, and if Matthew goes upstairs he will find him. He implies Bobadil was drunk, but when pressed, says he deals with water, not wine.

Matthew decides he must chasten Bobadil for staying here at such a place. Tib, Cob's wife, shows Matthew up to Bobadil.

After they are gone, Cob ruminates on Matthew. Cob sees him frequently at Kitely's where he pours water. Matthew is in love with Bridget, Cob's master's sister. There one can hear Matthew reading "abominable, vile . . . rascally verses . . . and speaking of interludes, 'twill make a man burst to hear him" (20). Matthew is not the only one who annoys Cob, though; he also scoffs at his guest Bobadil, who owes his wife forty shillings and smokes "filthy, roguish tobacco" (20).

Scene 4

Bobadil is lying on his bench. Tib enters and tells him a gentleman is here to see him. Bobadil tells her to tell the man he is not here, but Tib says Cob already said he was upstairs. Bobadil curses.

Matthew enters the room. Bobadil graciously asks him to sit, and says he was at a gathering of Wellbred's last night where they spoke of Matthew and toasted him. He groans that he got home very late and is only newly risen. He asks if Matthew would refrain from telling people where he is lodging, as he does not want too many visitors. Matthew agrees with alacrity.

Bobadil asks Matthew what volume he carries and sees it is Thomas Kyd's *Spanish Tragedy*. Both men exult over it and Matthew quotes a few lines. Matthew then asks if Bobadil will take a look at his own work—the "infancy of my Muses!" (22). He ventures a compliment on Bobadil's boot as well.

This makes Matthew then confess he is not on good terms with Wellbred's brother, Squire Downright, because the other day Matthew was discoursing on something and Downright criticized his work. Bobadil scoffs angrily that Downright has no wisdom whatsoever, no "good phrases" (23) in him, and he is better built for the manger.

Matthew adds that Downright bragged he would give him a bastinado (beating), a word that Bobadil is surprised Downright would use. Matthew said *he* used it for more color. Bobadil says they will send over the chartel, the written stipulations between two adversaries, and he will teach Matthew what he needs to know to best Downright.

At Bobadil's command, Tib brings another bedstaff. Bobadil shows Matthew how to move about and make thrusts with his makeshift sword. Bobadil becomes annoyed at Matthew's "facility or grace" (24), and says they will stop. He says they will go have food and drink and a bit of tobacco, and he will tell Matthew what he needs to know to "control any enemy's point i' the world" (24).

Analysis

Ben Jonson is known for his pioneering "comedy of humours," which consists of *Every Man in His Humour*, *Every Man Out of His Humor*, *Volpone*, and more. In these comedies, characters are driven by one humour more than others, meaning their behavior tends toward rashness or anger or jealousy or melancholy depending on which humour predominates (see "Other" in this study guide for more information on the humours). *Every Man in His Humour* is the first of such works, lauded by critics and audiences for its astute and amusing look at man's foibles and motivations as well as its engagement with such themes as what good poetry and drama are, class and gender, and youth v. old age. Jonson's prologue sets out his goals for the play, which consist of avoiding hyperbole and histrionics to focus on the way real people live and speak and think. The narrator claims to show "an image of the times" and "sport with human follies, not with crimes" (7). He encourages the audience to behave rationally and pragmatically, which he will reinforce by bringing out characters who most decidedly *do not*. Critic A. Richard Dutton explains that *Every Man in His Humour* is part of Jonson's turn to more "realistic depiction," which naturally "relinquished . . . loudly proclaimed moral purposes." He strives for "an increased psychological realism," accomplished through "local and verbal realism—familiar settings, topical allusions, and a wider use of colloquial idioms."

With this humours comedy, Jonson seeks to (gently, and wittily) condemn certain traits. Dutton writes that in this play Jonson "reveals a fully-engaged concern for humanity, for a sane and rational society, in his determination to ridicule and destroy manifestations of folly, which he regards as socially divisive and morally degenerate." Right from the beginning this is clear through almost every character who steps on the stage. Stephen is greedy, telling a servant he is his uncle's heir if his cousin Edward dies, and that he hopes he will. He picks a fight with the placid servant, going into a rage when he finds that the "whorson scanderbag / rogue" (15) left without getting a beating by his hand. He is inordinately proud of his dress, asking Brainworm to compliment him on his leg and silk hose.

As for Knowell, he knowingly reads a letter addressed to his son and makes certain conclusions about his son and his son's friends. He does exhibit a bit of rationality as he tells himself to be patient and modest because "There is a way of winning, more by love, / And urging of modesty, than fear" (14), but he will soon abandon such counsels to himself and seek to confront his son about his putative behavior.

Matthew and Bobadil join Stephen as being some of the most obnoxious characters in the text. Both are braggarts, Matthew about his poetry (which we later learn isn't even his) and Bobadil about his fighting skills. When Matthew says Squire Downright criticized his poetry, Bobadil launches into a scourge of the man and promises Matthew "you shall kill him with at pleasure" (23). We also learn from Cob that Bobadil has borrowed money and not paid it back. These characters' foibles and absurdities will only grow more conspicuous as the play continues.

The topic of poetry is ubiquitous in the text. Matthew, as stated, believes himself a great poet and loves to try and impress women with his verse. Cob calls Matthew's work "abominable, vile" and "rascally" (20). Bobadil glorifies his work but clearly has no idea what he's talking about. Later Edward and Wellbred will rib him for it, while Downright will roll his eyes and say he'd rather be in the stocks than have to listen to it. Knowell seems worried that his son is interested in poetry, but Edward has no overweening hubris regarding his own abilities. At the end of the play Clement discovers that Matthew does not write his own words but cribs from others, and punishes him by burning his papers. He concludes by suggesting that good poets are not common, certainly something the audience would agree with after having the pleasure of listening to Jonson's work.

ACT II

SCENE I.-The Old Jewry. A Hall in KITELY'S House.

Enter KITELY, CASH, and DOWNRIGHT.

Kit. Thomas, come hither.
There lies a note within upon my desk;
Here take my key: it is no matter neither.—-
Where is the boy?

Cash. Within, sir, in the warehouse.

Kit. Let him tell over straight that Spanish gold,
And weigh it, with the pieces of eight. Do you
See the delivery of those silver stuffs
To Master Lucar: tell him, if he will,
He shall have the grograns, at the rate I told him,
And I. will meet him on the Exchange anon.

Cash. Good, sir. [*Exit.*

Kit. Do you see that fellow, brother Downright?

Dow. Ay, what of him?

Kit. He is a jewel, brother.
I took him of a child up at my door,
And christen'd him, gave him mine own name, Thomas:
Since bred him at the Hospital; where proving
A toward imp, I call'd him home, and taught him
So much, as I have made him my cashier,
And giv'n him, who had none, a surname, Cash:
And find him in his place so full of faith,
That I durst trust my life into his hands.

Dow. So would not I in any bastard's, brother,
As it is like he is, although I knew
Myself his father. But you said you had somewhat
To tell me, gentle brother: what is't, what is't?

Kit. Faith, I am very loath to utter it,
As fearing it may hurt your patience:
But that I know your judgment is of strength,
Against the nearness of affection—-

Dow. What need this circumstance? pray you, be direct.

Kit. I will not say how much I do ascribe
Unto your friendship, nor in what regard
I hold your love; but let my past behaviour,
And usage of your sister, [both] confirm
How well I have been affected to your—-
Dow. You are too tedious; come to the matter, the matter.
Kit. Then, without further ceremony, thus.
My brother Wellbred, sir, I know not how,
Of late is much declined in what he was,
And greatly alter'd in his disposition.
When he came first to lodge here in my house,
Ne'er trust me if I were not proud of him:
Methought he bare himself in such a fashion,
So full of man, and sweetness in his carriage,
And what was chief, it shew'd not borrow'd in him,
But all he did became him as his own,
And seem'd as perfect, proper, and possest,
As breath with life, or colour with the blood.
But now, his course is so irregular,
So loose, affected, and deprived of grace,
And he himself withal so far fallen off
From that first place, as scarce no note remains,
To tell men's judgments where he lately stood.
He's grown a stranger to all due respect,
Forgetful of his friends; and not content
To stale himself in all societies,
He makes my house here common as a mart,
A theatre, a public receptacle
For giddy humour, and deceased riot;
And here, as in a tavern or a stews,
He and his wild associates spend their hours,
In repetition of lascivious jests,
Swear, leap, drink, dance, and revel night by night,
Control my servants; and, indeed, what not?
Dow. 'Sdeins, I know not what I should say to him, in the whole

world! He values me at a crack'd three-farthings, for aught I see.
It will never out of the flesh that's bred in the bone. I have
told him enough, one would think, if that would serve; but
counsel
to him is as good as a shoulder of mutton to a sick horse. Well!
he knows what to trust to, for George: let him spend, and spend,
and domineer, till his heart ake; an he think to be relieved by
me, when he is got into one O' your city pounds, the counters,
he
has the wrong sow by the ear, i'faith; and claps his dish at the
wrong man's door: I'll lay my hand on my halfpenny, ere I part
with it to fetch him out, I'll assure him.'
Kit. Nay, good brother, let it not trouble you thus.
Dow. 'Sdeath! he mads me; I could eat my very spur leathers for
anger! But, why are you so tame? why do you not speak to him,
and
tell him how he disquiets your house?
Kit. O, there are divers reasons to dissuade me.
But, would yourself vouchsafe to travail in it
(Though but with plain and easy circumstance),
It would both come much better to his sense,
And savour less of stomach, or of passion.
You are his elder brother, and that title
Both gives and warrants your authority,
Which, by your presence seconded, must breed
A kind of duty in him, and regard:
Whereas, if I should intimate the least,
It would but add contempt to his neglect,
Heap worse on ill, make up a pile of hatred,
That in the rearing would come tottering down,
And in the ruin bury all our love.
Nay, more than this, brother; if I should speak,
He would be ready, from his heat of humour,
And overflowing of the vapour in him,
To blow the ears of his familiars

With the false breath of telling what disgraces,
And low disparagement's, I had put upon him.
Whilst they, sir, to relieve him in the fable,
Make their loose comments upon every word,
Gesture, or look, I use; mock me all over,
From my flat cap unto my shining shoes;
And, out of their impetuous rioting phant'sies,
Beget some slander that shall dwell with me.
And what would that be, think you? marry, this:
They would give out, because my wife is fair,
Myself but lately married; and my sister '.
Here sojourning a virgin in my house,
That I were jealous I—-nay, as sure as death,
That they would say: and, how that I had quarrell'd,
My brother purposely, thereby to find
An apt pretext to banish them my house.
Dow. Mass, perhaps so; they're like enough to do it.
Kit. Brother, they would, believe it; so should I,
Like one of these penurious quack-salvers,
But set the bills up to mine own disgrace,
And try experiments upon myself;
Lend scorn and envy opportunity
To stab my reputation and good name—
Enter Master MATHEW struggling with BOBADILL.
Mat. I will speak to him.
Bob. Speak to him! away! By the foot of Pharaoh, you shall not! you
shall not do him that grace.—The time of day to you, gentleman O'
the house. Is master Wellbred stirring?
Dow. How then? what should he do?
Bob. Gentleman of the house, it is to you: is he within, sir?
Kit. He came not to his lodging to-night, sir, I assure you.
Dow. Why, do you hear? you!
Bob. The gentleman citizen hath satisfied me;

I'll talk to no scavenger. *[Exeunt Bob. and Mat.*

Dow. How! scavenger! stay, sir, stay!

Kit. Nay, brother Downright.

Dow. 'Heart! stand you away, an you love me.

Kit. You shall not follow him now, I pray you, brother, good faith you shall not; I will overrule you.

Dow. Ha! scavenger! well, go to, I say little: but, by this good day (God forgive me I should swear), if I put it up so, say I am the rankest cow that ever pist. 'Sdeins, an I swallow this, I'll ne'er draw my sword in the sight of Fleet-street again while I live; I'll sit in a barn with madge-howlet, and catch mice first. Scavenger! heart!—and I'll go near to fill that huge tumbrel-slop of yours with somewhat, an I have good luck: your Garagantua breech

cannot carry it away so.

Kit. Oh, do not fret yourself thus: never think on't.

Dow. These are my brother's consorts, these! these are his camerades, his walking mates! he's a gallant, cavaliero too, right hangman cut! Let me not live, an I could not find in my heart

to swinge the whole gang of 'em, one after another, and begin with

him first. I am grieved it should be said he is my brother, and take these courses: Well, as he brews, so shall he drink, for George, again. Yet he shall hear on't, and that tightly too, an I live, i'faith.

Kit. But, brother, let your reprehension, then,
Run in an easy current, not o'er high
Carried with rashness, or devouring choler;
But rather use the soft persuading way,
Whose powers will work more gently, and compose
The imperfect thoughts you labour to reclaim;
More winning, than enforcing the consent.

Dow. Ay, ay, let me alone for that, I warrant you.

Kit. How now! [Bell rings.] Oh, the bell rings to breakfast.

Brother, I pray you go in, and bear my wife company till I come;
I'll but give order for some despatch of business to my servants.
[Exit Downright. Enter COB, with his tankard.
Kit. What, Cob! our maids will have you by the back, i'faith, for
coming so late this morning.
Cob. Perhaps so, sir; take heed somebody have not them by the
belly,
    for walking so late in the evening. *[Exit.*
Kit. Well; yet my troubled spirit's somewhat eased,
Though not reposed in that security
As I could wish: but I must be content,
Howe'er I set a face on't to the world.
Would I had lost this finger at a venture,
So Wellbred had ne'er lodged within my house.
Why't cannot be, where there is such resort
Of wanton gallants, and young revellers,
That any woman should be honest long.
Is't like, that factious beauty will preserve
The public weal of chastity unshaken,
When such strong motives muster, and make head
Against her single peace? No, no: beware.
When mutual appetite doth meet to treat,
And spirits of one kind and quality
Come once to parley in the pride of blood,
It is no slow conspiracy that follows.
Well, to be plain, if I but thought the time
Had answer'd their affections, all the world
Should not persuade me but I were a cuckold.
Marry, I hope they have not got that start;
For opportunity hath balk'd them yet,
And shall do still, while I have eyes and ears
To attend the impositions of my heart.
My presence shall be as an iron bar,
'Twixt the conspiring motions of desire:
Yea, every look or glance mine eye ejects

Shall check occasion, as one doth his slave,
When he forgets the limits of prescription.
Enter Dame KITELY and BRIDGET.
Dame K. Sister Bridget, pray you fetch down the rose-water,
above in the closet.—-
[Exit Bridget.
Sweet-heart, will you come in to breakfast?
Kit. An she have overheard me now!—-
Dame K. I pray thee, good muss, we stay for you.
Kit. By heaven, I would not for a thousand angels.
Dame K. What ail you, sweet-heart? are you not well? speak, good

muss.
Kit. Troth my head akes extremely on a sudden.
Dame K. [putting her hand to his forehead.] O, the Lord!
Kit. How now! What?
DameK. Alas, how it burns! Muss, keep you warm; good truth it is

this new disease. There's a number are troubled withal. For love's

sake, sweetheart, come in, out of the air.
Kit. How simple, and how subtle are her answers!
A new disease, and many troubled with it?
Why true; she heard me, all the world to nothing.
Dame K. I pray thee, good sweet-heart, come in; the air will do you

harm, in troth.
Kit. The air! she has me in the wind.—Sweet-heart, I'll come to
you presently; 'twill away, I hope.
Dame K. Pray Heaven it do. *[Exit.*
Kit. A new disease! I. know not, new or old,
But it may well be call'd poor mortals' plague;
For, like a pestilence, it doth infect
The houses of the brain. First it begins
Solely to work upon the phantasy,

Filling her seat with such pestiferous air,
As soon corrupts the judgment; and from thence,
Sends like contagion to the memory:
Still each to other giving the infection.
Which as a subtle vapour spreads itself
Confusedly through every sensive part,
Till not a thought or motion in the mind
Be free from the black poison of suspect.
Ah! but what misery is it to know this?
Or, knowing it, to want the mind's erection
In such extremes? Well, I will once more strive,
In spite of this black cloud, myself to be,
And shake the fever off that thus shakes me. *[Exit.*

SCENE II.—-Moorfields.

Enter BRAINWORM disguised like a maimed Soldier.

Brai. 'Slid, I cannot choose but laugh to see myself translated
thus, from a poor creature to a creator; for now must I create an
intolerable sort of lies, or my present profession loses the grace:
and yet the lie, to a man of my coat, is as ominous a fruit as the
fico. O, sir, it holds for good polity ever, to have that outwardly
in vilest estimation, that inwardly is most dear to us: so much for
my borrowed shape. Well, the troth is, my old master intends to
follow my young master, dry-foot, over Moorfields to London,
this
morning; now, I knowing of this hunting-match, or rather
conspiracy,
and to insinuate with my young master (for so must we that are
blue
waiters, and men of hope and service do, or perhaps we may
wear
motley at the year's end, and who wears motley, you know),
have got
me afore in this disguise, determining here to lie in ambuscado,
and intercept him in the mid-way. If I can but get his cloke, his
purse, and his hat, nay, any thing to cut him off, that is, to stay

his journey, Veni, vidi, vici, I may say with captain Caesar, I am made for ever, i'faith. Well, now I must practise to get the true garb of one of these lance-knights, my arm here, and my—Odso! my young master, and his cousin, master Stephen, as I am true counterfeit man of war, and no soldier!

Enter E. KNOWELL and STEPHEN.

E. Know. So, sir! and how then, coz?

Step. 'Sfoot! I have lost my purse, I think.

E. Know. How! lost your purse? where? when had you it?

Step. I cannot tell; stay.

Brai. 'Slid, I am afraid they will know me: would I could get by them!

E. Know. What, have you it?

Step. No; I think I was bewitched, I— [*Cries.*

E. Know. Nay, do not weep the loss: hang it, let it go.

Step. Oh, it's here: No, an it had been lost, I had not cared, but for a jet ring mistress Mary sent me.

E. Know. A jet ring! O the poesie, the poesie?

Step. Fine, i'faith.

Though Fancy sleep,

My love is deep.

Meaning, that though I did not fancy her, yet she loved me dearly.

E. Know. Most excellent!

Step. And then I sent her another, and my poesie was,

The deeper the sweeter,

I'll be judg'd by St. Peter.

E. Know. How, by St. Peter? I do not conceive that.

Step. Marry, St. Peter, to make up the metre.

E. Know. Well, there the saint was your good patron, he help'd you at your need; thank him, thank him.

Brai. I cannot take leave on 'em so; I will venture, come what will. [Comes forward.] Gentlemen, please you change a few crowns

for a very excellent blade here? I am a poor gentleman, a soldier, one that, in the better state of my fortunes, scorned so mean a refuge; but now it is the humour of necessity to have it so. You seem to be gentlemen well affected to martial men, else I should rather die with silence, than live with shame: however, vouchsafe

to remember it is my want speaks, not myself; this condition agrees

not with my spirit—

E. Know. Where hast thou served?

Brai. May it please you, sir, in all the late wars of Bohemia, Hungary, Dalmatia, Poland, where not, sir? I have been a poor servitor by sea and land any time this fourteen years, and followed

the fortunes of the best commanders in Christendom. I was twice,

shot at the taking of Aleppo, once at the relief of Vienna; I have been at Marseilles, Naples, and the Adriatic gulf, a gentleman-slave in the gallies, thrice; where I was most dangerously shot in the head, through both the thighs; and yet, being thus maimed, I am void of maintenance, nothing left me but my

scars, the noted marks of my resolution.

Step. How will you sell this rapier, friend?

Brai. Generous sir, I refer it to your own judgment; you are a gentleman, give me what you please.

Step. True, I am a gentleman, I know that, friend; but what though!

I pray you say, what would you ask?

Brai. I assure you, the blade may become the side or thigh of the best prince in Europe.

E. Know. Ay, with a velvet scabbard, I think.

Step. Nay, an't be mine, it shall have a velvet scapbard, coz, that's flat; I'd not wear it, as it is, an you would give me an angel,

Brai. At your worship's pleasure, sir; nay, 'tis a most pure Toledo.

Step. I had rather it were a Spaniard. But tell me, what shall I give you for it? An it had a silver hilt

E. Know. Come, come, you shall not buy it: hold, there's a shilling, fellow; take thy rapier.

Step. Why, but I will buy it now, because you say so; and there's another shilling, fellow; I scorn to be out-bidden. What, shall I walk with a cudgel, like Higginbottom, and may have a rapier for money.

E. Know. You may buy one in the city.

Step. Tut! I'll buy this i' the field, so I will: I have a mind to't, because 'tis a field rapier. Tell me your lowest price.

E. Know. You shall not buy it, I. say.

Step. By this money, but I will, though I give more than 'tis worth.

E. Know. Come away, you are a fool.

Step. Friend, I am a fool, that's granted; but I'll have it, for that word's sake. Follow me for your money.

Brai. At your service, sir.

[Exeunt.

SCENE III.—-Another Part of Moorfields.

Enter KNOWELL.

Know. I cannot lose the thought yet of this letter,
Sent to my son; nor leave t' admire the change
Of manners, and the breeding of our youth
Within the kingdom, since myself was one—-
When I was young, he lived not in the stews
Durst have conceived a scorn, and utter'd it,
On a gray head; age was authority
Against a buffoon, and a man had then
A certain reverence paid unto his years,
That had none due unto his life: so much

The sanctity of some prevail'd for others.
But now we all are fallen; youth, from their fear,
And age, from that which bred it, good example.
Nay, would ourselves were not the first, even parents,
That did destroy the hopes in our own children;
Or they not learn'd our vices in their cradles,
And suck'd in our ill customs with their milk;
Ere all their teeth be born, or they can speak,
We make their palates cunning; the first words
We form their tongues with, are licentious jests:
Can it call whore? cry bastard? O, then, kiss it!
A witty child! can't swear? the father's darling!
Give it two plums. Nay, rather than't shall learn
No bawdy song, the mother herself will teach it!—-
But this is in the infancy, the days
Of the long coat; when it puts on the breeches,
It will put off all this: Ay, it is like,
When it is gone into the bone already!
No, no; this dye goes deeper than the coat,
Or shirt, or skin; it stains into the liver,
And heart, in some; and, rather than it should not,
Note what we fathers do! look how we live!
What mistresses we keep! at what expense,
In our sons' eyes! where they may handle our gifts,
Hear our lascivious courtships, see our dalliance,
Taste of the same provoking meats with us,
To ruin of our states! Nay, when our own
Portion is fled, to prey on the remainder,
We call them into fellowship of vice;
Bait 'em with the young chamber-maid, to seal,
And teach 'em all bad ways to buy affliction.
This is one path: but there are millions more,
In which we spoil our own, with leading them.
Well, I thank heaven, I never yet was he
That travell'd with my son, before sixteen,

To shew him the Venetian courtezans;
Nor read the grammar of cheating I had made,
To my sharp boy, at twelve; repeating still
The rule, Get money; still, get money, boy;
No matter by what means; money will do
More, boy, than my lord's letter. Neither have I
Drest snails or mushrooms curiously before him,
Perfumed my sauces, and taught him how to make them;
Preceding still, with my gray gluttony,
At all the ord'naries, and only fear'd
His palate should degenerate, not his manners.
These are the trade of fathers now; however,
My son, I hope, hath met within my threshold
None of these household precedents, which are strong,
And swift, to rape youth to their precipice.
But let the house at home be ne'er so clean
Swept, or kept sweet from filth, nay dust and cobwebs,
If he will live abroad with his companions,
In dung and leystals, it is worth a fear;
Nor is the danger of conversing less
Than all that I have mention'd of example.
Enter BRAIN WORM, disguised as before.
Brai. My master! nay, faith, have at you; I am flesh'd now, I have
sped so well. [Aside.] Worshipful sir, I beseech you, respect the
estate of a poor soldier; lam ashamed of this base course of
life,—God's my comfort—but extremity provokes me to't: what
remedy?
Know. I have not for you, now.
Brai. By the faith I bear unto truth, gentleman, it is no ordinary
custom in me, but only to preserve manhood. I protest to you, a
man
I have been: a man I may be, by your sweet bounty.
Know. Pray thee, good friend, be satisfied.
Brai. Good sir, by that hand, you may do the part of a kind

gentleman, in lending a poor soldier the price of two cans of beer,
  a matter of small value: the king of heaven shall pay you, and I
  shall rest thankful: Sweet worship—
  Know. Nay, an you be so importunate
  Brai. Oh, tender sir! need will have its course: I was not made to
  this vile use. Well, the edge of the enemy could not have abated
me
  so much: it's hard when a man hath served in his prince's cause,
  and be thus. [Weeps.] Honourable worship, let me derive a small
  piece of silver from you, it shall not be given in the course of
  time. By this good ground, I was fain to pawn my rapier last
night
  for a poor supper; I had suck'd the hilts long before, am a pagan
  else: Sweet honour—
  Know. Believe me, I am taken with some wonder,
  To think a fellow of thy outward presence,
  Should, in the frame and fashion of his mind,
  Be so degenerate, and sordid-base.
  Art thou a man? and sham'st thou not to beg,
  To practise such a servile kind of life?
  Why, were thy education ne'er so mean,
  Having thy limbs, a thousand fairer courses
  Offer themselves to thy election.
  Either the wars might still supply thy wants,
  Or service of some virtuous gentleman,
  Or honest labour; nay, what can I name,
  But would become thee better than to beg:
  But men of thy condition feed on sloth,
  As cloth the beetle on the dung she breeds in;
  Nor caring how the metal of your minds
  Is eaten with the rust of idleness.
  Now, afore me, whate'er he be, that should
  Relieve a person of thy quality,
  While thou insist'st in this loose desperate course,

I would esteem the sin not thine, but his.

Brai. Faith, sir, I would gladly find some other course, if so—-

Know. Ay, You'd gladly find it, but you will not seek it.

Brai. Alas, sir, where should a man seek? in the wars; there's no ascent by desert in these days; but—and for service, would it were as soon purchased, as wished for! the air's my comfort.—- [Sighs.]—-l know what I would say.

Know. What's thy name?

Brai. Please you, Fitz-Sword, sir.

Know. Fitz-Sword!

Say that a man should entertain thee now,

Wouldst thou be honest, humble, just, and true?

Brai. Sir, by the place and honour of a soldier—-

Know. Nay, nay, I like not these affected oaths; speak plainly, man, what think'st thou of my words?

Brai. Nothing, sir, but wish my fortunes were as happy as my service should be honest.

Know. Well, follow me; I'll prove thee, if thy deeds

Will carry a proportion to thy words. *[Exit.*

Brai. Yes, sir, straight; I'll but garter my hose. Oh that my belly were hoop'd now, for I am ready to burst with laughing! never was

bottle or bagpipe fuller. 'Slid, was there ever seen a fox in years to betray himself thus! now shall I be possest of all his counsels; and, by that conduit, my young master. Well, he is resolved to prove my honesty; faith, and I'm resolved to prove his patience: Oh, I shall abuse him intolerably. This small piece of service will bring him clean out of love with the soldier for ever. He will never come within the sign of it, the sight of a cassock, or a musket-rest again. He will hate the musters at Mile-end for it, to his dying day. It's no matter, let the world think me a bad counterfeit, if I cannot give him the slip at an instant: why, this is better than to have staid his journey: well, I'll follow him. Oh, how I long to be employed!

[Exit.

**Every Man in His Humour Summary and Analysis of Act II
Summary**

Act II

Scene 1

<u>Kitely</u>, his man <u>Cash</u>, and <u>Downright</u> enter. Kitely asks Cash to take care of a bit of his merchant business, and Cash accedes. After he leaves, Kitely tells Downright he took Cash in when he was a child and gave him his own first name, Thomas, and trusts him with his own life.

Downright listens politely but asks his brother-in-law what he said he had to tell him. Kitely is reluctant, trying Downright's patience. Kitely begins by saying Downright's brother, <u>Wellbred</u>, has declined of late. When he came to stay with Kitely, he was marked by sweetness and elegance, but now his "course is so irregular" (26). He is "loose, affected, and depriv'd of grace" (26). He seems a stranger, and makes Kitely's house common and tawdry, a place where "He and his wild associates spend their hours, / In repetition of lascivious jests, / Swear, leap, drink, dance, and revel night by night" (26).

Downright asks why Kitely thinks he would be any help. He has talked to Wellbred before, and "counsel to him is as good as a shoulder of mutton to a sick horse" (27). He suggests just letting the man do what he wants to do, and reap the consequences. He then asks why Kitely does not say something if he is so bothered. Kitely explains that Downright is Wellbred's elder brother and the title gives authority. Wellbred would feel a sense of duty if Downright spoke to him, but if Kitely did, then "He would be ready from his heat of humour" (27). He would be mocking and scornful and claim Kitely was jealous of him.

Before the men can continue, <u>Bobadil</u> and Matthew burst in. Bobadil tells Matthew he will not speak to Downright at the moment, and asks after Wellbred. Kitely replies that he did not come in. Bobadil and Mathew leave.

Downright is vexed at the appearance of Matthew, but Kitely implores him not to follow him. Downright cannot believe these men are his brother's friends; he wishes he could just get rid of them all. Kitely encourages him to calm down and not let himself be controlled by choler; instead, "rather use the soft persuading way, / Whose powers work more gently" (29).

A bell rings, and Kitely says it is breakfast. He says for Downright to go in and sit with his wife for now, and Downright exits.

Kitely reflects on his situation, wishing Wellbred had not lodged in his house. He thinks women cannot resist such "wanton gallants, and young revelers" (30), and is certain that he is being cuckolded. He plans to be like "an iron bar" between the "conspiring motions of desire" (30).

Dame Kitely and Bridget enter, and Dame Kitely tells her husband they've been waiting for him to begin their meal. He says his head aches and his wife is immediately solicitous. After the women leave, he grumbles to himself that he does have a disease—the "poor mortals' plague" which infects "the houses of the brain" (31). It begins in the mind, fills it with phantasy, and touches every thought and motion in the mind with "the black poison of suspect" (31).

Scene 2

Brainworm enters, disguised. He is pleased with his appearance and his plan, which is to intercept his young master before the old master arrives. He espies Edward and Stephen coming his way.

Stephen is telling Edward he seems to have lost his purse, but then discovers he still has it. it would be bad, he says, for he has a jet ring his mistress Mary sent him. He sent her poems in return.

Brainworm reveals himself to the men, and asks if they'd like to exchange a few crowns for a good blade he is selling. He introduces himself as a poor gentleman and soldier who is reduced to a state of poverty. Edward asks where he served, and Brainworm mentions a number of places and a number of times he was shot.

Stephen asks what he would sell the rapier for. Both Stephen and Edward are interested in it, and Brainworm assures them it is a real Toledo. Edward tells his cousin it will not be his, and hands

Brainworm a shilling. Stephen is angry that he was outbid, and the men argue. Stephen says he will pay more than it is worth, and gestures for Brainworm to follow him.

Scene 3

<u>Knowell</u> bitterly reflects on what the letter's tone and content suggests about youth today. He recalls how there was a time when age was authority, when an older man received reverence. Yet now, all are fallen—youth from their fear, and age from good example. He believes all have a role to play in this state of affairs, though, for parents make their children's "palates cunning" because "the first words / We form their tongues with are licentious jests!" (35). Children repeat words like "whore" and "bastard" and parents laugh and praise them.

Furthermore, Knowell bemoans, the way fathers live should be censured. The mistresses, the "lascivious courtships" (35), the bringing their sons into such things—this is problematic. There are so many ways that parents "spoil our own" (35), and it seems all children are taught is to get money. Knowell hopes he has done better by *his* son, but he is not sure.

Brainworm enters, disguised still as the soldier-beggar. He sycophantically asks for a bit of money and begins weeping dramatically, saying he had to part with his rapier. Knowell is disgusted by him and excoriates him for living this sort of life. He tells the disguised Brainworm that there are so many forms of honest labor he could be undertaking.

Brainworm replies that he would love to find another course, and Knowell replies sharply that he would love to *find* it, but not *seek* it. Knowell asks his name and Brainworm says he is "Fitz-Sword." Knowell asks Brainworm to work for him, and to follow him to see if Brainworm's deeds "will carry a proportion to thy words" (38).

After Knowell leaves, Brainworm starts laughing. He cannot believe this "fox" betrayed himself thusly. He knows that being Knowell's confidante will help him become "possess'd of all his counsels: and, by that conduit, my / young master" (38). He plans to "bring him clean out of love with the soldier for ever" and "abuse him intolerably" (38).

Analysis

The second major household in the play is that of Kitely. He and his wife reside with his sister, Bridget, and their visitor Wellbred (Dame Kitely's brother). Wellbred's presence means the presence of diverse young men, here to smoke and carouse with their friends. Kitely is frustrated with this, and asks Wellbred's older brother, Squire Downright, to intervene. Kitely's main reasons, as he tells Downright, are that Wellbred is no longer who he used to be—now he is "loose, affected, and depriv'd of grace" (26)—and that he has ruined Kitely's house—"He makes my house common, as a mart, / A theatre, a public receptacle / For giddy humour, and diseased riot" (26). A staid, rather dour man himself, Kitely cannot countenance how Wellbred and "his wild associates spend their hours, / In repetition of lascivious jests, / Swear, leap, drink, dance, and revel night by night" (26).

Perhaps more importantly, though, is that Kitely is desperately jealous of these men and assume his wife will fall prey to their advances. He doesn't tell this to Downright explicitly, preferring to say that he assumes he will be *called* jealous, but after Downright leaves, Kitely admits to himself that he does indeed feel the intense stirrings of jealousy permeating his mind—"like a pestilence, it doth infect / The houses of the brain . . . Till not a thought, or motion, in the mind, / Be free from the black poison of suspect" (31). Kitely's preponderant humor seems to be melancholy, as he convinces himself that his lovely wife cannot be faithful to him.

In this second act Brainworm begins to don his disguises. He intends to do so to show his loyalty to his young master, but he also knows there is more at stake. He says, "now must / I create an intolerable sort of lies, or my present profession / loses the grace" (32). He also must wear disguises to make his way in the world, and the money he gets from these encounters helps sustain him. His first disguise is that of a soldier-beggar, and he tricks Stephen into buying his sword, an otherwise unimportant blade that he claims is a Toledo.

Brainworm's stated desire to protect Edward from his father derives from Knowell's consternation over his son's perceived dissolute behavior. In a moving passage, Knowell wonders if he went wrong somewhere as a parent. He is perspicacious in his condemnation of the way fathers can corrupt their sons almost from the cradle with their curses, jests, flaunting of mistresses, advice to make money above all else, etc. He thinks he did a decent job, but worries nonetheless.

Knowell is like many parents and those of the older generation who think that the youth are corrupted, perhaps forgetting their own dalliances and adventures now that they are gray-haired. Knowell's words are a little pitiful and very universal in their suggestion of how the old in most places and most times view the young: "[I cannot] leave t'admire the change / Of manners, and the breeding of our youth, / Within the kingdom, since myself was one. / When I was young, he liv'd not in the stews / Durst have conceiv'd a scorn, and utter'd it, / On a grey head; age was authority / Against a buffoon: and a man had, then, / A certain reverence paid unto his years, / That had none due unto his life . . . But, now, we all are fall'n; youth, from their fear, / And age, from that which bred it, good example" (34). Scholar A. Richard Dutton suggests that there's even more in Knowell's characterization, writing, "Old Kno'well is not simply an abstract 'humour'—he is a manifestation of the London in the play, where suspicious, rather cynical old age is out of tune with regenerative nature and society, represented here by the playful vitality of the young men."

ACT III

SCENE I.-The Old Jewry. A Room in the Windmill Tavern.
Enter Master MATHEW, WELLBRED, and BOBADILL.
Mat. Yes, faith, sir, we were at your lodging to seek you too.
Wel; Oh, I came not there to-night.
Bob. Your brother delivered us as much.

Wel. Who, my brother Downright?

Bob. He. Mr. Wellbred, I know not in what kind you hold me; but let

me say to you this: as sure as honour, I esteem it So much out of

the sunshine of reputation, to throw the least beam of regard

upon

such a—

Wel. Sir, I must hear no ill words of my brother.

Bob. I protest to you, as I have a thing to be saved about me, I

never saw any gentlemanlike part—

Wel. Good captain, faces about to some other discourse.

Bob. With your leave, sir, an there were no more men living

upon

th' face of the earth, I should not fancy him, by St. George!

Mat. Troth, nor I; he is of a rustical cut, I know not how: he doth

not carry himself like a gentleman of fashion.

Wel. Oh, master Mathew, that's a grace peculiar but to a few,

quos

aequus amavit Jupiter.

Mat. I understand you, sir.

Wel. No question, you do,—or do you not, sir.

Enter E. KNOWELL and Master STEPHEN.

Ned Knowell! by my soul, welcome: how dost thou, sweet spirit,

my

genius? 'Slid, I shall love Apollo and the mad Thespian girls the

better, while I live, for this, my dear Fury; now, I see there's

some love in thee. Sirrah, these be the two I writ to thee of: nay,

what a drowsy humour is this now! why dost thou not speak?

E. Know. Oh, you are a fine gallant; you sent me a rare letter.

Wel. Why, was't not rare?

E. Know. Yes, I'll be sworn, I was ne'er guilty of reading the

like; match it in all Pliny, or Symmachus's epistles, and I'll have

my judgment burn'd in the ear for a rogue: make much of thy

vein,

for it is inimitable. But I marle what camel it was, that had the

carriage of it; for, doubtless, he was no ordinary beast that
brought it.

Wel. Why?

E. Know. Why, say'st thou! why, dost thou think that any reasonable

creature, especially in the morning, the sober time of the day too,

could have mistaken my father for me?

Wel. 'Slid, you jest, I hope.

E. Know. Indeed, the best use we can turn it to, is to make a jest
on't; now: but I'll assure you, my father had the full view of your
flourishing style some hour before I saw it.

Wel. What a dull slave was this! but, sirrah, what said he to it,
i'faith?

E. Know. Nay, I know not what he said; but I have a shrewd guess
what he thought.

Wel. What, what?

E. Know. Marry, that thou art some strange, dissolute young fellow,

and I—a grain or two better, for keeping thee company.

Wel. Tut! that thought is like the moon in her last quarter, 'twill
change shortly: but, sirrah, I pray thee be acquainted with my two

hang-by's here; thou wilt take exceeding pleasure in them if thou
hear'st 'em once go; my wind-instruments; I'll wind them up—But

what strange piece of silence is this, the sign of the Dumb Man?

E. Know. Oh, sir, a kinsman of mine, one that may make your music

the fuller, an he please; he has his humour, sir.

Wel. Oh, what is't, what is't?

E. Know. Nay, I'll neither do your judgment nor his folly that
wrong, as to prepare your apprehension: I'll leave him to the mercy

of your search; if you can take him, so!

Wel. Well, captain Bobadill, master Mathew, pray you know this gentleman here; he is a friend of mine, and one that will deserve your affection. I know not your name, sir, [to Stephen.] but I shall be glad of any occasion to render me more familiar to you.

Step. My name is master Stephen, sir; I am this gentleman's own cousin, sir; his father is mine uncle, sir: I am somewhat melancholy, but you shall command me, sir, in whatsoever is incident to a gentleman.

Bob. Sir, I must tell you this, I am no general man; but for master Wellbred's sake, (you may embrace it at what height of favour you please,) I do communicate with you, and conceive you to be a gentleman of some parts; I love few words.

E. Know. And I fewer, sir; I have scarce enough to thank you.

Mat. But are you, indeed, sir, so given to it?

Step. Ay, truly, sir, I am mightily given to melancholy.

Mat. Oh, it's your only fine humour, sir: your true melancholy breeds your perfect fine wit, sir. I am melancholy myself, diver times, sir, and then do I no more but take pen and paper, presently, and overflow you half a score, or a dozen of sonnets at a sitting.

E. Know. Sure he utters them then by the gross. [Aside.

Step. Truly, sir, and I love such things out of measure.

E. Know. I'faith, better than in measure, I'll undertake.

Mat. Why, I pray you, sir, make use of my study, it's at your service.

Step. I thank you, sir, I shall be bold I warrant you; have you a stool there to be melancholy upon?

Mat. That I have, sir, and some papers there of mine own doing, at idle hours, that you'll say there's some sparks of wit in 'em, when you see them,

Wel. Would the sparks would kindle once, and become a fire amongst them! I might see self-love burnt for her heresy. [Aside.

Step. Cousin, is it well? am I melancholy enough?

E. Know, Oh ay, excellent.

Wel. Captain Bobadill, why muse you so?

E. Know. He is melancholy too.

Bob. Faith, sir, I was thinking of a most honourable piece of service, was performed to-morrow, being St. Mark's day, shall be some ten years now.

E. Know. In what place, captain?

Bob. Why, at the beleaguering of Strigonium, where, in less than two hours, seven hundred resolute gentlemen, as any were in Europe,

lost their lives upon the breach. I'll tell you, gentlemen, it was the first, but the best leaguer that ever I beheld with these eyes, except the taking in of—what do you call it?—last year, by the Genoways; but that, of all other, was the most fatal and dangerous

exploit that ever I was ranged in, since I first bore arms before the face of the enemy, as I am a gentleman and a soldier!

Step. So! I had as lief as an angel I could swear as well as that gentleman.

E. Know. Then, you were a servitor at both, it seems; at Strigonium, and what do you call't?

Bob. O lord, sir! By St. George, I was the first man that entered the breach; and had I not effected it with resolution, I had been slain if I had had a million of lives.

E. Know. 'Twas pity you had not ten; a cat's and your own, i'faith.

But, was it possible?

Mat. Pray you mark this discourse, sir.

Step. So I do.

Bob. I assure' you, upon my reputation, 'tis true, and you shall confess.

E. Know. You must bring me to the rack, first. [Aside.

Bob. Observe me judicially, sweet sir; they had planted me three demi-culverins just in the mouth of the breach; now, sir, as we were to give on, their master-gunner (a man of no mean skill and mark, you must think,) confronts me with his linstock, ready to give fire; I, spying his intendment, discharged my petronel in his bosom, and with these single arms, my poor rapier, ran violently upon the Moors that guarded the ordnance, and put them pell-mell,

to the sword.

Wel. To the sword! To the rapier, captain.

E. Know. Oh, it was a good figure observed, sir: but did you all this, captain, without hurting your blade?

Bob. Without any impeach O' the earth: you shall perceive, sir. [Shews his rapier.] It is the most fortunate weapon that ever rid on poor gentleman's thigh. Shall I tell you, sir? You talk of Morglay, Excalibur, Durindana, or so; tut! I lend no credit to that is fabled of 'em: I know the virtue of mine own, and therefore I dare the boldlier maintain it.

Step. I marle whether it be a Toledo or no.

Bob. A most perfect Toledo, I assure you, sir. Step. I have a countryman of his here.

Mat. Pray you, let's see, sir; yes, faith, it is.

Bob. This a Toledo! Pish!

Step. Why do you pish, captain?

Bob. A Fleming, by heaven! I'll buy them for a guilder a-piece. An

I would have a thousand of them.

E. Know. How say you, cousin? I told you thus much.

Wel. Where bought you it, master Stephen?

Step. Of a scurvy rogue soldier: a hundred of lice go with him! He

swore it was a Toledo.

Bob. A poor provant rapier, no better.

Mat. Mass, I think it be indeed, now I look on't better.

E. Know. Nay, the longer you look on't, the worse. Put it up, put it up.

Step. Well, I will put it up; but by—I have forgot the captain's oath, I thought to have sword! by it,—an e'er I meet him—

Wel. O, it is past help now, sir; you must have patience.

Step. Whoreson, coney-hatching rascal! I could eat the very hilts for anger.

E. Know. A sign of good digestion; you have an ostrich stomach, Cousin.

Step. A stomach! would I had him here, you should see an I had a

stomach.

Wel. It's better as it is.—Come, gentlemen, shall we go?

Enter BRAINWORM, disguised as before.

E. Know. A miracle, cousin; look here, look here!

Step. Oh—'Od's lid. By your leave, do you know me, sir?

Brai. Ay, sir, I know you by sight.

Step. You sold me a rapier, did you not?

Brai. Yes, marry did I, sir.

Step. You said it was a Toledo, ha?

Brai. True, I did so.

Step. But it is none.

Brai. No, sir, I confess it; it is none.

Step. Do you confess it? Gentlemen, bear witness, he has confest it:—'Od's will, an you had not confest it.===

E. Know. Oh, cousin, forbear, forbear! Step. Nay, I have done, cousin.

Wel. Why, you have done like a gentleman; he has confest it, what

would you more?

Step. Yet, by his leave, he is a rascal, under his favour, do you see.

E. Know. Ay, by his leave, he is, and under favour: a pretty piece of civility! Sirrah, how dost thou like him?

Wel. Oh, it's a most precious fool, make much on him: I can compare

him to nothing more happily than a drum; for every one may play upon him.

E. Know. No, no, a child's whistle were far the fitter.

Brai. Shall I intreat a word with you?

E. Know. With me, sir? you have not another Toledo to sell, have you?

Brai. You are conceited, sir: Your name is Master Knowell, as I take it?

E. Know. You are in the right; you mean not to proceed in the catechism, do you?

Brai. No, sir; I am none of that coat.

E. Know. Of as bare a coat, though: well, say, sir.

Brai. *[taking E. Know. aside.]* Faith, sir, I am but servant to the drum extraordinary, and indeed, this smoky varnish being washed off, and three or four patches removed, I appear your worship's in reversion, after the decease of your good father, Brainworm.

E. Know. Brainworm'! 'Slight, what breath of a conjurer hath blown thee hither in this shape?

Brai. The breath of your letter, sir, this morning; the same that blew you to the Windmill, and your father after you.

E. Know. My father!

Brai. Nay, never start, 'tis true; he has followed you over the fields by the foot, as you would do a hare in the snow.

E. Know. Sirrah Wellbred, what shall we do, sirrah? my father is come over after me.

Wel. Thy father! Where is he?

Brai. At justice Clement's house, in Coleman-street, where he but stays my return; and then—

Wel. Who's this? Brainworm!

Brai. The same, sir.

Wel. Why how, in the name of wit, com'st thou transmuted thus?

Brai. Faith, a device, a device; nay, for the love of reason,
gentlemen, and avoiding the danger, stand not here; withdraw,
and
I'll tell you all.
Wel. But art thou sure he will stay thy return?
Brai. Do I live, sir? what a question is that!
Wel. We'll prorogue his expectation, then, a little: Brainworm,
thou shalt go with us.—Come on, gentlemen.==-Nay, I pray thee,
sweet Ned, droop not; 'heart, an our wits be so wretchedly dull,
that one old plodding brain can outstrip us all, would we were
e'en
prest to make porters of, and serve out the remnant of our days
in
Thames-street, or at Custom-house key, in a civil war against the
carmen!
Brai. Amen, amen, amen, say I. [*Exeunt.*
SCENE II—-The Old Jewry. KITELY'S Warehouse.
Enter KITELY and CASH.
Kit. What says he, Thomas? did you speak with him?
Cash. He will expect you, sir, within this half hour.
Kit. Has he the money ready, can you tell?
Cash. Yes, sir, the money was brought in last night.
Kit. O, that is well; fetch me my cloak, my cloak!—- [*Exit Cash.*
Stay, let me see, an hour to go and come;
Ay, that will be the least; and then 'twill be
An hour before I can dispatch with him,
Or very near; well, I will say two hours.
Two hours! ha! things never dreamt of yet,
May be contrived, ay, and effected too,
In two hours' absence; well, I will not go.
Two hours! No, fleering Opportunity,
I will not give your subtilty that scope.
Who will not judge him worthy to be robb'd,
That sets his doors wide open to a thief,
And shews the felon where his treasure lies?

Again, what earthly spirit but will attempt
To taste the fruit of beauty's golden tree,
When leaden sleep seals up the dragon's eyes?
I will not go. Business, go by for once.
No, beauty, no; you are of too good caract,
To be left so, without a guard, or open,
Your lustre, too, 'll inflame at any distance,
Draw courtship to you, as a jet doth straws;
Put motion in a stone, strike fire from ice,
Nay, make a porter leap you with his burden.
You must be then kept up, close, and well watch'd,
For, give you opportunity, no quick-sand
Devours or swallows swifter! He that lends
His wife, if she be fair, or time or place,
Compels her to be false. I will not go!
The dangers are too many;—-and then the dressing
Is a most main attractive! Our great heads
Within this city never were in safety
Since our wives wore these little caps: I'll change 'em;
I'll change 'em straight in mine: mine shall no more
Wear three-piled acorns, to make my horns ake.
Nor will I go; I am resolved for that.
Re-enter CASH with a cloak.
Carry in my cloak again. Yet stay. Yet do, too:
I will defer going, on all occasions.
Cash. Sir, Snare, your scrivener, will be there with the bonds
Kit. That's true: fool on me! I had clean forgot it;
I must go. What's a clock?
Cash. Exchange-time, sir.
Kit.
'Heart, then will Wellbred presently be here too,
With one or other of his loose consorts.
I am a knave, if I know what to say,
What course to take, or which way to resolve.
My brain, methinks, is like an hour-glass,

Wherein my imaginations run like sands,
Filling up time; but then are turn'd and turn'd:
So that I know not what to stay upon,
And less, to put in act.—-It shall be so.
Nay, I dare build upon his secrecy,
He knows not to deceive me.—-Thomas!
Cash. Sir.
Kit. Yet now I have bethought me too, I will not.—-
Thomas, is Cob within?
Cash. I think he be, sir.
Kit.
But he'll prate too, there is no speech of him.
No, there were no man on the earth to Thomas,
If I durst trust him; there is all the doubt.
But should he have a clink in him, I were gone.
Lost in my fame for ever, talk for th' Exchange!
The manner he hath stood with, till this present,
Doth promise no such change: what should I fear then?
Well, come what will, I'll tempt my fortune once.
Thomas—-you may deceive me, but, I hope—-
Your love to me is more—-
Cash. Sir, if a servant's
Duty, with faith, may be call'd love, you are
More than in hope, you are possess'd of it.
Kit. I thank you heartily, Thomas: give me your hand:
With all my heart, good Thomas. I have, Thomas,
A secret to impart unto you—-but,
When once you have it, I must seal your lips up;
So far I tell you, Thomas.
Cash. Sir, for that—-
Kit. Nay, hear me out. Think I esteem you, Thomas,
When I will let you in thus to my private.
It is a thing sits nearer to my crest,
Than thou art 'ware of, Thomas; if thou should'st
Reveal it, but—-

Cash. How, I reveal it?
Kit. Nay,
I do not think thou would'st; but if thou should'st,
'Twere a great weakness.
Cash. A great treachery:
Give it no other name.
Kit. Thou wilt not do't, then?
Cash. Sir, if I do, mankind disclaim me ever!
Kit. He will not swear, he has some reservation,
Some conceal'd purpose, and close meaning sure;
Else, being urg'd so much, how should he choose
But lend an oath to all this protestation?
He's no precisian, that I'm certain of,
Nor rigid Roman Catholic: he'll play
At fayles, and tick-tack; I have heard him swear.
What should I think of it? urge him again,
And by some other way! I will do so.
Well, Thomas, thou hast sworn not to disclose:—-
Yes, you did swear?
Cash. Not yet, sir, but I will,
Please you—-
Kit. No, Thomas, I dare take thy word,
But, if thou wilt swear, do as thou think'st; good;
I am resolv'd without It; at thy pleasure.
Cash. By my soul's safety then, sir, I protest,
My tongue shall ne'er take knowledge of a word
Deliver'd me in nature of your trust.
Kit. It is too much; these ceremonies need not:
I know thy faith to be as firm as rock.
Thomas, come hither, near; we cannot be
Too private in this business. So it is,—-
Now he has sworn, I dare the safelier venture. *[Aside.*
I have of late, by divers observations—-
But whether his oath can bind him, yea, or no,
Being not taken lawfully? ha! say you?

I will ask council ere I do proceed:—— [*Aside.*
Thomas, it will be now too long to stay,
I'll spy some fitter time soon, or to-morrow.
Cash. Sir, at your pleasure.
Kit. I will think:-and, Thomas,
I pray you search the books 'gainst my return,
For the receipts 'twixt me and Traps.
Cash. I will, sir.
Kit. And hear you, if your mistress's brother, Wellbred,
Chance to bring hither any gentleman,
Ere I come back, let one straight bring me word.
Cash. Very well, sir.
Kit. To the Exchange, do you hear?
Or here in Coleman-street, to justice Clement's.
Forget it not, nor be not out of the way.
Cash. I will not, sir.
Kit. I pray you have a care on't.
Or, whether he come or no, if any other,
Stranger, or else; fail not to send me word.
Cash. I shall not, sir.
Kit. Be it your special business
Now to remember it.
Cash. Sir, I warrant you.
Kit. But, Thomas, this is not the secret, Thomas,
I told you of.
Cash. No, sir; I do suppose it.
Kit. Believe me, it is not.
Cash. Sir, I do believe you.
Kit. By heaven it is not, that's enough: but, Thomas,
I would not you should utter it, do you see,
To any creature living; yet I care not.
Well, I must hence. Thomas, conceive thus much;
It was a trial of you, when I meant
So deep a secret to you, I mean not this,
But that I have to tell you; this is nothing, this.

But, Thomas, keep this from my wife, I charge you,
Lock'd up in silence, midnight, buried here.—-
No greater hell than to be slave to fear. [*Exit.*
Cash. Lock'd up in silence, midnight, buried here!
Whence should this flood of passion, trow, take head? ha!
Best dream no longer of this running humour,
For fear I sink; the violence of the stream
Already hath transported me so far,
That I can feel no ground at all: but soft—-
Oh, 'tis our water-bearer: somewhat has crost him now.
Enter COB, hastily.
Cob. Fasting-days! what tell you me of fasting days? 'Slid, would
they were all on a light fire for me! they say the whole world
shall be consumed with fire one day, but would I had these
Ember-weeks and villanous Fridays burnt in the mean time, and
then—
Cash. Why, how now, Cob? what moves thee to this choler, ha?
Cob. Collar, master Thomas! I scorn your collar, I, sir; I am none
O' your cart-horse, though I carry and draw water. An you offer
to
ride me with your collar or halter either, I may hap shew you a
jade's trick, sir.
Cash. O, you'll slip your head out of the collar? why, goodman
Cob,
you mistake me.
Cob. Nay, I have my rheum, and I can be angry as well as
another,
sir.
Cash. Thy rheum, Cob! thy humour, thy humour—thou
misstak'st.
Cob. Humour! mack, I think it be so indeed; what is that
humour?
some rare thing, I warrant.
Cash. Marry I'll tell thee, Cob: it is a gentlemanlike monster,
bred in the special gallantry of our time, by affectation; and fed

by folly.

Cob. How! must it be fed?

Cash. Oh ay, humour is nothing if it be not fed: didst thou never hear that? it's a common phrase, feed my humour.

Cob. I'll none on it: humour, avaunt! I know you not, be gone! let who will make hungry meals for your monstership, it shall not be I.

Feed you, quoth he! 'slid, I have much ado to feed myself;

especially on these lean rascally days too; an't had been any other

day but a fasting-day—a plague on them all for me! By this light,

one might have done the commonwealth good service, and have drown'd

them all in the flood, two or three hundred thousand years ago. O,

I do stomach them hugely. I have a maw now, and 'twere for sir Bevis his horse, against them.

Cash. I pray thee, good Cob, what makes thee so out of love with fasting days?

Cob. Marry, that which will make any man out of love with 'em, I

think; their bad conditions, an you will needs know. First they are

of a Flemish breed, I am sure on't, for they raven up more butter than all the days of the week beside; next, they stink of fish and leek-porridge miserably; thirdly, they'll keep a man devoutly hungry all day, and at night send him supperless to bed.

Cash. Indeed, these are faults, Cob.

Cob. Nay, an this were all, 'twere something; but they are the only

known enemies to my generation. A fasting-day no sooner comes, but

my lineage goes to wrack; poor cobs! they smoak for it, they are made martyrs O' the gridiron, they melt in passion: and your maids

to know this, and yet would have me turn Hannibal, and eat my own

flesh and blood. My princely coz, [pulls out a red herring] fear

nothing; I have not the heart to devour you, an I might be made as

rich as king Cophetua. O that I had room for my tears, I could weep

salt-water enough now to preserve the lives of ten thousand

thousand of my kin! But I may curse none but these filthy

almanacks; for an't were not for them, these days of persecution

would never be known. I'll be hang'd an some fish-monger's son do

not make of 'em, and puts in more fasting-days than he should do,

because he would utter his father's dried stock—fish and stinking

conger.

Cash. 'Slight peace! thou'lt be beaten like a stock-fish else:
here's master Mathew.

**Enter WELLIBRED, E. KNOWELL, BRAINWORM,
MATHEW, BOBADILL, and STEPHEN.**

Now must I look out for a messenger to my master.

[Exit with Cob.]

Wel, Beshrew me, but it was an absolute good jest, and
exceedingly

well carried!

E. Know. Ay, and our ignorance maintain'd it as well, did it not?

Wel. Yes, faith; but was it possible thou shouldst not know him?
I

forgive master Stephen, for he is stupidity itself.

E. Know. 'Fore God, not I, an I might have been join'd patten with

one of the seven wise masters for knowing him. He had so writhen himself into the habit of one of your poor infantry, your decayed;

ruinous, worm-eaten gentlemen of the round; such as have vowed to

sit on the skirts of the city, let your provost and his half-dozen of halberdiers do what they can; and have translated begging out of

the old hackney-pace to a fine easy amble, and made it run as smooth off the tongue as a shove-groat shilling. Into the likeness of one of these reformados had he moulded himself so perfectly, observing every trick of their action, as, varying the accent, swearing with an emphasis, indeed, all with so special and exquisite a grace, that, hadst thou seen him, thou wouldst have sworn he might have been sergeant-major, if not lieutenant-colonel

to the regiment.

Wel. Why, Brainworm, who would have thought thou hadst been such an

artificer?

E. Know. An artificer! an architect. Except a man had studied begging all his life time, and been a weaver of language from his infancy for the cloathing of it, I never saw his rival.

Wel. Where got'st thou this coat, I marle?

Brai. Of a Hounsditch man, sir, one of the devil's near kinsmen, a

broker.

Wel. That cannot be, if the proverb hold; for 'A crafty knave needs

no broker.'

Brai. True, sir; but I did need a broker, ergo—

Wel. Well put off:—no crafty knave, you'll say.

E. Know. Tut, he has more of these shifts.

Brai. And yet, where I have one the broker has ten, sir.

Reenter CASH

Cash. Francis! Martin! ne'er a one to be found now? what a spite's

this!

Wel. How now, Thomas? Is my brother Kitely within?

Cash. No, sir, my master went forth e'en now; but master Downright

is within.—Cob! what, Cob! Is he gone too?

Wel. Whither went your master, Thomas, canst thou tell?

Cash. I know not: to justice Clement's, I think, sir—Cob!

[Exit

E. Know. Justice Clement! what's he?

Wel. Why, dost thou not know him? He is a city-magistrate, a justice

here, an excellent good lawyer, and a great scholar; but the only

mad, merry old fellow in Europe. I shewed him you the other day.

E. Know. Oh, is that he? I remember him now. Good faith, and he is

a very strange presence methinks; it shews as if he stood out of

the rank from other men: I have heard many of his jests in the

University. They say he will commit a man for taking the wall of

his horse

Wel. Ay, or wearing his cloak on one shoulder, or serving of God;

any thing, indeed, if it come in the way of his humour.

Re-enter CASH.

Cash. Gasper! Martin! Cob! 'Heart, where should they be trow?

Bob. Master Kitely's man, pray thee vouchsafe us the lighting of this match.

[Exit.

Cash. Fire on your match! no time but now to vouchsafe?—Francis!

Cob!

Bob. Body O' me! here's the remainder of seven pound since yesterday was seven-night. 'Tis your right Trinidado: did you never

take any master Stephen?

Step. No, truly, sir; but I'll learn to take it now, since you commend it so.

Bob. Sir, believe me, upon my relation for what I tell you, the world shall not reprove. I have been in the Indies, where this herb

grows, where neither myself, nor a dozen gentlemen more of my knowledge, have received the taste of any other nutriment in the world, for the space of one and twenty weeks, but the fume of this

simple only: therefore, it cannot be, but 'tis most divine. Further, take it in the nature, in the true kind; so, it makes an antidote, that, had you taken the most deadly poisonous plant in all Italy, it should expel it, and clarify you, with as much ease as I speak. And for your green wound,—your Balsamum and your St.

John's wort, are all mere gulleries and trash to it, especially your Trinidado: your Nicotian is good too. I could say what I know

of the virtue of it, for the expulsion of rheums, raw humours, crudities, obstructions, with a thousand of this kind; but I profess myself no quack-salver. Only thus much; by Hercules, I do

hold it, and will affirm it before any prince in Europe, to be the most sovereign and precious weed that ever the earth tendered to

the use of man.

E. Know. This speech would have done decently in a tobacco-trader's

mouth.

Re-enter CASH with COB.

Cash. At justice Clement's he is, in the middle of Coleman-street.

Cob. Oh, oh!

Bob. Where's the match I gave thee, master Kitely's man?

Cash. Would his match and he, and pipe and all, were at Sancto Domingo! I had forgot it.

[Exit.

Cob. 'Od's me, I marle what pleasure or felicity they have in taking this roguish tobacco. It's good for nothing but to choke a man, and fill him full of smoke and embers: there were four died out of one house last week with taking of it, and two more the bell

went for yesternight; one of them, they say, will never scape it;

he voided a bushel of soot yesterday, upward and downward. By the

stocks, an there were no wiser men than I, I'd have it present

whipping, man or woman, that should but deal with a tobacco pipe:

why, it will stifle them all in the end, as many as use it; it's

little better than ratsbane or rosaker.

[Bobadill beats him.

All. Oh, good captain, hold, hold!

Bob. You base cullion, you!

Re-enter CASH.

Cash. Sir, here's your match. Come, thou must needs be talking too,

thou'rt well enough served.

Cob. Nay, he will not meddle with his match, I warrant you: well, it shall be a dear beating, an I live.

Bob. Do you prate, do you murmur?

E. Know. Nay, good captain, will you regard the humour of a fool?

Away, knave.

Wel. Thomas, get him away. *[Exit Cash with Cob.*

Bob. A whoreson filthy slave, a dung-worm, an excrement! Body O'

Caesar, but that I scorn to let forth so mean a spirit, I'd have stabb'd him to the earth.

Wel. Marry, the law forbid, sir!

Bob. By Pharaoh's foot, I would have done it.

Step. Oh, he swears most admirably! By Pharaoh's foot! Body O' Caesar!—I shall never do it, sure. Upon mine honour, and by St. George!—No, I have not the right grace.

Mat. Master Stephen, will you any? By this air, the most divine tobacco that ever I drunk.

[Practises at the post.

As I am a gentleman! By— *[Exeunt Bob. and Mat.*

Step. None, I thank you, sir. O, this gentleman does it rarely, too: but nothing like the other. By this air!

Brai.*[pointing to Master Stephen.]* Master, glance, glance! master Wellbred!

Step. As I have somewhat to be saved, I protest—

Wel. You are a fool; it needs no affidavit.

E. Know. Cousin, will you any tobacco?

Step. I, sir! Upon my reputation—

E. Know. How now, cousin!

Step. I protest, as I am a gentleman, but no soldier, indeed—

Wel. No, master Stephen! As I remember, your name is entered in the
artillery-garden.

Step. Ay, sir, that's true. Cousin, may I swear, as I am a soldier, by that?

E. Know. O yes, that you may; it is all you have for your money.

Step. Then, as I am a gentleman, and a soldier, it is "divine tobacco!"

Wel. But soft, where's master Mathew! Gone?

Brai. No, sir; they went in here.

Wel. O let's follow them: master Mathew is gone to salute his mistress in verse; we shall have the happiness to hear some of his
poetry now; he never comes unfinished.—Brainworm!

Step. Brainworm! Where? Is this Brainworm?

E. Know. Ay, cousin; no words of it, upon your gentility.

Step. Not I, body of me! By this air! St. George! and the foot of Pharaoh!

Wel. Rare! Your cousin's discourse is simply drawn out with oaths.

E. Know. 'Tis larded with them; a kind of French dressing, if you love it.

[Exeunt.

SCENE III-Coleman-Street. A Room in Justice CLEMENT'S House.

Enter KITELY and COB.

Kit. Ha! how many are there, say'st thou?

Cob. Marry, sir, your brother, master Wellbred—

Kit. Tut, beside him: what strangers are there, man?

Cob. Strangers? let me see, one, two; mass; I know not well,— there are so many.

Kit. How! so many?

Cob. Ay, there's some five or six of them at the most.

Kit. A swarm, a swarm!

Spite of the devil...how they sting my head

With forked stings, thus wide and large!

But, Cob, How long hast thou been coming hither, Cob?

Cob. A little while, sir.

Kit. Didst thou come running?

Cob. No, sir.

Kit. Nay, then I am familiar with thy haste.

Bane to my fortunes! what meant I to marry?

I, that before was rank'd in such content,

My mind at rest too, in so soft a peace,

Being free master of mine own free thoughts,

And now become a slave? What! never sigh;

Be of good cheer, man; for thou art a cuckold:

'Tis done, 'tis done! Nay, when such flowing-store,

Plenty itself, falls into my wife's lap,

The cornucopiae will be mine, I know.—But, Cob,

What entertainment had they? I am sure
My sister and my wife would bid them welcome: ha?
Cob. Like enough, sir; yet I heard not a word of it.
Kit. No;
Their lips were seal'd with kisses, and the voice,
Drown'd in a flood of joy at their arrival,
Had lost her motion, state and faculty.—
Cob,
Which of them was it that first kiss'd my wife,
My sister, I should say?—My wife, alas!
I fear not her: ha! who was it say'st thou?
Cob. By my troth, sir, will you have the truth of it?
Kit. Oh, ay, good Cob, I pray thee heartily.
Cob. Then I am a vagabond, and fitter for Bridewell than your
worship's company, if I saw any body to be kiss'd, unless they
would have kiss'd the post in the middle of the warehouse; for
there I left them all at their tobacco, with a pox!
Kit. How! were they not gone in then ere thou cam'st?
Cob. O no, sir.
Kit. Spite of the devil! what do I stay here then? Cob, follow me.
[Exit.
Cob. Nay, soft and fair; I have eggs on the spit; I cannot go yet,
sir. Now am I, for some five and fifty reasons, hammering,
hammering revenge: oh for three or four gallons of vinegar, to
sharpen my wits! Revenge, vinegar revenge, vinegar and
mustard
revenge! Nay, an he had not lien in my house, 'twould never have
grieved me; but being my guest, one that, I'll be sworn, my wife
has lent him her smock off her back, while his own shirt has
been
at washing; pawned her neck-kerchers for clean bands for him;
sold
almost all my platters, to buy him tobacco; and he to turn
monster
of ingratitude, and strike his lawful host! Well, I hope to raise

up an host of fury for't: here comes justice Clement.

Enter Justice CLEMENT, KNOWELL, and FORMAL.

Clem. What's master Kitely gone, Roger?

Form. Ay, sir.

Clem. 'Heart O' me! what made him leave us so abruptly?—How now,

sirrah! what make you here? what would you have, ha?

Cob. An't please your worship, I am a poor neighbour of your worship's—

Clem. A poor neighbour of mine! Why, speak, poor neighbour.

Cob. I dwell, sir, at the sign of the Water-tankard, hard by the Green Lattice: I have paid scot and lot there any time this eighteen years.

Clem. To the Green Lattice?

Cob. No, sir, to the parish: Marry, I have seldom scaped scot-free at the Lattice.

Clem. O, well; what business has my poor neighbour with me?

Cob. An't like your worship, I am come to crave the peace of your

worship.

Clem. Of me, knave! Peace of me, knave! Did I ever hurt thee, or threaten thee, or wrong thee, ha?

Cob. No, sir; but your worship's warrant for one that has wrong'd

me, sir: his arms are at too much liberty, I would fain have them bound to a treaty of peace, an my credit could compass it with your

worship.

Clem. Thou goest far enough about for't, I am sure.

Kno. Why, dost thou go in danger of thy life for him, friend?

Cob. No, sir; but I go in danger of my death every hour, by his means; an I die within a twelve-month and a day, I may swear by the

law of the land that he killed me.

Clem. How, how, knave, swear he killed thee, and by the law? What

pretence, what colour hast thou for that?

Cob. Marry, an't please your worship, both black and blue; colour

enough, I warrant you. I have it here to shew your worship.

Clem. What is he that gave you this, sirrah?

Cob. A gentleman and a soldier, he says, he is, of the city here.

Clem. A soldier of the city! What call you him?

Cob. Captain Bobadill.

Clem. Bobadill! and why did he bob and beat you, sirrah? How began

the quarrel betwixt you, ha? speak truly, knave, I advise you.

Cob. Marry, indeed, an't please your worship, only because I spake

against their vagrant tobacco, as I came by them when they were

taking on't; for nothing else.

Clem. Ha! you speak against tobacco? Formal, his name.

Form. What's your name, sirrah

Cob. Oliver, sir, Oliver Cob, sir.

Clem. Tell Oliver Cob he shall go to the jail, Formal.

Form. Oliver Cob, my master, justice Clement, says you shall go to

the jail.

Cob. O, I beseech your worship, for God's sake, dear master justice!

Clem. 'Sprecious! an such drunkards and tankards as you are, come

to dispute of tobacco once, I have done: away with him!

Cob, O, good master justice! Sweet old gentleman! [To Knowell.

Know. "Sweet Oliver," would I could do thee any good!—justice

Clement, let me intreat you, sir.

Clem. What! a thread-bare rascal, a beggar, a slave that never

drunk out of better than piss-pot metal in his life! and he to

deprave and abuse the virtue of an herb so generally received in the courts of princes, the chambers of nobles, the bowers of sweet

ladies, the cabins of soldiers!—Roger, away with him! 'Od's precious—I say, go to.

Cob. Dear master justice, let me be beaten again, I have deserved it: but not the prison, I beseech you.

Know. Alas, poor Oliver!

Clem. Roger, make him a warrant:—he shall not go, but I fear the knave.

Form. Do not stink, sweet Oliver, you shall not go; my master will

give you a warrant.

Cob. O, the Lord maintain his worship, his worthy worship!

Clem. Away, dispatch him. [Exeunt Formal and Cob;] How now, master

Knowell, in dumps, in dumps! Come, this becomes not.

Know. Sir, would I could not feel my cares.

Clem. Your cares are nothing: they are like my cap, soon put on, and as soon put off. What! your son is old enough to govern himself: let him run his course, it's the only way to make him a staid man. If he were an unthrift, a ruffian, a drunkard, or a licentious liver, then you had reason; you had reason to take care:

but, being none of these, mirth's my witness, an I had twice so many cares as you have, I'd drown them all in a cup of sack. Come,

come, let's try it: I muse your parcel of a soldier returns not all this while.

[Exeunt.

Every Man in His Humour Summary and Analysis of Act III Summary

Act III

Scene 1

In the Old Jewry at the Windmill Tavern, Matthew, Wellbred, and Bobadil convene. Matthew tells Wellbred they were looking for him and Bobadil cuts in to say something of <u>Downright</u>, but Wellbred will hear no ill words about his brother. Matthew tells Wellbred he thinks Downright does not "carry himself like a gentleman of / fashion" (39) but Wellbred laughs that few do.

Edward and Stephen enter. Wellbred greets Edward jovially, and Edward laughs that the letter Wellbred sent him was surely something. He also says the man who brought him the letter was certainly "no ordinary beast" (39), for how could anyone confuse himself and his father? He tells Wellbred his father saw the letter before he did.

Amused, Wellbred asks what <u>Knowell</u> thought. Edward replies he does not know, but can guess the old man thinks they are both dissolute. Wellbred dismisses that, saying such a thought will soon vanish. He turns to his two "hang-by's" (40) but then asks who the silent man is with Edward. Everyone is introduced, and Stephen proclaims himself "somewhat / melancholy" but that "you [Wellbred] shall command me, sir, in whatsoever / is incident to a gentleman" (40).

Matthew asks Stephen if he is really given to melancholy, and when Stephen says yes, Matthew ventures that it is only "your fine humour, sir, your true / melancholy breeds your perfect fine wit, sir" (41). As for himself, he adds, when he gets a bit of melancholy he takes up his pen to write. Matthew suggests Stephen take up his study to be melancholy within.

Wellbred asks Bobadil why he seems so pensive, and Edward notes that Bobadil is melancholy as well. Bobadil explains that he was thinking of something that took place ten years ago tomorrow: seven hundred men lost their lives at the "beleag'ring of Strigonium" (41). Edward asks if he was truly there, and Bobadil replies that he was the first to enter the breach and was almost slain.

Bobadil continues to narrate his experience, and shows them his trusty Toledo rapier. Stephen comments that he has one too, and when he shows Bobadil, Bobadil laughs that it is not one. Wellbred asks Stephen where he bought it, and Stephen grumbles that it was from a "scurvy rogue soldier" (43). He is extremely angry, and threatens harm to the man if he ever meets him again.

Brainworm enters, disguised as before. Stephen confronts him about the rapier and Brainworm promptly confesses. Briainworm asks Edward for a word. Amused, Edward asks if he has another fake Toledo to sell him. Brainworm pulls him aside and tells him who he really is, and that Edward's father is on his way.

Edward announces to Wellbred that Knowell is coming, and that this man is actually Brainworm. Wellbred decides Brainworm will come with them and that Edward ought to keep his spirits high, because there is no way their wits can be so dull that "one old plodding brain can outstrip / us all" (45).

Scene 2

In the Old Jewry at Kitely's warehouse, Kitely asks Cash if his client is ready for him and has the money, and Cash says yes. Cash leaves to fetch his master's cloak.

Kitely continues to bemoan his situation, chastising himself: "Who will not judge him worthy to be robb'd / That sets his doors wide open to a thief / And shows the felon where his treasure lies?" (45). He decides he cannot leave, but when Cash returns and tells him the scrivener will be there with the bonds, he is in agony over what to do.

Finally Kitely turns to Cash and asks if he can trust him as he thinks he can. Cash proclaims that if a servant's duty can be called love, then Kitely has it. After some wavering, Kitely finally decides to trust him, but is concerned that for some reason Cash does not want to swear not to say anything. Perhaps he has some concealed purpose, for why would he not "choose / But lend an oath to all this protestation?" (47). After all, Kitely muses, he has heard Cash wear before.

Kitely finally asks outright if he will swear and Cash says later. Kitely decides he knows Cash well enough and tells him that if Wellbred brings other gentlemen to the house, to let him know at Justice Clement's straight away. He does not have time to tell him the whole secret, which he reminds Cash of, but he still must not say anything at all about this conversation to Dame Kitely.

Kitely leaves, and Cash is left alone. He sees <u>Cob</u> enter, complaining about fasting days. Kitely asks him about his choler, which Cob interprets as "collar." Cash has no time for Cob's whining, though, for he sees Matthew and other men come in with Wellbred, and knows he has to send a messenger to Kitely.

Wellbred and Edward are marveling and laughing over Brainworm's disguise and duping of Stephen. Cash pops back in, anguished that he cannot find a messenger. Wellbred asks if Kitely is within and Cash replies no but Downright is. Wellbred asks where Kitely is and Cash says he thinks Justice Clement's. Cash leaves again.

Edward asks who Clement is, and Wellbred replies that he is a "city magis- / trate, a Justice here, an excellent good lawyer, and a great / scholar: but the only mad, merry old fellow in Europe!" (52). Edward remembers Wellbred pointing him out the other day, and says he had a "strange presence" (52).

Cash wanders in again, calling for the servants. Bobadil asks him to light a match for them but Cash says he has no time, and wanders out again.

Bobadil takes out the Trinidado weed, and extols its merits to the men as "the most sovereign / and precious weed that ever the earth tendered to the use / of man" (53). Edward laughs that "This speech would ha' done decently in a tobacco / trader's mouth!" (53).

Cash re-enters with Cob, telling Cob where to find Kitely. Cash then runs out. Cob looks at the men getting ready to smoke and grumbles that he finds no merit in it, for all it does is "choke a man and fill him full of smoke and / embers" (54). Four people died last week, he recalls, and thinks "it will stifle them all in the end, / as many as use it" (54).

Enraged at these comments, Bobadil starts to hit Cob with a cudgel and the others yell at him to stop. Cash comes back with a match, and is ordered to take Cob away. Bobadil rages that Cob is a "whorson filthy slave, a dung-worm, an excre- / ment" (54).

The men smoke, and wonder where Matthew went. Wellbred says he must have gone to salute his mistress with verse, and they all decide to go listen.

Scene 3

On Colman Street at Justice Clement's house, Cob, acting as messenger, is telling Kitely who is at his house. Kitely mourns that it is a "swarm, a swarm" (56). He wishes he had never married because before he was free, and now he is a slave and a cuckold. He asks Cob how his wife and sister welcomed them and Cob says he does not know. He asks Cob which one kissed his wife first and Cob responds that he does not know, and left the men only with their tobacco. Kitely thinks there might still be time, then, and orders Cob to come with him. Kitely exits.

Cob says aloud that he is preparing his revenge against Bobadil, who laid in his house and borrowed money from his wife all so he could buy such filthy tobacco.

Justice Clement, Knowell, and Clement's man Roger Formal enter. Clement is surprised Kitely is gone, and Cob introduces himself as a poor neighbor of his worship's. He says he dwells at the sign of the water-tankard and comes here to "crave the / the peace of your worship" (58)—specifically, a warrant.

Clement is intrigued and asks for further information. Cob says the man is Captain Bobadil and he has wronged him. Clement asks how the quarrel began and Cob says all he did is speak about the tobacco the man and others were using. Clement asks what Cob's name is, and after Cob replies, Clement turns to Formal and tells him to arrest Cob.

Cob is stunned and begins protesting heatedly. Clement declares that one cannot rail against "the virtue of an herb so / generally receiv'd in the courts of princes, the chambers / of nobles, the bowers of sweet ladies, the cabins of soldiers!" (59). Cob cries out for justice again, and Clement sighs that Cob will not go to jail and can have his warrant.

After Formal leads out Cob, Clement tells Knowell to stop bothering him about his son, who is old enough to live his own life. He suggests letting Edward run his course, which is the only way to "make him a staid man" (59).

Analysis

In Act Three, Kitely worries further about his wife, descending more and more into jealousy. Bobadil, Matthew, and Stephen continue to prove themselves ridiculous in their boasting, hubris, and ignorance. Wellbred and Edward delight in Brainworm's disguises and schemes, and Cob makes his case against tobacco to the Judge.

In regards to this last plot point, Cob's distaste for tobacco and Clement's response about its ubiquity and popularity are telling of this moment in the late 16th century. Returning from his voyage to the New World, Christopher Columbus brought some of this "weed" back home to Europe. It was not only pleasant to smoke but was also believed to harbor medicinal value. Thus, the production, distribution, and consumption of tobacco exploded during the subsequent century of exploration and colonization of the New World, forming a cornerstone of the increasing trans-Atlantic trade. Cob gives voice to tobacco's dangerous qualities (which, ironically, come across as obnoxious and petty in the text but actually bear out as true when we consider the health hazards of smoking), saying, "It's good for / nothing but to choke a man and fill him full of smoke and / embers: there were four died of one house, last week, / with taking of it, and two more the bell went for, yester- / night" (54). Clement has no patience for such a ridiculous complaint, frightening Cob for his silliness by threatening to put him in jail and claiming that it is absurd to "deprave and abuse the virtue of an herb so / generally receiv'd in the courts of princes, the chambers / of nobles, the bowers of sweet ladies, the cabins of soldiers!" (59).

Clement's appearance in the play signals that there is someone of import, of authority, who might eventually have to intervene to keep the humour-motivated characters in line. He lives on Colman Street, a known respectable neighborhood in London, and by providing that bit of information, Jonson shows just how important moving the play to London from Florence (its initial 1598 setting) was for appealing to the audience's knowledge and sensibilities and heightening their enjoyment and amusement.

Critic Ralph Alan Cohen takes each of the main characters and explains what their location means for them. To return to Clement, he explains that the area was known as a Puritan one, and was close to the Guildhall; this links Clement "more closely to the religion and government of mercantile London" and bestows upon him a "particularly civic responsibility." Knowell lives in Hoxton, a suburb north of London. He is well-to-do, and this geographic association "[enhances] Knowell's character as a plain country gentleman suspicious of the city and its temptations." Brainworm is from the Moorfields, an area south of Hoxton and once a retreat/resort of sorts now become "a haunt of beggars, specifically lunatics from Bedlam, adjacent to the fields." The place has connotations of "soldiering, rascality, and beggary," which are all "embodied in the protean figure of Brainworm (whose name even suggests the lunacy of Bedlam." Cob's house does not have an exact location, but it is described by various characters as obscure but tidy, most likely near the conduit within Moorgate because it was a water source.

As for the young men, Wellbred is "true London gallant." He took up frequent residence in the Windmill Tavern, an actual popular tavern familiar to the London audience. Bobadil is a Paulsman, a disreputable and notorious disgraced soldier. Jonson contrasts "between the hardworking and honest laborer [Cob] who keeps a poor but 'cleanly' house and the fraudulent parasite [Bobadil] who sleeps there on a bench and does not pay his rent."

Kitely and Downright represent the "quintessence of London's bourgeois society, the urban counterpart to Knowell." They are very middle-class, and Kitely seems suspicious of the leisure class. He is also in Old Jewry Lane, reinforcing his role as a merchant. The audience of the time would see that "the grasping and parsimonious nature of the jealous merchant fits the Renaissance stereotype of the Jew."

Jonson's very specific locating of his characters also makes their movement from place to place more plausible and unifies the action: "By locating all the persons and actions in a small area, Jonson creates the illusion of a naturally evolving and unified plot."

ACT IV

SCENE I—-A Room in KITELY'S House.

Enter DOWNRIGTIT and Dame KITELY.

Dow. Well, sister, I tell you true; and you'll find it so in the end.

DameK. Alas, brother, what would you have me to do? I cannot help

it; you see my brother brings them in here; they are his friends.

Dow. His friends! his fiends. 'Slud! they do nothing but haunt him

up and down like a sort of unlucky spirits, and tempt him to all
manner of villainy that can be thought of. Well, by this light, a
little thing would make me play the devil with some of them: an
'twere not more for your husband's sake than anything else, I'd
make the house too hot for the best on 'em; they should say, and
swear, hell were broken loose, ere they went hence. But, by God's

will, 'tis nobody's fault but yours; for an you had done as you
might have done, they should have been parboiled, and baked too,

every mother's son, ere they should have come in, e'er a one of
them.

Dame K. God's my life! did you ever hear the like? what a strange

man is this! Could I keep out all them, think you? I should put
myself against half a dozen men, should I? Good faith, you'd mad
the patien'st body in the world; to hear you talk so, without any
sense or reason.

*Enter Mistress BRIDGET, Master MATHEW, and BOBADILL;
followed, at a distance, by WELLBRED, E. KNOWELL,
STEPHEN, and BRAINWORM.*

Brid. Servant, in troth you are too prodigal

Of your wit's treasure, thus fu pour it forth

Upon so mean a subject as my worth.

Mat. You say well, mistress, and I mean as well.

Dow. Hoy-day, here is stuff!

Wel. O, now stand close; pray Heaven, she can get him to read! he

should do it of his own natural impudency.

Brid. Servant, what is this same, I pray you?

Mat. Marry, an elegy, an elegy, an odd toy—

Dow. To mock an ape withal! O, I could sew up his mouth, now.

Dame K. Sister, I pray you let's hear it.

Dow. Are you rhyme-given too?

Mat. Mistress, I'll read it if you please.

Brid. Pray you do, servant.

Dow. O, here's no foppery! Death! I can endure the stocks better.

[Exit]

E. Know. What ails thy brother? can he not hold his water at reading of a ballad?

Wel. O, no; a rhyme fu him is worse than cheese, or a bag-pipe; but

mark; you lose the protestation.

Mat. Faith, I did it in a humour; I know not how it is; but please you come near, sir. This gentleman has judgment, he knows how to

censure of a—pray you, sir, you can judge?

Step. Not I, sir; upon my reputation, and by the foot of Pharaoh!

Wel. O, chide your cousin for swearing.

E. Know. Not I, so long as he does not forswear himself.

Bob. Master Mathew, you abuse the expectation of your dear mistress, and her fair sister: fie! while you live avoid this prolixity.

Mat. I shall, sir, well; incipere dulce.

E. Know. How, insipere duke! a sweet thing to be a fool, indeed!

Wel. What, do you take incipere in: that sense?

E. Know. You do not, you! This was your villainy, to gull him with

a motte.

Wel. O, the benchers' phrase: pauca verba, pauca verba!

Mat. Rare creature, let me speak without offence,
Would God my rude words had the influence
To rule thy thoughts, as thy fair looks do mine,
Then shouldst thou be his prisoner, who is thine.
E. Know. This is Hero and Leander.
Wel. O, ay: peace, we shall have more of this.
Mat. Be not unkind and fair: misshapen stuff
Is of behaviour boisterous and rough.
Wel. How like you that, sir? [Master Stephen shakes his head.
E. Know. 'Slight, he shakes his head like a bottle, to feel an there
be any brain in it.
Mat. But observe the catastrophe, now:
And I in duty will exceed all other,
As you in beauty do excel Love's mother.
E. Know. Well, I'll have him free of the wit-brokers, for he
utters nothing but stolen remnants.
Wel. O, forgive it him.
E. Know. A filching rogue, hang him!—-and from the dead! it's
worse than sacrilege.
*WELLBRED, E. KNOWELL, and Master STEPHEN, come
forward.*
Wel. Sister, what have you here, verses? pray you let's see: who
made these verses? they are excellent good.
Mat. O, Master Wellbred, 'tis your disposition to say so, sir. They
were good in the morning: I made them ex tempore this
morning.
Wel. How! ex tempore?
Mat. Ay, would I might be hanged else; ask Captain Bobadill: he
saw
me write them, at the—pox on it!—the Star, yonder.
Brai. Can he find in his heart to curse the stars so?
E. Know. Faith, his are even with him; they have curst him
enough
already.
Step. Cousin, how do you like this gentleman's verses?

E. Know. O, admirable! the best that ever I heard, coz.

Step. Body O' Caesar, they are admirable! the best that I ever heard, as I am a soldier!

Re-enter DOWNRIGHT.

Dow. I am vext, I can hold ne'er a bone of me still: 'Heart, I think they mean to build and breed here

Wet. Sister, you have a simple servant here, that crowns your beauty with such encomiums and devices; you may see what it is to

be the mistress of a wit, that can make your perfections so

transparent, that every blear eye may look through them, and see

him drowned over head and ears in the deep well of desire: Sister

Kitely. I marvel you get you not a servant that can rhyme, and do tricks too.

Dow. O monster! impudence itself! tricks!

Dame K. Tricks, brother! what tricks?

Brid. Nay, speak, I pray you what tricks?

Dame K. Ay, never spare any body here; but say, what tricks.

Brid. Passion of my heart, do tricks!

Wel. 'Slight, here's a trick vied and revied! Why, you monkeys, you, what a cater-wauling do you keep! has he not given you rhymes

and verses and tricks?

Dow. O, the fiend!

Wel. Nay, you lamp of virginity, that take it in snuff so, come, and cherish this tame poetical fury in your servant; you'll be begg'd else shortly for a concealment: go to, reward his muse. You

cannot give him less than a shilling in conscience, for the book he

had it out of cost him a teston at least. How now, gallants! Master Mathew! Captain! what, all sons of silence, no spirit?

Dow. Come, you might practise your ruffian tricks somewhere else,

and not here, I wuss; this is no tavern or drinking-school, to vent your exploits in.

Wel. How now; whose cow has calved?

Dow. Marry, that has mine, sir. Nay, boy, never look askance at me for the matter; I'll tell you of

it, I, sir; you and your companions mend yourselves when I have done.

Wel. My companions!

Dow. Yes, sir, your companions, so I say; I am not afraid of you, nor them neither; your hang-byes here. You must have your poets and

your potlings, your soldados and foolados to follow you up and down

the city; and here they must come to domineer and swagger. Sirrah,

you ballad-singer, and slops your fellow there, get you out, get you home; or by this steel, I'll cut off your ears, and that presently.

Wel. 'Slight, stay, let's see what he dare do; cut off his ears! cut a whetstone. You are an ass, do you see; touch any man here, and by this hand I'll run my rapier to the hilts in you.

Dow. Yea, that would I fain see, boy.

[They all draw.]

Dame K. O Jesu! murder! Thomas! Gasper!

Brid. Help, help! Thomas!

Enter CASH and some of the house to part them.

E. Know. Gentlemen, forbear, I pray' you.

Bob. Well, sirrah, you Holofernes; by my hand, I will pink your flesh full of holes with my rapier for this; I will, by this good heaven! nay, let him come, let him come, gentlemen; by the body of

St. George, I'll not kill him.

[Offer to fight again, and are parted].

Gash. Hold, hold, good gentlemen. Dow. You whoreson, bragging
coystril!
Enter KITELY.
Kit. Why, how now! what's the matter, what's the stir here?
Whence springs the quarrel? Thomas! where is he?
Put up your weapons, and put off this rage:
My wife and sister, they are the cause of this.
What, Thomas! where is the knave?
Gash. Here, sir.
Wel. Come, let's go: this is one of my brother's ancient humours, this.
Step. I am glad nobody was hurt by his ancient humour.
[Exeunt Wellbred, Stephen, E. Knowell, Bobadill, and Brainworm].
Kit. Why, how now, brother, who enforced this brawl?
Dow. A sort of lewd rake-hells, that care neither for God nor the
devil And they must come here to read ballads, and roguery, and
trash! I'll mar the knot of 'em ere I sleep, perhaps; especially
Bob there, he that's all manner of shapes: and songs and sonnets,
his fellow.
Brid. Brother, indeed you are too violent,
Too sudden in your humour: and you know
My brother Wellbred's temper will not bear
Any reproof, chiefly in such a presence,
Where every slight disgrace he should receive
Might wound him in opinion and respect.
Dow. Respect! what talk you of respect among such, as have no
spark
of manhood, nor good manners? 'Sdeins, I am ashamed to hear
you'!
respect!
[Exit].
Brid. Yes, there was one a civil gentleman,
And very worthily demeaned himself.
Kit. O, that was some love of yours, sister.

Brid. A love of mine! I would it were no worse, brother;
You'd pay my portion sooner than you think for.
Dame K. Indeed he seem'd to be a gentleman of a very exceeding
fair disposition, and of excellent good parts.
[Exeunt Dame Kitely and Bridget].
Kit. Her love, by heaven! my wife's minion.
Fair disposition! excellent good parts!
Death! these phrases are intolerable.
Good parts! how should she know his parts?
His parts! Well, well, well, well, well, well;
It is too plain, too clear: Thomas, come hither.
What, are they gone?
Cash. Ay, sir, they went in.
My mistress and your sister—
Kit. Are any of the gallants within?
Cash. No, sir, they are all gone.
Kit. Art thou sure of it—-?
Cash. I can assure you, sir.
Kit. What gentleman was that they praised so, Thomas?
Cash. One, they call him Master Knowell, a handsome young
gentleman, sir.
Kit. Ay, I thought so; my mind gave me as much:
I'll die, but they have hid him in the house,
Somewhere, I'll go and search; go with me, Thomas:
Be true to me, and thou shalt find me a master.
[Exeunt].
SCENE II.—-The Lane before COB'S House.
Enter COB
Cob. [knocks at the door.] What, Tib! Tib, I say!
Tib. [within.] How now, what cuckold is that knocks so hard?
Enter Tib.
O, husband! is it you? What's the news?
Cob. Nay, you have stunn'd me, i'faith; you have, given me a
knock O' the forehead will stick by me. Cuckold! 'Slid, cuckold!
Tib. Away, you fool! did I know it was you that knocked?

Come, come, you may call me as bad when you list.

Cob. May I? Tib, you are a whore.

Tib. You lie in your throat, husband.

Cob. How, the lie! and in my throat tool do you long to be stabb'd, ha?

Tib. Why, you are no soldier, I hope.

Cob. O, must you be stabbed by a soldier? Mass, that's true! when

was Bobadill here, your captain? that rogue, that foist, that fencing Burgullion? I'll tickle him, i'faith.

Tib. Why, what's the matter, trow?

Cob. O, he has basted me rarely, sumptuously! but I have it here in

black and white, [pulls out the warrant.] for his black and blue shall pay him. O, the justice, the honestest old brave Trojan in London; I do honour the very flea of his dog. A plague on him, though, he put me once in a villanous filthy fear; marry, it vanished away like the smoke of tobacco; but I was smoked soundly

first. I thank the devil, and his good angel, my guest. Well, wife, or Tib, which you will, get you in, and lock the door; I charge you

let nobody in to you, wife; nobody in to you; those are my words: not Captain Bob himself, nor the fiend in his likeness. You are a woman, you have flesh and blood enough in you to be tempted; therefore keep the door shut upon all comers.

Tib. I warrant you, there shall nobody enter here without my consent.

Cob. Nor with your consent, sweet Tib; and so I leave you.

Tib. It's more than you know, whether you leave me so.

Cob. How?

Tib. Why, sweet.

Cob. Tut, sweet or sour, thou art a flower.

Keep close thy door, I ask no more.

[Exeunt].

SCENE III.-A Room in the Windmill Tavern.

Enter E. KNOWELL, WELLBRED, STEPHEN, and
BRAINWORM,
disguised as before.

E. Know. Well, Brainworm, perform this business happily, and thou

makest a purchase of my love for ever.

Wel. I'faith, now let thy spirits use their best faculties: but, at

any hand, remember the message to my brother; for there's no other

means to start him.

Brai. I warrant you, sir; fear nothing; I have a nimble soul has

waked all forces of my phant'sie by this time, and put them in true

motion. What you have possest me withal, I'll discharge it amply,

sir; make it no question.

[Exit].

Wel. Forth, and prosper, Brainworm. Faith, Ned, how dost thou

approve of my abilities in this device?

E. Know. Troth, well, howsoever; but it will come excellent if it take.

Wel. Take, man! why it cannot choose but take, if the circumstances

miscarry not: but, tell me ingenuously, dost thou affect my sister Bridget as thou pretend'st?

E. Know. Friend, am I worth belief?

Wel. Come, do not protest. In faith, she is a maid of good

ornament, and much modesty; and, except I conceived very worthily

of her, thou should'st not have her.

E. Know. Nay, that I am afraid, will be a question yet, whether I shall have her, or no.

Wel. 'Slid, thou shalt have her; by this light thou shalt.

E. Know. Nay, do not swear.

Wel. By this hand thou shalt have her; I'll go fetch her presently.

'Point but where to meet, and as I am an honest man I'll bring her.

E. Know. Hold, hold, be temperate.

Wel. Why, by—what shall I swear by? thou shalt have her, as I am—

E. Know. Praythee, be at peace, I am satisfied; and do believe thou

wilt omit no offered occasion to make my desires complete.

Wel. Thou shalt see, and know, I will not.

[Exeunt].

SCENE IV.-The Old Jewry.

Enter FORMAL and KNOWELL.

Form. Was your man a soldier, sir?

Know. Ay, a knave

I took him begging O' the way, this morning,

As I came over Moorfields.

Enter BRAINWORM. disguised as before.

O, here he is!—-you've made fair speed, believe me,

Where, in the name of sloth, could you be thus?

Brai. Marry, peace be my comfort, where I thought I should have

had little comfort of your worship's service.

Know. How so?

Brai. O, sir, your coming to the city, your entertainment of me,

and your sending me to watch—-indeed all the circumstances either

of your charge, or my employment, are as open to your son, as to

yourself.

Know. How should that be, unless that villain, Brainworm,

Have told him of the letter, and discover'd

All that I strictly charg'd him to conceal?

'Tis so.

Brai. I am partly O' the faith, 'tis so, indeed.

Know. But, how should he know thee to be my man?

Brai. Nay, sir, I cannot tell; unless it be by the black art. Is
not your son a scholar, sir?

Know. Yes, but I hope his soul is not allied
Unto such hellish practice: if it were,
I had just cause to weep my part in him,
And curse the time of his creation.
But, where didst thou find them, Fitz-Sword?

Brai. You should rather ask where they found me, sir; for I'll
be sworn, I was going along in the street, thinking nothing,
when,
    of a sudden, a voice calls, Mr. Knowell's man! another cries,
    Soldier! and thus half a dozen of them, till they had call'd me
    within a house, where I no sooner came, but they seem'd men,
and
    out flew all their rapiers at my bosom, with some three or four
    score oaths to accompany them; and all to tell me, I was but a
    dead man, if I did not confess where you were, and how I was
    employed, and about what; which when they could not get out
of
    me, (as, I protest, they must have dissected, and made an
anatomy
    of me first, and so I told them,) they lock'd me up into a room
    in the top of a high house, whence by great miracle (having a
    light heart) I slid down by a bottom of packthread into the
    street, and so 'scaped. But, sir, thus much I can assure you,
    for I heard it while I was lock'd up, there were a great many
    rich merchants and brave citizens' wives with them at a feast;
    and your son, master Edward, withdrew with one of them, and
has
    'pointed to meet her anon at one Cob's house a water-bearer
    that dwells by the Wall. Now, there your worship shall be sure
    to take him, for there he preys, and fail he will not.

Know. Nor will I fail to break his match, I doubt not.
Go thoualong with justice Clement's man,
And stay there for me. At one Cob's house, say'st thou?

Brai. Ay, sir, there you shall have him. [Exit Knowell.] Yes—invisible! Much wench, or much son! 'Slight, when he has staid there thrcc or four hours, travailing with the expectation of wonders, and at length be deliver'd of air! O the sport that I should then take to look on him, if I durst! But now, I mean to appear no more afore him in this shape: I have another trick to act

yet. O that I were so happy as to light on a nupson now of this justice's novice!—Sir, I make you stay somewhat long.

Form. Not a whit, sir. Pray you what do you mean, sir?

Brai. I was putting up some papers.

Form. You have been lately in the wars, sir, it seems.

Brai. Marry have I, sir, to my loss, and expense of all, almost.

Form. Troth, sir, I would be glad to bestow a bottle of wine on you, if it please you to accept it—

Brai, O, sir

Form. But to hear the manner of your services, and your devices

in

the wars; they say they be very strange, and not like those a man reads in the Roman histories, or sees at Mile-end.

Brai. No, I assure you, sir; why at any time when it please you, I shall be ready to discourse to you all I know;—and more too somewhat. [Aside.]

Form. No better time than now, sir; we'll go to the Windmill:

there

we shall have a cup of neat grist, we call it. I pray you, sir, let me request you to the Windmill.

Brai. I'll follow you, sir;—and make grist of you, if I have good luck. [Aside.]

[Exeunt].

SCENE V.-Moorfields.

Enter MATHEW, E. KNOWELL, BOBADILL, and STEPHEN.

Mat. Sir, did your eyes ever taste the like clown of him where we were to-day, Mr. Wellbred's half-brother? I think the whole

earth

cannot shew his parallel, by this daylight.

E. Know. We were now speaking of him: captain Bobadill tells me he

is fallen foul of you too.

Mat. O, ay, sir, he threatened me with the bastinado.

Bob. Ay, but I think, I taught you prevention this morning, for that: You shall kill him beyond question; if you be so generously minded.

Mat. Indeed, it is a most excellent trick.

[*Fences*].

Bob: O, you do not give spirit enough to your motion, you are too

tardy, too heavy! O, it must be done like lightning, hay!

[*Practises at a post with his cudgel.*]

Mat. Rare, captain!

Bob. Tut! 'tis nothing, an't be not done in a—punto. E. Know. Captain, did you ever prove yourself upon any of our masters of defence here?

Mat. O good sir! yes, I hope he has.

Bob. I will tell you, sir. Upon my first coming to the city, after my long travel for knowledge, in that mystery only, there came three or four of them to me, at a gentleman's house, where it was my chance to be resident at that time, to intreat my presence at their schools: and withal so much importuned me, that I protest to

you, as I am a gentleman, I was ashamed of their rude demeanour out

of all measure: Well, I told them that to come to a public school, they should pardon me, it was opposite, in diameter, to my humour;

but if so be they would give their attendance at my lodging, I protested to do them what right or favour I could, as I was a gentleman, and so forth.

E. Know. So, sir! then you tried their skill?

Bob. Alas, soon tried: you shall hear, sir. Within two or three

days after, they came; and, by honesty, fair sir, believe me, I
graced them exceedingly, shewed them some two or three tricks
of
prevention have purchased them since a credit to admiration:
they
cannot deny this; and yet now they hate me, and why? because I
am
excellent; and for no other vile reason on the earth.

E. Know. This is strange and barbarous, as ever I heard.

Bob. Nay, for a more instance of their preposterous natures; but
note; sir. They have assaulted me some three, four, five, six of
them together, as I have walked alone in divers skirts it'll town,
as Turnbull, Whitechapel, Shoreditch, which were then my
quarters;
and since, upon the Exchange, at my lodging, and at my
ordinary:
where I have driven them afore me the whole length of a street,
in
the open view of all our gallants, pitying to hurt them, believe
me. Yet all this lenity will not overcome their spleen; they will
be doing with the pismire, raising a hill a man may spurn abroad
with his foot at pleasure. By myself, I could have slain them all,
but I delight not in murder. I am loth to bear any other than this
bastinado for them: yet I hold it good polity not to go disarmed,
for though I be skilful, I may be oppressed with multitudes.

E. Know. Ay, believe me, may you, sir: and in my conceit, our
whole
nation should sustain the loss by it, if it were so.

Bob. Alas, no? what's a peculiar man to a nation? not seen.

E. Know. O, but your skill, sir.

Bob. Indeed, that might be some loss; but who respects it? I will
tell you, sir, by the way of private, and under seal; I am a
gentleman, and live here obscure, and to myself; but were I
known

to her majesty and the lords,—observe me,—I would undertake, upon

this poor head and life, for the public benefit of the state, not only to spare the entire lives of her subjects in general; but to save the one half, nay, three parts of her yearly charge in holding war, and against what enemy soever. And how would I do it, think

you?

E. Know. Nay, I know not, nor can I conceive.

Bob. Why thus, sir. I would select nineteen more, to myself. throughout the land; gentlemen they should be of good spirit, strong and able constitution; I would choose them by an instinct, a

character that I have: and I would teach these nineteen the special

rules, as your punto, your reverso, your stoccata, your imbroccato,

your passada, your montanto; till they could all play very near, or

altogether as well as myself. This done, say the enemy were forty thousand strong, we twenty would come into the field the tenth of

March, or thereabouts; and we would challenge twenty of the enemy;

they could not in their honour refuse us: Well, we would kill them;

challenge twenty more, kill them; twenty more, kill them; twenty

more, kill them too; and thus would we kill every man his twenty a

day, that's twenty score; twenty score that's two hundred; two hundred a day, five days a thousand: forty thousand; forty times five, five times forty, two hundred days kills them all up by computation. And this will I venture my poor gentlemanlike carcase to perform, provided there be no treason practised upon us, by fair

and discreet manhood; that is, civilly by the sword.

E. Know. Why, are you so sure of your hand, captain, at all times?

Bob. Tut! never miss thrust, upon my reputation with you.

E. Know. I would not stand in Downright's state then, an you meet

him, for the wealth of anyone street in London.

Bob. Why, sir, you mistake me: if he were here now, by this welkin,

I would not draw my weapon on him. Let this gentleman do his mind:

but I will bastinado him, by the bright sun, wherever I meet him.

Mat. Faith, and I'll have a fling at him, at my distance.

E. Know. 'Od's, so, look where he is! yonder he goes.

[Downright crosses the stage].

Dow. What peevish luck have I, I cannot meet with these bragging

rascals?

Bob. It is not he, is it?

E. Know. Yes, faith, it is he.

Mat. I'll be hang'd then if that were he.

E. Know. Sir, keep your hanging good for some greater matter, for I

assure you that were he.

Step. Upon my reputation, it was he.

Bob. Had I thought it had been he, he must not have gone so: but I

can hardly be induced to believe it was he yet.

E. Know. That I think, sir.

Re-enter DOWNRIGHT.

But see, he is come again.

Dow. O, Pharaoh's foot, have I found you? Come, draw to your tools;

draw, gipsy, or I'll thrash you.

Bob. Gentleman of valour, I do believe in thee; hear me—

Dow. Draw your weapon then.

Bob. Tall man, I never thought on it till now—Body of me, I had a warrant of the peace served on me, even now as I came along, by a water-bearer; this gentleman saw it, Master Mathew.

Dow. 'Sdeath! you will not draw then?

[Disarms and beats him. Mathew runs away].

Bob. Hold, hold! under thy favour forbear!

Dow. Prate again, as you like this, you whoreson foist you! You'll control the point, you! Your consort is gone; had he staid he had shared with you, sir.

[Exit].

Bob. Well, gentlemen, bear witness, I was bound to the peace, by this good day.

E. Know. No, faith, it's an ill day, captain, never reckon it other: but, say you were bound to the peace, the law allows you to defend yourself: that will prove but a poor excuse.

Bob. I cannot tell, sir; I desire good construction in fair sort. I never sustain'd the like disgrace, by heaven! Sure I was struck with a planet thence, for I had no power to touch my weapon.

E. Know. Ay, like enough; I have heard of many that have been beaten under a planet: go, get you to a surgeon. 'Slid! An these be your tricks, your passadoes, and your montantos, I'll none of them.

[Exit Bobadill.] O, manners! That this age should bring forth such creatures! That nature should be at leisure to make them! Come, coz.

Step. Mass, I'll have this cloak.

E. Know. 'Od's will, 'tis Downright's.

Step. Nay, it's mine now, another might have ta'en it up as well: I'll wear it, so I will.

E. Know. How an he see it? He'll challenge it, assure yourself.

Step. Ay, but he shall not have it: I'll say I bought it.

E. Know. Take heed you buy it not too dear, coz.

[Exeunt.]

SCENE IV.-A Room in KITELY'S House.

Enter KITELY, WELLBRED, Dame KITELY, and BRIDGET,

Kit. Now, trust me, brother, you were much to blame,

T' incense his anger, and disturb the peace

Of my poor house, where there are sentinels

That every minute watch to give alarms

Of civil war, without adjection

Of your assistance or occasion.

Wel. No harm done, brother, I warrant you: since there is no harm

done, anger costs a man nothing; and a tall man is never his own

man till he be angry. To keep his valour in obscurity, is to keep

himself as it were in a cloak bag. What's a musician, unless he

play? What's a tall man unless he fight? For, indeed, all this my

wise brother stands upon absolutely; and that made me fall in with

him so resolutely.

Dame K. Ay, but what harm might have come of it, brother?

Wel. Might, sister? so might the good warm clothes your husband

wears be poisoned, for any thing he knows: or the wholesome wine he

drank, even now at the table.

Kit. Now, God forbid! O me! now I remember

My wife drank to me last, and changed the cup,

And bade me wear this cursed suit to-day.

See, if Heaven suffer murder undiscover'd!

I feel me ill; give me some mithridate,

Some mithridate and oil, good sister, fetch me:

O, I am Sick at heart, I burn. I burn.

If you will save my life, go fetch it me.

Wel. O strange humour! my very breath has poison'd him.

Brid. Good brother be content, what do you mean?

The strength of these extreme conceits will kill you.

DameK. Beshrew your heart, blood, brother Wellbred, now,

For putting such a toy into his head!

Wel. Is a fit simile a toy? will he be poison'd with a simile?

Brother Kitely, what a strange and idle imagination is this! For

shame, be wiser. O' my soul there's no such matter.

Kit. Am I not sick? how am I then not poison'd? Am I not

poison'd?

how am I then so sick?

Dame K. If you be sick, your own thoughts make you sick.

Wel. His jealousy is the poison he has taken.

Enter BRAINWORM, disguised in FORMAL'S clothes.

Brai. Master Kitely, my master, justice Clement salutes you; and

desires to speak with you with all possible speed.

Kit. No time but now, when I think I am sick, very sick! well, I

will wait upon his worship. Thomas! Cob! I must seek them out,

and

set them sentinels till I return. Thomas! Cob! Thomas!

[Exit. Wel.]

This is perfectly rare, Brainworm; [takes him aside.] but how

got'st thou this apparel of the justice's man?

Brai. Marry, sir, my proper fine pen-man would needs bestow

the

grist on me, at the Windmill, to hear some martial discourse;

where

I so marshall'd him, that I made him drunk with admiration; and,

because too much heat was the cause of his distemper, I stript

him

stark naked as he lay along asleep, and borrowed his suit to

deliver this counterfeit message in, leaving a rusty armour, and

an

old brown bill to watch him till my return; which shall be, when I

have pawn'd his apparel, and spent the better part O' the money, perhaps.

Wel. Well, thou art a successful merry knave, Brainworm: his absence will be a good subject for more mirth. I pray thee return to thy young master, and will him to meet me and my sister Bridget

at the Tower instantly; for here, tell him the house is so stored with jealousy, there is no room for love to stand up'right in. We must get our fortunes committed to some larger prison, say; and than the Tower, I know no better air, nor where the liberty of the

house may do us more present service. Away.

Exit Brai.

Re-enter KITELY, talking aside to CASH.

Kit. Come hither, Thomas. Now my secret's ripe,
And thou shalt have it: lay to both thine ears.
Hark what I say to thee. I must go forth, Thomas;
Be careful of thy promise, keep good watch,
Note every gallant, and observe him well,
That enters in my absence to thy mistress:
If she would shew him rooms, the jest is stale,
Follow them, Thomas, or else hang on him,
And let him not go after; mark their looks;
Note if she offer but to see his band,
Or any other amorous toy about him;
But praise his leg, or foot: or if she say
The day is hot, and bid him feel her hand,
How hot it is; O, that's a monstrous thing!
Note me all this, good Thomas, mark their sighs,
And if they do but whisper, break 'em off:
I'll bear thee out in it. Wilt thou do this?
Wilt thou be true, my Thomas?
Cash. As truth's self, sir.

Kit. Why, I believe thee: Where is Cob, now? Cob!
[Exit].

Dame K. He's ever calling for Cob: I wonder how he employs Cob so.

Wel. Indeed, sister, to ask how he employs Cob, is a necessary question for you that are his wife, and a thing not very easy for you to be satisfied in; but this I'll assure you, Cob's wife is an excellent bawd, sister, and oftentimes your husband haunts her house; marry, to what end? I cannot altogether accuse him; imagine
you what you think convenient: but I have known fair hides have foul hearts ere now, sister.

Dame K. Never said you truer than that, brother, so much I can tell
you for your learning. Thomas, fetch your cloak and go with me. *[Exit Gash.]* I'll after him presently: I would to fortune I could take him there, i'faith, I'd return him his own, I warrant him!
[Exit].

Wel. So, let 'em go; this may make sport anon. Now, my fair sister-in-law, that you knew but how happy a thing it were to be fair and beautiful.

Brid. That touches not me, brother.

Wel. That's true; that's even the fault of it; for indeed, beauty stands a woman in no stead, unless it procure her touching.—But,
sister, whether it touch you or no. It touches your beauties; and I
am sure they will abide the touch; an they do not, a plague of all ceruse, say I! and it touches me too in part, though not in the—Well, there's a dear and respected friend of mine, sister, stands very strongly and worthily affected toward you, and hath vowed to inflame whole bonfires of zeal at his heart, in honour of
your perfections. I have already engaged my promise to bring you

where you shall hear him confirm much more. Ned Knowell is the man,

sister: there's no exception against the party. You are ripe for a husband; and a minute's loss to such all occasion, is a great trespass in a wise beauty. What say you, sister? On 'my soul he loves you; will you give him the meeting?

Brid. Faith, I had very little confidence in mine own constancy, brother, if I durst not meet a man; but this motion of yours savours of an old knight adventurer's servant a little too much, methinks.

Wel. What' s that, sister?

Brid. Marry, of the squire.

Wel. No matter if it did, I would be such an one for my friend. But

see, who is return'd to hinder us!

Reenter KITELY.

Kit. What villainy is this? call'd out on a false message!

This was some plot; I was not sent for.—-Bridget,

Where is your sister?

Brid. I think she be gone forth, sir.

Kit. How! is my wife gone forth? whither, for God's sake?

Brid. She's gone abroad with Thomas.

Kit.

Abroad with Thomas! Oh, that villain dors me:

Beast that I was, to trust him! whither, I pray you,

Went she?

Brid. I know not, sir.

Wel. I'll tell you, brother, Whither I suspect she's gone;

Kit. Whither, good brother?

Wel. To Cob's house, I believe: but, keep my counsel.

Kit. I will, I will: to Cob's house! doth she haunt Cob's?

She's gone a purpose now to cuckold me,

With that lewd rascal, who, to win her favour,

Hath told her all.

[Exit.]

Wel. Come, he is once more gone,

Sister, let's lose no time; the affair is worth it. *[Exeunt.]*

SCENE VII.—-A Street.

Enter MATHEW and BOBADILL.

Mat. I wonder, captain, what they will say of my going away, ha?

Bob. Why, what should they say; but as of a discreet gentleman; quick, wary, respectful of nature's fair lineaments? and that's all.

Mat. Why so! but what can they say of your beating

Bob. A rude part, a touch with soft wood, a kind of gross battery used, laid on strongly, borne most patiently; and that's all.

Mat. Ay, but would any man have offered it in Venice, as you say?

Bob. Tut! I assure you, no: you shall have there your nobilis, your gentilezza, come in bravely upon your reverse, stand you close, stand you firm, stand you fair, save your retricato with his left leg, come to the assalto with the right, thrust with brave steel, defy your base wood! But wherefore do I awake this remembrance? I was fascinated, by Jupiter; fascinated, but I will be unwitch'd and revenged by law.

Mat. Do you hear? is it not best to get a warrant, and have him arrested and brought before justice Clement?

Bob. It were not amiss; would we had it!

Enter BRAINWORM disguised as FORMAL.

Mat. Why, here comes his man; let's speak to him.

Bob. Agreed, do you speak,

Mat. Save you, sir.

Brai. With all my heart, sir.

Mat. Sir, there is one Downright hath abused this gentleman and myself, and we determine to make our amends by law: now, if you would do us the favour to procure a warrant to bring him afore your master, you shall be well considered, I assure you, sir.

Brai. Sir, you know my service is my living; such favours as these
gotten of my master is his only preferment, and therefore you must
consider me as I may make benefit of my place.

Mat. How is that, Sir?

Brai. Faith, sir, the thing is extraordinary, and the gentleman may
be of great account; yet, be he what he will, if you will lay me
down a brace of angels in my hand you shall have it, otherwise not.

Mat. How shall we do, captain? he asks a brace of angels, you have
no money?

Bob. Not a cross, by fortune.

Mat. Nor I, as I am a gentleman, but twopence left of my two
shillings in the morning for wine and radish: let's find him some
pawn.

Bob. Pawn! we have none to the value of his demand.

Mat. O, yes; I'll pawn this jewel in my ear, and you may pawn your
silk stockings, and pull up your boots, they will ne'er be mist: it
must be done now.

Bob. Well, an there be no remedy, I'll step aside and pull them
off.

[Withdraws.]

Mat. Do you hear, sir? we have no store of money at this time, but
you shall have good pawns; look you, sir, this jewel, and that
gentleman's silk stockings; because we would have it dispatch'd ere
we went to our chambers.

Brai. I am content, sir; I will get you the What's his name, say
you? Downright?

Mat. Ay, ay, George Downright.

Brai. What manner of man is he?

Mat. A tall big man, sir; he goes in a cloak most commonly of silk-russet, laid about with russet lace.

Brai. 'Tis very good, sir.

Mat. Here, Sir, here's my jewel.

Bob. [returning.] And here are my stockings.

Brai. Well, gentlemen, I'll procure you this warrant presently; but

who will you have to serve it?

Mat. That's true, captain: that must be considered.

Bob. Body O' me, I know not; 'tis service of danger.

Brai. Why, you were best get one O' the varlets of the city, a serjeant: I'll appoint you one, if you please.

Mat. Will you, sir? why, we can wish no better.

Bob. We'll leave it to you, sir.

[Exeunt Bob. and Mat.]

Brai. This is rare! Now will I go and pawn this cloak of the justice's man's at the broker's, for a varlet's suit, and be the varlet myself; and get either more pawns, or more money of Downright, for the arrest.

[Exit.]

SCENE VIII.-The Lane before COB'S House.

Enter KNOWELL.

Know. Oh, here it is; I am glad I have found it now;

Ho! who is within here?

Tib. [within.] I am within, sir; what's your pleasure?

Know. To know who is within beside yourself.

Tib. Why, sir, you are no constable, I hope?

Know. O, fear you the constable? then I doubt not,

You have some guests within deserve that fear;

I'll fetch him straight.

Enter TIB.

Tib. O' God's name, sir!

Know. Go to: come tell me, is not young Knowell here?

Tib. Young Knowell! I know none such, sir, o' mine honesty.

Know. Your honesty, dame! it flies too lightly from you.

There is no way but fetch the constable.
Tib. The constable! the man is mad, I think.
[Exit, and claps to the door.]
Enter Dame KITELY and CASH.
Cash. Ho! who keeps house here?
Know. O, this is the female copesmate of my son:
Now shall I meet him straight.
DameK. Knock, Thomas, hard.
Cash. Ho, goodwife!
Re-enter TIB.
Tib. Why, what's the matter with you?
Dame K. Why, woman, grieves it you to ope your door?
Belike you get something to keep it shut.
Tib. What mean these questions, pray ye?
DameK. So strange you make it! is not my husband here?
Know. Her husband!
Dame K. My tried husband, master Kitely?
Tib. I hope he needs not to be tried here.
Dame K. No, dame, he does it not for need, but pleasure.
Tib. Neither for need nor pleasure is he here.
Know. This is but a device to balk me withal:
Enter KITELY, muffled in his cloak.
Soft, who is this? 'tis not my son disguised?
DameK. *[spies her husband, and runs to him.]*
O, sir, have I fore-stall'd your honest market,
Found your close walks? You stand amazed now, do you?
I'faith, I am glad I have smok'd you yet at last.
What is your jewel, trow? In, come, let's see her;
Fetch forth your housewife, dame; if she be fairer,
In any honest judgment, than myself,
I'll be content with it: but she is change,
She feeds you fat, she soothes your appetite,
And you are well! Your wife, an honest woman,
Is meat twice sod to you, sir! O, you treachour!
Know. She cannot counterfeit thus palpably.

Kit. Out on thy more than strumpet impudence!
Steal'st thou thus to thy haunts? and have I taken
Thy bawd and thee, and thy companion,
This hoary-headed letcher, this old goat,
Close at your villainy, and would'st thou 'scuse it
With this stale harlot's jest, accusing me?
O, old incontinent, [to Knowell.] dost thou not shame,
When all thy powers in chastity are spent,
To have a mind so hot? and to entice,
And feed the enticements of a lustful woman?
DameK. Out, I defy thee, I, dissembling wretch!
Kit. Defy me, strumpet! Ask thy pander here,
Can he deny it; or that wicked elder?
Know. Why, hear you, sir.
Kit. Tut, tut, tut; never speak:
Thy guilty conscience will discover thee.
Know. What lunacy is this, that haunts this man?
Kit. Well, good wife bawd, Cob's wife, and you,
That make your husband such a hoddy-doddy;
And you, young apple-squire, and old cuckold-maker;
I'll have you every one before a justice:
Nay, you shall answer it, I charge you go.
Know. Marry, with all my heart, sir, I go willingly;
Though I do taste this as a trick put on me,
To punish my impertinent search, and justly,
And half forgive my son for the device.
Kit. Come, will you go?
Dame K. Go! to thy shame believe it.
Enter Cob.
Cob. Why, what's the matter here, 'what's here to do?
Kit. O; Cob, art thou come? I have been abused,
And in thy house; was never man so wrong'd!
Cob. 'Slid, in my house, my master Kitely! who wrongs you in
my house? '
Kit. Marry, young lust in old, and old in young here:

Thy wife's their bawd, here have I taken them.

Cob. How, bawd! is my house come to that? Am I preferr'd thithcr?

Did I not charge you to keep your doors shut, Isbel? and—-you let them lie open for all comers! [Beats his wife.

Know. Friend, know some cause, before thou beat'st thy wife. This is madness in thee.

Cob. Why, is there no cause?

Kit. Yes, I'll shew cause before the justice, Cob:

Come, let her go with me.

Cob. Nay, she shall go.

Tib. Nay, I will go. I'll see an you may be allowed to make a bundle of hemp of your right and lawful wife thus, at every cuckoldy knave's pleasure. Why do you not go?

Kit. A bitter quean! Come, we will have you tamed.
[Exeunt.]

SCENE IX.—-A Street.

Enter BRAINWORM, disguised as a City Serjeant.

Brai. Well, of all my disguises yet, now am I most like myself, being in this serjeant's gown. A man of my present profession never

counterfeits, till he lays hold upon a debtor, and says, he rests him; for then he brings him to all manner of unrest. A kind of little kings we are, bearing the diminutive of a mace, made like a young artichoke, that always carries pepper and salt in itself.

Well, I know not what danger I undergo by this exploit; pray Heaven

I come well off!

Enter MATHEW and BOBADILL.

Mat. See, I think, yonder is the varlet, by his gown.

Bob. Let's go in quest of him.

Mat. 'Save you, friend! 'are not you here by appointment of justice

Clement's man?

Brai. Yes, an't please you, sir; he told me, two gentlemen had will'd him to procure a warrant from his master, which I have about

me, to be served on one Downright.

Mat. It is honestly done of you both; and see where the party comes

you must arrest; serve it upon him quickly afore he be aware.

Bob. Bear back, master Mathew.

Enter STEPHEN in DOWNRIGHT'S cloak.

Brai. Master Downright, I arrest you in the queen's name, and must

carry you afore a justice by virtue of this warrant:

Step. Me, friend! I am no Downright, I; I am master Stephen; You do

not well to arrest me, I tell you, truly; I am in nobody's bonds nor books, I would you should know it. A plague on you heartily, for making me thus afraid afore my time!

Brai. Why, now you are deceived, gentlemen.

Bob. He wears such a cloak, and that deceived us: but see, here a'

comes indeed; this is he; officer.

Enter DOWNRIGHT.

Dow. Why how now, signior gull! are you turn'd filcher of late! Come, deliver my cloak.

Step. Your cloak, sir! I bought it even now, in open market.

Brai. Master Downright, I have a warrant I must serve upon you, procured by these two gentlemen.

Dow. These gentlemen! these rascals!

[Offers to beat them.]

Brai. Keep the peace, I charge you in her majesty's name.

Dow. I obey thee. What must I do, officer?

Brai. Go before master justice Clement; to answer that they can object against you, sir: I will use you kindly, sir.

Mat. Come, let's before, and make the justice, captain.

Bob. The varlet's a tall man, afore heaven!

[Exeunt Bob. and Mat.]

Dow. Gull, you'll give me my cloak.

Step. Sir, I bought it, and I'll keep it.

Dow. You will?

Step. Ay, that I will.

Dow. Officer, there's thy fee, arrest him.

Brai. Master Stephen I must arrest you.

Step. Arrest me! I scorn it. There, take your cloak, I'll none on't.

Dow. Nay, that shall not serve your turn now, sir. Officer, I'll go with thee to the justice's; bring him along.

Step. Why, is not here your cloak? what would you have?

Dow. I'll have you answer it, sir.

Brai. Sir, I'll take your word, and this gentleman's too, for his appearance.

Dow. I'll have no words taken: bring him along.

Brai. Sir, I may choose to do that, I may take bail.

Dow. 'Tis true, you may take bail, and choose at another time: but

you shall not now, varlet: bring him along, or I'll swinge you.

Brai. Sir, I pity the gentleman's case: here's your money again.

Dow. 'Sdeins, tell not me of my money; bring him away, I say.

Brai. I warrant you he will go with you of himself, sir.

Dow. Yet more ado?

Brai. I have made a fair mash on't;

Aside.

Step. Must I go?

Brai. I know no remedy, master Stephen.

Dow. Come along afore me here; I do not love your hanging look behind.

Step. Why, sir, I hope you cannot hang me for it: can he, fellow?

Brai. I think not, sir; it is but a whipping matter, sure.

[*Exeunt.*]

Every Man in His Humour Summary and Analysis of Act IV

Summary

Act IV

Scene 1

In <u>Kitely</u>'s house, <u>Dame Kitely</u> is protesting to <u>Downright</u> that there's nothing she could do—these are her brother's friends. Downright scoffs that they are not good friends at all but tempt him to bad behavior. Dame Kitely sighs that she cannot keep them all out.

<u>Bridget</u>, Matthew, and <u>Bobadil</u> enter, followed by <u>Wellbred</u>, Edward, Stephen, and <u>Brainworm</u>. Bridget is complimenting Matthew's verses to her, and Dame Kitely asks to hear them. Downright leaves, saying he'd prefer the stocks. Matthew proceeds with some lines from *Hero and Leander*.

Wellbred asks how they all like it, and Stephen shakes his head. Edward jokes that he shakes his head like a bottle to see if there is anything in it. Matthew adds that he wrote some verses this morning at Bobadil's desk. Stephen asks how Edward likes them, and when Edward says they're the best he's ever heard, Stephen quickly proclaims the same.

Downright returns, grumbling that the men are still here and orders all of them out of the house. Wellbred laughs and tells him he is an ass, and draws his rapier. Downright and the others do as well. Dame Kitely calls for servants and Edward tries to calm the men down. <u>Cash</u> and the servants come and part the men, holding them back.

Kitely enters and asks what is going on. He assumes it is his wife and sister who have caused this mayhem. Downright spits out that it was "A sort of lewd rake-hells, that care neither for / God, nor the Devil! And they must come here to read / ballads, and roguery, and trash!" (64). Bridget tries to calm him, saying he is too violent in his words and Wellbred will not tolerate such insults and reproofs. Downright scoffs that he has no desire to respect a man without manners or manhood. He exits.

After he departs, Bridget and Dame Kitely mention that there was one man who behaved himself admirably.

They depart as well, and Kitely jealously asks Cash who the man was whom they praised. He says it was <u>Edward Knowell</u>, "a handsome / young gentlemen, sir" (64). Kitely is upset and decides to search for him, assuming he is somewhere secreted away in the house.

Scene 2

In the lane before his house, Cob calls up to Tib. He warns her to stay inside and not let any gentlemen inside.

Scene 3

In a room at the Windmill Tavern, Edward praises Brainworm. Wellbred asks Edward if he is interested in Bridget. Edward demurs, but Wellbred proclaims he shall have her, and he only ought to say where Wellbred should bring her. Edward tells him he believes his ardor, and thanks him.

Scene 4

It is a street in the Old Jewry where Formal and Knowell converse. Formal is asking Knowell if his man was a soldier, and Brainworm, disguised as Fitz-sword, arrives. Brainworm informs Knowell his son knows everything, but he cannot say how he knows that. Knowell rues this, and asks where he found Edward and his companions.

Brainworm explains that they found *him*, actually, and surrounded him with their rapiers drawn and demanded he tell them where Knowell was. They locked him up but he managed to escape. Edward is planning to meet one of the wives of the rich merchants at Cob's house.

Upon hearing this, Knowell proclaims he will go there and intercept his son. He sends Cob to Clement's place. After Knowell is gone, Brainworm smiles to himself that he wishes he could see Knowell waiting there for hours like a fool. He cannot, though, and takes up Formal's invitation to get a drink at the Windmill.

Scene 5

Matthew, Edward, Bobadil, and Stephen come together at Moorfields. Matthew criticizes Downright and Bobadil boasts that he taught Matthew a trick to kill him. Edward asks if Bobadil ever proved himself to people in the town, and Bobadil says yes, he invited a few people to learn from him. The men did, but now hate him because he is "excellent, and for no / other vile reason on the earth" (71). Bobadil adds that sometimes they insult him in the street and he could have slain them all, but he does not delight in murder. He likes to be a gentleman and live obscurely here, but if he could, he would tell her Majesty and the Lords how he would manage to take down an entire army of an enemy.

Edward entertains him further by asking about his plan. Bobadil says he would select nineteen men along with himself, choosing them because they have the same wonderful instinct he does. He and his men would challenge the enemy to send out their best twenty men, and the enemy could not refuse. Then Bobadil and his men would slay the twenty, then twenty more, and so on until there are no enemies left. Edward, amused, asks if he is so sure of his hand. Bobadil replies that yes, he never misses, and if Downright were here right now, he'd draw his weapon on him.

At that moment, Downright walks by. He is annoyed to see these "peevish rascals" (73) again. He curses that Bobadil ought to draw his blade. Bobadil protests that he actually has a command of the peace served on him so he cannot fight. Downright beats him and disarms him. Matthew runs away in fear. Downright lets Bobadil go, and leaves.

Edward tells Bobadil that if he were really bound to the peace, then law says he can still *defend* himself. Bobadil replies that it was as if he'd been struck by a planet and had no ability to touch his weapon. He leaves.

Edward rolls his eyes that "this age should bring forth such creatures! that Nature / should be at leisure to make 'em!" (74). Stephen sees Downright's cloak on the ground and says he will take it; if Downright challenges him, he will say he bought it.

Scene 6

At Kitely's house, Kitely, Dame Kitely, Wellbred, and Bridget gather. Kitely is chiding Wellbred for disturbing the peace of his house, and Wellbred is acknowledging that there was, and is, no harm done. Dame Kitely asks what harm he's talking about, and Wellbred shrugs that Kitely could have been poisoned.

Upon hearing this, Kitely becomes convinced he is feeling ill, and calls for mithridate. Bridget and Dame Kitely roll their eyes, and Dame Kitely says Wellbred should not have put "such a toy into his head" (75). Kitely insists he is sick and his wife replies that if he is, it is of his own doing.

Brainworm, disguised as Clement's man Formal, enters. He announces Clement wishes to see Kitely. Wellbred pulls Brainworm aside and asks how he got this costume. Brainworm replies that he got Formal drunk and then took his clothes. Wellbred is impressed and asks if he could go to Edward and tell him to meet Bridget and Wellbred at the Tower. Brainworm agrees, and leaves.

Kitely is preparing to leave and tells Cash that he must be vigilant and watch for Dame Kitely showing any of the young men rooms, or speaking of their looks, or even just whispering with them. He must intervene, Kitely implores. Cash agrees.

After Kitely leaves, calling aloud for Cob, Dame Kitely muses aloud that her husband always seems to be employing Cob and ordering him about. Wellbred suggests slyly that Cob has a bawdy wife and oftentimes Kitely haunts her house. Dame Kitely is affronted and says she will go there now with Cash.

Wellbred laughs to himself at this sport he's made. He then turns to Bridget and tells him of Edward's affection for her, and reminds her that she is "ripe for a husband" (78). Bridget agrees to meet with Edward.

Kitely returns, angry at the false message he received. He asks where his wife is and Bridget says she went out with Thomas Cash. Kitely is convinced that he was wrong to trust Cash, and decides to go to Cob's house to confront her.

Scene 7

Matthew and Bobadil walk together in the street. Matthew is planning on going away but first they must secure a warrant against Downright to arrest him and bring him before Clement.

Brainworm, disguised as Formal, enters. Matthew and Bobadil approach him and say they need the warrant for Downright because he abused them. Brainworm agrees, but says it costs money. The men have none, but they take off their jewelry and silk stockings eagerly. Brainworm thanks them and says he will go out now to procure the warrant, which will be served by one of the city varlets.

Scene 8

Outside of Cob's house, Knowell calls up to know who is inside. Tib answers and wonders if he is a constable. Knowell asks if his son is there and she says she does not know him. Knowell thinks she is lying and that he must fetch the constable.

Dame Kitely and Cash arrive now, and Dame Kitely asks Tib why she will not open the door and if her husband is here. Tib says no. Knowell is confused by Dame Kitely's presence.

Kitely himself, muffled in his cloak, arrives. Dame Kitely rushes over to him, triumphantly proclaiming that she's found out his bad behavior. She bitterly wonders if the woman he's meeting is prettier than herself. Kitely retorts that *he* has found out *her* behavior. He says that Knowell is her paramour, which causes Knowell to declare Kitely a lunatic. Kitely swears he will bring them all before a judge, and both Knowell and Dame Kitely huffily agree.

Cob enters, and Kitely immediately tells him he has been wronged here at Cob's house. Cob is shocked that his wife has allowed their home to become a brothel, and grabs her and beats her. Tib and Cob also decide to go to Justice Clement's to sort this out.

Scene 9

Brainworm is now disguised as a varlet, or city servant; he feels like this disguise is closest to who he really is. When Matthew and Bobadil enter and espy him, they approach and Brainworm says he has the warrant.

Stephen wearing Downright's cloak walks by, and Brainworm accosts him and says he is arrested. Stephen proclaims that he is not Downright, and rebukes Brainworm for scaring him. Bobadil sees Downright himself coming, though, and points out the man.

Brainworm announces to Downright that he is arrested and must go before Justice Clement. Bobadil and Matthew eagerly leave to Clement's house.

Downright sees Stephen with his cloak and asks for it, but Stephen says it is his and he bought it. Downright calls for Stephen's arrest so Brainworm moves to do so. All of them plan to go to Clement's.

Analysis

Brainworm's plots and jokes and tricks begin to accelerate in this section, and by the act's end Cob and Tib and Kitely and Dame Kitely are estranged, swords have been drawn, warrants have been issued, and jealousy, anger, and irrationality have preponderated. Bobadil and Matthew are guided by their choler and lassitude, Stephen his choler and melancholy, Kitely his jealousy and ridiculousness, and Downright his impatience. These characters seem to be on mostly preordained paths, and it will take a Justice Clement figure to intervene and salvage their relationships and reputations.

For now, though, Brainworm gets to continue as he sees fit. He is one of Jonson's most compelling creations, and is more than a simple servant or trickster. Rather, as Matthew Kendrick suggests, he embodies the anxieties at the time regarding the lower classes. So-called vagrants or beggars or debtors were considered problematic in society and there were numerous measures in the late 16th century to "deal" with them. Brainworm, though, does not allow himself to be oppressed by his status and instead is a protean figure who adapts, evades, and fools others in order to keep himself afloat economically. Kendrick begins his exposition of the character by explaining that if humouralism suggests the body is influenced by the outside world, then Brainworm's "'humour of necessity' that sanctioned his trickery and deception describes a subjectivity that corresponds to the impoverished body that, locked in a struggle against a harsh economic environment, must continually adapt in order to survive." While some characters will be offended or consider themselves injured by Brainworm, others, including Clement, admire his skill and mutability.

The London of the play is one "thrown into chaos by the unsettling of traditional social boundaries." Jonson puts humours into economic context as well as social, creating in Brainworm a lower-class character whose subjectivity is tied to his economic standing. It might be easy to look at Brainworm's deeds and conclude he is a trickster, but this role is not "archetypal but rather contingent on the particular socioeconomic conditions of Elizabethan London." He feels he *has* to do what he does, for example choosing to undermine Knowell because his more solid employment is with Edward.

Brainworm's disguise as a former-soldier-now-turned beggar is an astute commentary on the complexities of begging. Kendrick sees his intentional adoption of a new identity as a way to maintain control over his circumstances. As Fitz-Sword Brainworm gets to "transvalue the status of beggar or vagrant, interpreting it as a source of agency and empowerment, a form of labor in its own right. In the disguise of a beggar, Brainworm can anticipate and attempt to prevent his decline to the status of an actual 'motley' beggar."

Brainworm's encounter with Knowell while he is in this guise also reveals common stereotypes held by those who cannot understand, or refuse to understand, why people cannot always succeed economically. Knowell articulates those as he says to Brainworm in Act Two, "Art thou a man? and sham'st thou not to beg? / To practice such a servile kind of life?", and subsequently suggests that "a thousand fairer courses / Offer themselves to thy election" (37). He does think Brainworm and others like him "care how the metal of your minds / Is eaten with the rust of idleness" (37) and sees his "choice" to live like this as a "loose desperate" course (37). And when Brainworm says he would gladly find some other course if he could, Knowell retorts rudely, "Aye, you'd gladly find it, but you will not seek / it" (37). He makes no attempt to see how capital oppresses labor, and how most of those in straitened circumstances are not there simply because they lack will or direction. Brainworm will endeavor to prove to Knowell that he is wrong in his assumptions, and while he most likely doesn't succeed in forever altering such assumptions, at the end of Act Five there is at least a glimmer of a shift in Knowell.

ACT V

SCENE I.-Coleman Street.

A Hall in Justice CLEMENT'S House.

Enter CLEMENT, KNOWELL, KITELY, Dame K., TIB., CASH, COB, and Servants.

Step. Why then let him do his worst, I am resolute.

Clem. Nay, but stay, stay, give me leave: my chair, sirrah. You, master Knowell, say you went thither to meet your son?

Know. Ay, sir.

Clem. But who directed you thither?

Know. That did mine own man, sir.

Clem. Where is he?

Know. Nay, I know not now; I left him with your clerk, and appointed him to stay here for me.

Clem. My clerk! about what time was this?

Know. Marry, between one and two, as I take it.

Clem. And what time came my man with the false message to you,

master Kitely?

Kit. After two, sir.

Clem. Very good: but, mistress Kitely, how chance that you were at

Cob's, ha?

Dame K. An't please you, sir, I'll tell you: my brother Wellbred told me, that Cob's house was a suspected place—

Clem. So it appears, methinks: but on.

Dame K. And that my husband used thither daily.

Clem. No matter, so he used himself well, mistress.

Dame K. True, sir: but you know what grows by such haunts oftentimes.

Clem. I see rank fruits of a jealous brain, mistress Kitely: but did you find your husband there, in that case as you suspected?

Kit. I found her there, sir.

Clem. Did you, so! that alters the case. Who gave you knowledge of

your wife's being there?

Kit. Marry, that did my brother Wellbred.

Clem. How, Wellbred first tell her; then tell you after! Where is Wellbred?

Kit. Gone with my sister, sir, I know not whither.

Clem. Why this is a mere trick, a device; you are gull'd in this most grossly all. Alas, poor wench! wert thou beaten for this?

Tib. Yell, most pitifully, an't please you.

Cob. And worthily, I hope, if it shall prove so.

Clem. Ay, that's like, and a piece of a sentence.—

Enter a Servant.

How now, sir! what's the matter?

Serv. Sir, there's a gentleman in the court without, desires to speak with your worship.

Clem. A gentleman! what is he?

Serv. A soldier, sir, he says.

Clem. A soldier! take down my armour, my sword quickly. A soldier

speak with me! Why, when, knaves? Come on, come on; [arms himself]

hold my cap there, so; give me my gorget, my sword: stand by, I will end your matters anon.—Let the soldier enter.

[Exit Servant.]

Enter BOBADILL, followed by MATHEW.

Now, sir, what have you to say to me? Bob. By your worship's favour—

Clem. Nay, keep out, sir; I know not your pretence. You send me word, sir, you are a soldier: why, sir, you shall be answer'd here: here be them that have been amongst soldiers. Sir, your pleasure.

Bob. Faith, sir, so it is, this gentleman and myself have been most uncivilly wrong'd and beaten by one Downright, a coarse fellow, about the town here; and for mine own part, I protest, being a man in no sort given to this filthy humour of quarrelling, he hath

assaulted me in the way of my peace, despoiled me of mine honour,

disarmed me of my weapons, and rudely laid me along in the open

streets, when I not so much as once offered to resist him.

Clem. O, God's precious! is this the soldier? Here, take my armour

off quickly, 'twill make him swoon, I fear; he is not fit to look

on't, that will put up a blow.

Mat. An't please your worship, he was bound to the peace.

Clem. Why, an he were, sir, his hands were not bound, were they?

Re-enter Servant.

Serv. There's one of the varlets of the city, sir, has brought two

gentlemen here; one, upon your worship's warrant.

Clem. My warrant!

Serv. Yes, sir; the officer says, procured by these two.

Clem. Bid him come in. [Exit Servant.] Set by this picture.

Enter DOWNRIGHT, STEPHEN, and BRAINWORM, disguised as before.

What, Master Downright! are you brought in at Mr. Freshwater's suit

here?

Dow. I'faith, sir, and here's another brought at my suit.

Clem. What are you, sir?

Step. A gentleman, sir. O, uncle!

Clem. Uncle! who, Master Knowell?

Know. Ay, sir; this is a wise kinsman of mine.

Step. God's my witness, uncle, I am wrong'd here monstrously, he

charges me with stealing of his cloak, and would I might never

stir, if I did not find it in the street by chance.

Dow. O, did you find it now? You said you bought it erestwhile.

Step. And you said, I stole it: nay, now my uncle is here, I'll do well enough with you.

Clem. Well, let this breathe awhile. You that have cause to complain there, stand forth: Had you my warrant for this gentleman's apprehension?

Bob. Ay, an't please your worship.

Clem. Nay, do not speak in passion so: where had you it?

Bob. Of your clerk, sir.

Clem. That's well! an my clerk can make warrants, and my hand not

at them! Where is the warrant-officer, have you it?

Brai. No, sir; your worship's man, Master Formal, bid me do it for

these gentlemen, and he would be my discharge.

Clem. Why, Master Downright, are you such a novice, to be ser'ved

and never see the warrant?

Dow. Sir, he did not serve it on me.

Clem. No! how then?

Dow. Marry, sir, he came to me, and said he must serve it, and he

would use me kindly, and so—

Clem. O, God's pity, was it so, sir? He must serve it! Give me my long sword there, and help me off. So, come on, sir varlet, I must cut off your legs, sirrah; [Brainworm kneels.] nay, stand up, I'll use you kindly, I must cut off your legs, I say.

[Flourishes over him with his long sword.]

Brai. O, good sir, I beseech you; nay, good master justice!

Clem. I must do it, there is no remedy; I must cut off your legs, sirrrah, I must cut off your ears, you rascal, I must do it: I must cut off your nose, I must cut off your head.

Brai. O, good your worship!

Clem. Well, rise; how dost thou do now? dost thou feel thyself well? hast thou no harm?

Brai. No, I thank your good worship, sir.

Clem. Why so! I said I must cut off thy legs, and I must cut off thy arms, and I must cut off thy head; but I did not do it: so you said you must serve this gentleman with my warrant, but you did not

serve him. You knave, you slave, you rogue, do you say you must, sirrah! away with him to the jail; I'll teach you a trick for your must, sir.

Brai. Good sir, I beseech you, be good to me.

Clem. Tell him he shall to the jail; away with him, I say.

Brai. Nay, sir, if you will commit me, it shall be for committing more than this: I will not lose by my travail any grain of my fame, certain.

[Throws off his serjeant's gown.]

Clem. How is this?

Know. My man Brainworm!

Step. O, yes, uncle; Brainworm has been with my cousin Edward and I

all this day.

Clem. I told you all there was some device.

Brai. Nay, excellent justice, since I have laid myself thus open to you, now stand strong for me; both with your sword and your balance.

Clem. Body O' me, a merry knave! give me a bowl of sack: if he belong to you, Master Knowell, I bespeak your patience.

Brai. That is it I have most need of; Sir, if you'll pardon me, only, I'll glory in all the rest of my exploits.

Know. Sir, you know I love not to have my favours come hard from

me. You have your pardon, though I suspect you shrewdly for being

of counsel with my son against me.

Brai. Yes, faith, I have, sir, though you retain'd me doubly this morning for yourself: first as Brainworm; after, as Fitz-Sword. I was your reform'd soldier, sir. 'Twas I sent you to Cob's upon the errand without end.

Know. Is it possible? or that thou should'st disguise thy language so as I should not know thee?

Brai. O, sir, this has been the day of my metamorphosis. It is not that shape alone that I have run through to-day. I brought this gentleman, master Kitely, a message too, in the form of master Justice's man here, to draw him out O' the way, as well as your worship, while master Wellbred might make a conveyance of mistress Bridget to my young master.

Kit. How! My sister stolen away? Know. My son is not married, I hope.

Brai. Faith, Sir, they are both as sure as love, a priest, and three thousand pound, which is her portion, can make them; and by this time are ready to bespeak their wedding-supper at the Windmill, except some friend here prevent them, and invite them home.

Clem. Marry, that will I; I thank thee for putting me in mind on't. Sirrah, go you and fetch them hither upon my warrant. [Exit Servant.] Neither's friends have cause to be sorry, if I know the young couple aright. Here, I drink to thee for thy good news. But I pray thee, what hast thou done with my man, Formal?

Brai. Faith, sir, after some ceremony past, as making him drunk, first with story, and then with wine, (but all in kindness,) and stripping him to his shirt, I left him in that cool vein; departed, sold your worship's warrant to these two, pawn'd his livery for that varlet's gown, to serve it in; and thus have brought myself by my activity to your worship's consideration.

Clem. And I will consider thee in another cup of sack. Here's to thee, which having drunk off this my sentence: Pledge me. Thou hast done, or assisted to nothing, in my judgment, but deserves to be pardon'd for the wit of the offence. If thy master, or any man

here, be angry with thee, I shall suspect his ingine, while I know
him, for't. How now, what noise is that?

Enter Servant.

Serv. Sir, it is Roger is come home.

Clem. Bring him in, bring him in.

Enter FORMAL in a suit of armour.

What! drunk? in arms against me? your reason, your reason for
this?

Form. I beseech your worship to pardon me; I happened into ill
company by chance, that cast me into a sleep, and stript me of
all
my clothes.

Clem. Well, tell him I am Justice Clement, and do pardon him:
but
what is this to your armour? what may that signify?

Form. An't please you, sir, it hung up in the room where I was
stript; and I borrow'd it of one of the drawers to come home in,
because I was loth to do penance through the street in my shirt.

Clem. Well, stand by a while.

Enter E. KNOWELL, WELLBRED, and BRIDGET.

Who be these? O, the young company; welcome, welcome! Give
you joy.

Nay, mistress Bridget, blush not; you are not so fresh a bride, but
the news of it is come hither afore you. Master bridegroom, I
have
made your peace, give me your hand: so will I for all the rest ere
you forsake my roof.

E. Know. We are the more bound to your humanity, sir.

Clem. Only these two have so little of man in them, they are no
part of my care.

Wel. Yes, sir, let me pray you for this gentleman, he belongs to
my
sister the bride.

Clem. In what place, sir?

Wel. Of her delight, sir, below the stairs, and in public: her poet, sir.

Clem. A poet! I will challenge him myself presently at extempore.

Mount up thy Phlegon, Muse, and testify,
How Saturn, sitting in an ebon cloud,
Disrobed his podex, white as ivory,
And through the welkin thunder'd all aloud.

Wel. He is not for extempore, sir: he is all for the pocket muse; please you command a sight of it.

Clem. Yes, yes, search him for a taste of his vein. [*They search Mathew's pockets.*

Wel. You must not deny the queen's justice, sir, under a writ of rebellion.

Clem. What! all this verse? body O' me, he carries a whole realm, a

commonwealth of paper in his hose: let us see some of his subjects.

[Reads.]
Unto the boundless ocean of thy face,
Runs this poor river, charg'd with streams of eyes.
How! this is stolen.

E. Know. A parody! a parody! with a kind of miraculous gift, to make it absurder than it was.

Clem. Is all the rest of this batch? bring me a torch; lay it together, and give fire. Cleanse the air. [*Sets the papers on fire.*] Here was enough to have infected the whole city, if it had not been taken in time. See, see, how our poet's glory shines! brighter and brighter! still it increases! O, now it is at the highest; and now it declines as fast. You may see, sic transit gloria mundi!

Know. There's an emblem for you, son, and your studies.

Clem. Nay, no speech or act of mine be drawn against such as profess it worthily. They are not born every year, as an alderman.

There goes more to the making of a good poet, than a sheriff.

Master Kitely, you look upon me!—though I live in the city here,
amongst you, I will do more reverence to him, when I meet him, than
I will to the mayor out of his year. But these paper-pedlars! these
ink-dabblers! they cannot expect reprehension or reproach; they
have it with the fact,

E. Know. Sir, you have saved me the labour of a defence.

Clem. It shall be discourse for supper between your father and me,
if he dare undertake me. But to dispatch away these, you sign O'
the soldier, and picture of the poet, (but both so false, I will
not have you hanged out at my door till midnight,) while we are at
supper, you two shall penitently fast it out in my court without;
and, if you will, you may pray there that we may be so merry within
as to forgive or forget you when we come out. Here's a third,
because we tender your safety, shall watch you, he is provided for
the purpose. Look to your charge, sir.

Step. And what shall I do?

Clem. O! I had lost a sheep an he had not bleated: why, sir, you
shall give master Downright his cloak; and I will intreat him to
take it. A trencher and a napkin you shall have in the buttery, and
keep Cob and his wife company here; whom I will intreat first to be
reconciled; and you to endeavour with your wit to keep them so.

Step. I'll do my best.

Cob. Why, now I see thou art honest, Tib, I receive thee as my dear
and mortal wife again.

Tib. And I you, as my loving and obedient husband

Clem. Good compliment! It will be their bridal night too. They are married anew. Come, I conjure the rest to put off all discontent.

You, master Downright, your anger; you, master Knowell, your cares;

Master Kitely and his wife, their jealousy.

For, I must tell you both, while that is fed,

Horns in the mind are worse than on the head.

Kit. Sir, thus they go from me; kiss me, sweetheart.

See what a drove of horns fly in the air,

Wing'd with my cleansed and my credulous breath!

Watch' em suspicious eyes, watch where they fall.

See, see! on heads that think they have none at all!

O, what a plenteous world of this will come!

When air rains horns, all may be sure of some!

I have learn'd so much verse out of a jealous man's part in a play.

Clem. 'Tis well, 'tis well! This night we'll dedicate to

friendship, love, and laughter. Master bridegroom, take your bride

and lead; every one a fellow. Here is my mistress, Brainworm! to

whom all my addresses of courtship shall have their reference:

whose adventures this day, when our grandchildren shall hear to be

made a fable, I doubt not but it shall find both spectators and applause.

[Exeunt.]

Every Man in His Humour Summary and Analysis of Act V
Summary

Act V

Scene 1

The scene is at Clement's house, and Clement, <u>Knowell</u>, <u>Kitely</u>, <u>Dame Kitely</u>, <u>Tib</u>, <u>Cash</u>, <u>Cob</u>, and various servants are present. Clement asks the parties—Knowell, Kitely, and Dame Kitely—why they were at Cob's house. Clement sees that Tib in particular has done nothing wrong because she did not solicit anyone coming to her house.

A servant announces that a soldier is here to see the Judge. Clement demands his armor and sword and arms himself. Bobadil and Matthew enter. Bobadil declares that he and Matthew have been wronged and beaten by Downright, a "coarse fellow about the town" (88). Clement is incredulous that this man is the "soldier," and takes his armor off in annoyed amusement.

The servant re-enters and says there is a varlet here and two gentlemen, brought hence by Clement's warrant. Clement is confused, but says to bring them in.

Downright, Stephen, and the disguised Brainworm appear. Stephen cries out to his uncle, and Knowell identifies him as a kinsman. Stephen complains that Downright accosted him for his cloak but he found it in the street by chance. Downright, disgusted, says he thought Stephen said he bought it.

Clement tells them to cease and asks to see the warrant. Downright admits he never saw it but allowed himself to be brought here. Clement flourishes his sword and tells Brainworm he must cut off his legs. Brainworm begs him not to. Clement shrugs and says he must cut off his legs, his ears, his nose, and his head. Then he declares Brainworm must go off to jail.

At this, Brainworm throws off his varlet's disguise and everyone gasps. Knowell recognizes his man, and Clement laughs that he knew there must be "some device" (90) at work. Brainworm asks Knowell for patience and pardon, and Knowell gives it, but says he suspects Brainworm of "being of counsel with my son against me" (91). Brainworm admits to it, and admits to being Fitz-sword and also the form of Formal. He did this to draw Kitely away so Wellbred could take Bridge to meet Edward.

Kitely and Knowell are surprised at this revelation and Brainworm says indeed they are married and are getting ready to have their wedding supper at the Windmill. Clement smiles and says they all ought to drink to this good news. He asks the couple to be brought here. He then asks where Formal is. Brainworm tells him, and Clement admires his wit.

A servant enters and says Formal has come home. When Formal enters, Clement lightly scolds him for being drunk but the distressed Formal tells him he was made drunk and then stripped of his clothes.

Edward, Bridget, and Wellbred arrive, and Clement welcomes them and wishes them joy. Edward says humbly that they are bound to his humanity. Wellbred points to Matthew and says that he "belongs to my sister, the bride" (92). Clement asks how so, and Wellbred says he is her poet. Clement says he shall challenge him without preparation, and quotes a few lines. Wellbred says that Matthew has to have preparation, and suggests searching his pockets.

They search Matthew's pockets and Clement laughs that Matthew "carries a whole realm, a commonwealth of paper, in's hose" (93). He reads two lines and proclaims that they're stolen.

Clement groans and asks for fire to set it all ablaze. As the flames flicker, he says that all should see "how our poet's glory shines! Brighter and brighter!" (93). Clement says that poets are not born every year like aldermen are, and there "goes more to the making of a good / poet, than a sheriff" (93). As an aspiring poet, Edward appreciates the support for his craft, and Clement tells him he will speak to Knowell more about it.

While they are talking, Stephen asks what he shall do. Clement tells him he needs to give Downright his cloak back. He also says Cob and Tib must be reconciled; it will "be their bridal night / too. They are married anew" (94). All others, he adds, must put off their discontent.

Clement gestures to Brainworm, calling him his mistress and the focus of all of his addresses. He praises his adventures and says in the future, grandchildren will love to hear his story.

Analysis

Act Five is short, but it brings together the estranged characters, calms disputes, unmasks Brainworm, and reasserts the values of justice, harmony, and balance. Almost all of this is due to the mediation of Justice Clement, commonly viewed as a *deus ex machina* figure in that he resolves all the disputes and delivers rewards and punishments. Clement redeems the wrongly accused Tib, pushes her and Cob and Kitely and Dame Kitely to reconcile, punishes the false poet Matthew, forces Stephen to give Downright his cloak back, chastises Downright for letting himself be brought in without seeing the warrant, tells Knowell to give Edward the benefit of the doubt, ridicules the pompous Bobadil, and congratulates Edward and Bridget on their union.

Clement also forces Brainworm to unmask himself but instead of being upset at him, calls him a "merry knave" and laughs, "I told you there was some device!" (90). And at the very end, he says, "Here is my mistress, Brainworm! to whom all my addresses of court- / ship shall have their reference. Whose adventures, this / day, when our grandchildren shall hear to be made a fable, / I doubt not, but it shall find both spectators, and applause" (94). Critic Matthew Kendrick explains that "by making Brainworm the 'reference' of courtship, Clement's remarks acknowledge the central importance of Brainworm's labor to the events of the play. And indeed, in terms of plot development, Brainworm's tricks have facilitated the events that lead to Clement's intervention and the 'friendship, love, and laughter' that conclude the play. To this extent, Brainworm has gone from signifying the 'diseased riot' that threatens London social order, to being the only person capable of preserving that social order."

In his article on the play, Lawrence A. Levin looks more closely at the character of Clement. His name, of course, refers to "clemency" or "mercy," and he does exhibit intelligence, rationality, and a strong understanding of what his job as a man of the law entails. His "experiential understanding of other individuals enables him intuitively to diagnose their merits and defects" and "his ability to pierce disguises and deal objectively with others . . . [makes him stand] out in sharp contrast to the irrational characters around him."

The play ends, Levin notes, "with a formal, ritualistic ceremony followed by an orderly procession off stage." The wedding, the renewing of vows, the meted justice—all of these emphasize Jonson's commitment to order, harmony, and balance. Levin sees Jonson claiming in this play that he is a "poet-reformer" whose attitude toward the public was different than others like Shakespeare. Poetry can instruct, uplift, and cure; bad poetry can inflict disease, misunderstanding, and corruption.

Summary of the Play:

The play opens with a prologue addressing the audience. This play will have no absurdities but instead will be realistic in events and language. It will not whisk the audience away to a foreign land, but will portray a contemporary place and time for people to laugh at.

The first act starts with old man Knowell at his house. Master Stephen, a country man who is easily deceived, has come to visit his uncle, Knowell, and his cousin, Edward Knowell (Knowell's son). A servant enters and after some conversation, Stephen leaves. This allows the servant to deliver a letter to Knowell that is meant for his son. The elder Knowell reads it, knowing it is not for him. Knowell is offended by how impolite and louche the letter's writer, a young man named Wellbred is, and calls in Brainworm to give the letter to his son and not tell him he read it. Knowell vows he will not force his son to be a good man, but will try to compel him to be one freely.

Brainworm brings Edward the letter and admits that Edward's father read it. Stephen enters, inquiring about the man that brought the letter. He wants to go after the man because of his perceived rudeness, but he is far gone. Edward asks Stephen if he would like to come with him to Wellbred's, and Stephen eagerly agrees.

Matthew arrives to Cob's the water-bearer's house looking for a Captain Bobadil. Cob says he is his guest. Mathew does not believe this, but Cob insists that the man fell asleep on his bench the night before. A servant of Cob's then takes Mathew to Bobadil. The scene ends with a monologue by Cob about the drama in his master Kitely's house and his annoyance with Bobadil, who owes his wife Tib money.

Bobadil and Matthew discuss the previous night's events. Bobadil asks to keep it a secret that he spent the night there, and Matthew agrees. Matthew shares a play he likes and then the conversation moves to Matthew's own work. <u>Downright</u>, Wellbred's brother, had insulted it and threatened to beat Matthew. Bobadil offers to teach Mathew how to fight, and the two head off to a tavern.

Act Two opens at the house of Kitely, a merchant at the Old Jewry. His man <u>Cash</u> and the squire Downright enter. Kitely gives his cashier some work to do. Next, Kitely hesitantly tells the squire that Wellbred, who is the brother of his own wife, <u>Dame Kitely</u>, has become disrespectful. While Wellbred's actions anger Downright, Kitely remains calm. Kitely says that he has no authority over Wellbred and that he cannot scold him for fear of backlash.

Bobadil and Matthew enter, but quickly leave when they do not find Wellbred. Downright wants to follow them and fight, but Kitely tells him not to go. The squire leaves, and Kitely reflects on the possibility of the women in his life—his wife and his sister—being overcome by these lecherous men who are spending time in his house.

In the Moorfields, the open areas of land in London, Brainworm is disguised as a soldier. He wants to interrupt Knowell's following of his son. Stephen and Edward enter. Stephen loses his purse, which holds a ring from a mistress. Brainworm appears and offers his sword for sale since he is reduced to poverty. Though Edward tries to discourage Stephen from buying a knife off of the "soldier," Stephen says he will buy it anyway.

Still in the Moorfields, Knowell is torn between disappointment due to the letter to his son, and memories of his own youth. His speech turns to the way that parents shape their children, often in a bad way. Knowell is happy he did not do so with his own son. Yet, he sees that his son has gone astray and is not pleased. Brainworm enters in his disguise as before and begs for beer and money. Knowell scolds the "soldier" for begging, and tells him to be a better gentleman. Brainworm claims to not know how to find work, but Knowell says he will show him.

The first scene of Act Three takes place in a tavern with Matthew, Bobadil, and Wellbred. Mathew and Bobadil speak of not liking Wellbred's brother, Downright. Edward Knowell and Stephen enter. Wellbred and Edward laugh about the letter Wellbred sent, and how it was wrongly delivered to the elder Knowell.

The conversation turns to the military service served by both Stephen and Bobadil. Bobadil in particular shares a story about fighting with his trusty rapier. He and Stephen compare their swords (Stephen's is the one he bought from Brainworm). They all insult his common sword, which makes Stephen angry. Just then, Brainworm enters still disguised. Brainworm admits to fooling Stephen into buying the knife. The group of men learn the elder Knowell is headed their way, and they leave in order to not be found. Brainworm also reveals his true identity to Edward, who is grateful to be looked after this way.

Cash helps Kitely prepare to conduct some suspicious business exchanging money. Kitely then wishes to tell Cash a secret, but he feels that Cash is hesitant to swear to keep it so he does not reveal it, and instead sends Cash to do another job. Before he leaves, Kitely asks his cashier to tell him if Wellbred comes to his house with the company of any other man. Additionally, he asks that Cash keep the whole business private from Dame Kitely.

Cob enters in distress. Cash tries to convince Cob that it is his "humour" making him so distressed. As he continues to speak of fear and persecution, Matthew, Bobadil, Stephen, Wellbred, Brainworm, and Edward enter. Cash and Cob exit. The group of men discuss Brainworm's clever trick earlier. Cash reenters looking for a servant to tell Kitely that men are here, and accidentally lets out that Kitely went to Justice Clement's. The men continue to talk, this time about tobacco, and Bobadil boasts about its many uses. Then Cob and Cash reenter and Cob begins talking about recent deaths attributed to tobacco. Bobadil beats the man, but the others pull him away.

At Justice Clement's house, Cob warns Kitely about the men at his house. Kitely is worried about his wife and sister giving into desire for the men. Cob tries to put his worries at bay. After Kitely leaves, Cob states that he wants revenge on Bobadil for smoking tobacco and borrowing money from his wife.

Justice Clement, his clerk Roger Formal, and Knowell enter. Clement and Cob converse about Cob's life and meager possessions. Cob then asks the Justice for peace by punishing Bobadil and tells him about the tobacco. Instead, the Justice orders his clerk to put Cob in jail for insulting tobacco and being a rascal. He relents, but Cob's plan for revenge is over.

In Act Four, Downright and Dame Kitely discuss the visiting men. Downright wants the lady to make the men leave, but she insists she has no power over them. Matthew, Bobadil, Wellbred, Edward Knowell, Stephen, Brainworm, and Kitely's sister Bridget enter. Mathew and Bridget talk a bit flirtatiously but are interrupted by the group of men arguing. Matthew tries to impress the group with his poetry but they have mixed reviews. Wellbred does not think that the poems are enough for Dame Kitely and Bridget but the ladies think they are. Downright tries to get the group of men to leave by threatening them. They all draw swords and start to fight but are pulled apart by Cash and some other men of the house. Kitely enters asking about the quarrel but the men all exit. Bridget and Dame Kitely admit to being impressed by Edward, who tried to stop the fighting, which makes Kitely greatly distressed. He decides to search for the rascal.

Cob and his Wife Tib bicker. Cob asks his wife to let no one in to the house and she agrees. At the tavern, Stephen, Edward, Wellbred, and Brainworm convene. Wellbred sends Brainworm, disguised as a soldier, to give a message to his brother. Edward and Wellbred converse about Bridget. Edward admits to being in love with her and Wellbred wants to bring them together, but Edward is not sure he should try.

In the Old Jewry, Roger Formal and Knowell are looking for the soldier that Knowell met earlier. Brainworm enters dressed again as the soldier, Fitz-well, and in the persona of Fitz-well working for Knowell, he admits to telling Matthew and the other men about Knowell going to Justice Clement's house. Knowell then sends him with Formal and he goes to Cob's house to find the group of men.

Back at the Moorfields, the group of men gossip about Downright. Matthew and Bobadil fence a little, which leads into Bobadil telling a story about fencing some young men and continually winning. He claims that he is doing the nation a favor by sparing the lives of those men that keep coming after him to fight. Bobadil says he would not draw his sword on Downright if he appeared, and coincidentally, Downright does come by just then. Downright tells Bobadil to fight, and Downright successfully disarms the man. To close the scene, Stephen picks up Downright's cloak that he left there and claims it as his own.

Back at Kitely's house with Kitely, Wellbred, Dame Kitely, and Bridget, Kitely scolds Wellbred for fighting with the men earlier. Brainworm enters dressed as Roger Formal and says Clement wants to see Kitely. Kitely privately tells Cash to keep an eye on his wife. When Kitely leaves, his wife wonders why he has been wanting Cob so much lately, and, to tease her, Wellbred says that Cob's wife is tawdry. She is perturbed and decides to bring Cash with her to track her husband to Cob and Tib's house.

This leaves Bridget and Wellbred alone to discuss Bridget's admirer, and she decides to meet with Edward. Kitely returns and interrupts them, becoming angry when he learns that his wife and Cash went somewhere together.

Matthew and Bobadil are in a street discussing their reputations after the previous events. Brainworm then enters dressed as Formal and the men try to get Downright in legal trouble. Brainworm says he will help the men for a price. Since Mathew and Bobadil have no money, they pawn some of their belongings to get him to agree.

Knowell is looking for his son at Cob's house. Cob's wife Tib is fearful that Knowell is a constable but speaks to him anyway. She shuts the door almost immediately when Dame Kitely and Cash arrive. The two ask for Kitely, but he is not there. Instead he arrives just then so Kitely and his wife argue. Each believes that they are being cheated on. Cob enters and believes what Kitely says about his place being a whorehouse.

Brainworm is dressed as a legal officer. He supposedly bears a warrant for Downright, which allows Bobadil and Matthew to arrest Downright. Stephen enters in Downright's cloak so the men mistakenly try to arrest him. He is then actually arrested by the disguised Brainworm for supposedly stealing Downright's cloak. All of the men head to Justice Clement.

Act Five is at Justice Clement's house. Clement, Knowell, Kitely, Dame Kitely, Tib, Cash, Cob and servants enter. They are sorting out the business of how each was given false messages by Clement's man. Clement realizes that they were both tricked to go to Cob's house. Bobadil and Matthew enter, and speak of their warrant for Downright. Then Stephen, Downright, and the disguised Brainworm enter. Those men bring forth their quarrel about the cloak, as well as the issue of Formal's supposed man who had the warrant for Downright's arrest. Clement wants to jail Brainworm for not having served the warrants correctly. Brainworm reveals himself, and the tricks he played are exposed. His tricks on Knowell and Kitely earlier are also revealed. Roger Formal then enters, apologetic that he got drunk and had his clothes stolen (Brainworm's doing, to pretend to be him).

Wellbred reveals Edward and Bridget's marriage, and Clement orders them to be brought here for congratulations. The men out Matthew's propensity for poetry and Clement recites some off the top of his head, but they realize that Matthew just reads others' work and passes it off as his own. Clement orders his collection of verses to be burned. He also makes Stephen give Downright his cloak back and urges Tib and Cob renew their vows. To end the play, Justice Clement tells each person to clean themselves of their overweening emotions, and they all celebrate.

Ben Jonson: (1572-1637, London) was an English Stuart dramatist, lyric poet and critic. He is generally regarded as the second most important English dramatist after William

Shakespeare, during the reign of James I. among his major plays are the comedies of *Everyman in His Humour (1598); Volepone (1605), Epicone;* or the *Silent Woman (1609), The Alchemist (1610)* and *Bartholomew Fair (1614)*.

The year 1598 marked an abrupt change in Jonson's status, when *Everyman in His Humour* was successfully presented by the Lord Chamberlain's theatrical company and his reputation was established. In this play Jonson tried to bring out the spirit and manner of Latin comedy to the English popular stage by presenting the story of a young an with an eye for a girl, who has difficulty with a phlegmatic father, is dependent on a clever servant, and is ultimately successful – in fact, the standard plot of the Latin dramatist Plautus. But at the same time Jonson sought to embody in four of the main characters the four "humours" of medieval and Renaissance medicine – choler, melancholy, phlegm and blood – which are thought to determine human physical and mental makeup.

The same year Jonson killed a fellow actor in a duel, and, though he escaped capital punishment by pleading "benefit of clergy" (the ability to read from the Latin Bible) he could not escape branding. During his brief imprisonment over the affairs he became a Roman Catholic.

Major Themes:

Everyman in His Humour popularized the 'comedy of humours'. Originally a medical term, 'humour' were the fluids believed to regulate the body and by extension the human temperament. The theory which can be traced to ancient times is that there are four distinct bodily fluids, or humours, causes a personality disturbance.

In *Everyman in His Humour* Jonson worked these theories into his drama to great effect – the characters in the work show clear evidence of their individual imbalances of humours. Although Jonson was not the first to employ the idea of humour in the play, his use of the conceit in *Everyman in His Humour* is considered exemplary. Commentators contend that key features of the play are derived from classical drama, particularly from Plautus's comedies in form and structure. Like those plays, the plot centers on an unlikely couple overcoming obstacles – particularly familial and social opposition – to marry. In addition the concept of a pair of stately, elderly people outwitted by a pair of clever young men can be traced back to Plautine comedy, as can the characters of the cunning servant and the braggart soldier. The work is also considered a predecessor of cosmic realism on the English stage.

CHAPTER FIVE

Every Man in His Humour: Questions & Answers

A BRIEF HISTORY OF ENGLISH COMEDY

It was under the direct influence of the Renaissance (the Revival of Learning) that English comedy and tragedy passed out of the preliminary phases of their development into forms of art. Men went back to the classics for inspiration and example in the drama, as in other fields of literary enterprise, though it was the work of the Latin, not of the Greek, playwrights that they took as their models. Plautus and Seneca provided the inspiration for the writing of comedy and tragedy respectively.

The earliest regular English comedy is *Gammer Gurton's Needle*, the authorship of which is not known. It was written about 1550 and was acted long after that date at Christ's College, Cambridge. It is a realistic farce, often coarse, and in long rhyming lines. The second regular English comedy was *Ralph Roister Doister*, also written around 1550, by Nicholas Udall.

The quarter century or so, which followed, was a period of vast experimentation in the English drama. There was a conflict between those who insisted on the classical tradition and those who wanted to cater to the strong national taste of the English public. In the end the national taste won, and just before Shakespeare began his career as a playwright, the romantic form of drama (as distinguished from the classical type) was definitely established. The establishing of this romantic drama was the achievement of

Shakespeare's immediate predecessors, a group of university men commonly known as the "university wits". They included John Lyly, Thomas Kyd, George Peele, Robert Greene, Christopher Marlowe, and Thomas Nash.

Shakespeare's comedies begin with the bright, frolicsome *Love's Labour's Lost*, full of jest and light hearted merriment. The play abounds in witty dialogue, and there is much satire on affectations. There are in it many ingenious conceits too, and the play is more in Lyly's style than any other of Shakespeare's dramas. *The Comedy of Errors* is a farce linked to a pathetic story of a sea-sorrow. Much of the humour is due to the confusion arising from mistaken identity. Shakespeare's comedies are essentially Romantic comedies, not only because of the mingling in them of the romantic love –interest with mirth and fun, but because they are also a mixture of serious, and even tragic, elements and comic elements, and further, because they do not observe any of the classical unities (of time, place and action). They are rich in characterization both as regards range or variety, and depth.

In a different key altogether are the comedies of Ben Jonson. Not only did Jonson call for an observance of the three classical unities, but he made war upon the fantastic and extravagant qualities of the romantic imagination, trying to replace them with classical sanity and restraint. In one respect at least the classical quality of Jonson's comedies gives them an interest that is permanent, and an influence that was far-reaching. One difference between the romantic spirit and the classic is that the former tends towards escape from the actual condition of life, while the latter tends to work realistically within them. This appears clearly when we compare *Twelfth Night* with *Every Man in His Humour*. Shakespeare's plays are full of glancing imagination and irresponsible fancy, while Jonson's move in the hard light of everyday London. This realism the vivid picture of London life, makes his comedies among the most informative plays of the period. From Jonson's comedies alone it would be possible to reconstruct whole areas of Elizabethan society.

Every Man in His Humour Quotes and Analysis

1. *Your son is old enough to govern himself...*

Clement, Act III, Scene 3

Knowell, Edward's father, is unsure of what to do with his son and whether he should allow him to rule over his own life or if he should continue to try and control him. Knowell does not trust his own judgment and as such he talks with someone whom he respects, namely Justice Clement, the person who has legal power in the city where Knowell lives. Clement uses the word "govern" to show that Edward is mature enough and old enough to be left on his own and for his father to be assured he is doing the right thing by giving his son freedom. The word is commonly used in relation with political power or with the power owned by the King and thus, Justice Clement is also suggesting that whether Knowell wants to admit or not, he no longer has any type of power over his son.

1. *He that is so respectless in his courses, / Oft sells his reputation at cheap market.*

Prologue

Jonson's famous prologue lays out his views on what a good play/ poetry does: it tells it like it is, essentially. He says he will not use antiquated or silly plots, and will use real language and speak of men's real deeds. In these lines he suggests that a playwright/poet who does not respect himself or his work will sell himself short, no doubt in terms of money but also in terms of his reputation. He will not be helping himself or his audience, and history will be less inclined to remember him.

3. *Nay, more than this, brother, if I should speak / He would be ready from the heat of humour / And over-flowing of the vapour in him, / To blow the ears of his familiars / With the false breath of telling what disgraces / And low disparagements I had put upon him.*

Kitely, Act II, Scene 1

The term "humour" is used several times in the play, this being one of the most conspicuous usages. Kitely is talking with Downright about Wellbred and suggesting it is his role as the elder brother to step in and tell Wellbred his behavior is inappropriate. Downright asks why Kitely does not do it himself, and this quote is Kitely's reply. He is essentially suggesting that Wellbred has a distinct humour that motivates him and overflows within him, and because of that Kitely already knows exactly how he will act. He knows Wellbred will become angry and prone to spreading lies about him, and Kitely certainly wants to preclude this. This quote thus articulates Jonson's comedy of humours, in which characters are driven by their excess humour and behave poorly.

4. *Now shall I / be possess'd of all his counsels: and, by that conduit, my / young master.*

Brainworm, Act II, Scene 3

Brainworm is a more complex character than he might initially appear to be. Certainly, yes, he seems to be a trickster of sorts, enjoying his machinations and his control over others. But this quote shows that there is much more to it: Brainworm has to look out for himself because he doesn't have money, property, or power, and he knows that if he throws his lot in with Edward, he is likely to be taken care of. His power over Knowell is ultimately, as

Brainworm knows, false, yet he still enjoys it while it lasts.

5. *For fear I sink! the violence of the stream / Already hath transported me so far, / That I can feel no ground at all!*

• 244 •

Kitely, Act III, Scene 2

Kitely is rather obnoxious and absurd, but he is still fascinating in that he is relatable to the audience/reader even if we do not wish it to be so. This is because Kitely is actually perspicacious and self-aware, knowing how his thoughts are tending and, as this quote suggests, that he has moved far from his ideal self. Yet, what makes him relatable is that he also knows he cannot stop himself. His thoughts are running away with him and he knows he's being ridiculous and unfair

but it seems impossible to listen to his rational self. This no doubt seems familiar to us in that we often know our conduct or thoughts are not conducive to a happy ending yet we feel as if we cannot alter their course.

6. *And they must come here to read / ballads, and roguery, and trash!*

Downright, Act IV, Scene 1

Downright has little patience for anything, it seems. He certainly has a legitimate reason to disapprove of his brother's behavior if it is disrupting a household, but much of Downright's complaints are similar to Knowell's in that they merely seem the ravings of one who does not like the young or the gallant or the fun-loving. In particular, he singles out "ballads" and calls them "roguery" and "trash." It's not hard to sympathize with him if he's talking about the absurd Matthew, but overall, Downright's disapproval of poetry seems unfair and representative of his own close-mindedness. Jonson ultimately makes a case for poetry, not only through the implicit condemnation of Downright and others who don't get it, but through Clement's promulgation of it at the end of the play.

7. *You are ripe for a husband; and a minute's loss / to such an occasion is a great trespass in a wise beauty.*

Wellbred, Act IV, Scene 6

It is not at all surprising that patriarchal assumptions and practices rule the day in a late 16th-century play—we really should expect no less—but that does not mean a contemporary audience/reader cannot pause to inspect the unfortunate and antiquated nature of Wellbred's words here. He essentially says that Bridget is nearing her expiration point, that her goal in life is to marry and that she must take advantage of the opportunities that come her way. Edward's putative love for her seems irrelevant; she is to marry and he's better than Matthew. Bridget and Dame Kitely are only in the play to be married or get married, to be suspicious or beguiling.

8. *O, god's precious! is this the soldier? here, take / my armour off quickly, 'twill make him swoon, I fear . . .*

Clement, Act V, Scene 1

Clement is clearly a wise, intelligent, and professional man, but what makes him appealing beyond that is his sometimes cutting sense of humor. Here, he sees Bobadil introduced as the "soldier" he'd been somewhat apprehensive about upon announcement—enough to don his own armor—but based on Bobadil's looks alone, Clement can see that he is essentially a fake. Clement scoffs that he should take this armor off immediately since it will both be unneeded and perhaps conducive to Bobadil becoming flustered at the sight of real power. It's an amusing moment, and one that shows why Clement really is the one to puncture the inflated pride of many of these characters.

9.   *. . . you sign o' the soldier, and picture o' the poet / (but, both so false, I will not ha' you hang'd out at my door / till midnight), while we are at supper, you two shall peni- / tently fast it out in my court, without . . .*

Clement, Act V, Scene 1

Clement resolves conflicts but also doles out appropriate punishments. Here he says that Bobadil and Matthew, the fake soldier and the fake poet, are not allowed to come in to supper because they need to meditate on their shortcomings. Clement is merciful here, not doing anything above and beyond keeping them out of a celebratory dinner, but his command is nonetheless, the audience assumes, effective. Those who create disharmony in society need to be punished so they do not continue to do so.

10.   *This night we'll dedicate to / friendship, love, and laughter.*

Clement, Act V, Scene 1

At the end of the play Clement helps resolve the various conflicts, misunderstandings, and grievances. He punishes bad behavior and sets courses aright. And, here, in this brief quote, he articulates what really matters in life—friendship, love, and laughter. Though everyone has tendencies toward bad behavior (on account of their humours, of course), they should work to

moderate those behaviors in order to promote a harmonious society. At the end of the day, Clement affirms, people really only want the same things.

"Every Man in His Humour" – (Quotes and Analysis):

1."He that is proud of his own works, is a fool. For what had he to do with them more than the carpenter's square, or the tailor's needle?" – Justice Clement.

Ben Jonson's "Every Man in His Humour" (1598) is a classic comedy of humours, showcasing exaggerated personality traits to critique human folly. The play satirizes London society through a vivid cast of characters, each dominated by a particular "humour" or temperament.

The quote above, spoken by Justice Clement—a voice of wisdom amidst the chaos—reflects Jonson's moral and philosophical concerns. Clement criticizes vanity and self-congratulation, suggesting that individuals are merely tools or instruments in the broader process of creation or success. Just as a carpenter's square or tailor's needle contributes to a finished product without claiming credit, people should not boast about their accomplishments as if they alone achieved them.

This quote encapsulates one of Jonson's recurring themes: humility versus arrogance. It mocks the self-important characters in the play—especially those like Kitely, who obsesses over honour and reputation, or Captain Bobadill, who boasts of martial glory without substance. Justice Clement, in contrast, represents rationality, balance, and a deeper understanding of human nature.

Jonson's use of humour is moral and corrective, aligning with classical comedic traditions. Through characters overwhelmed by their dominant "humours," he highlights the absurdity of imbalance in personality and social pretension.

Overall, this quote exemplifies the play's satirical edge and Jonson's belief in moderation, reason, and self-awareness as antidotes to foolishness and pride.

Some more quotes to look at:-

1. "I do call to mind now, that you told me once, you had a desire to travel."

— Edward Knowell to Stephen

? Analysis: This quote introduces Stephen's naive and affected interest in appearing cultured. Jonson mocks the Elizabethan trend of young men adopting superficial airs of sophistication, particularly through travel. It's a jab at those who confuse imitation with intelligence.

2. "Marry, I would have him do nothing but read, read, read."

— Old Knowell (about his son, Edward Knowell)

? Analysis: This satirical line highlights the older generation's rigid and unrealistic expectations. Jonson critiques the blind veneration of scholarship for its own sake, suggesting that balance in life is more important than obsessive study.

3. "A man must keep time in all."

— Wellbred

? Analysis: Wellbred represents wit and social awareness, often contrasting the uptight, paranoid characters like Kitely. This quote reminds us of the importance of timing and decorum in both social interactions and broader life conduct—one of Jonson's recurring comedic lessons.

4. "O, he is the courageous captain, you talk of; he is the very bull-beggar of all the suburbs, and stalks up and down like a walking lightning."

— Wellbred (about Bobadill)

? Analysis: This is a mock-heroic description of Captain Bobadill, the ridiculous braggart soldier. It exposes his empty bravado and Jonson's disdain for those who pretend to be more than they are—a central theme of the play.

1. "He that is proud of his own works, is a fool." — Justice Clement

This quote reflects Ben Jonson's deep-rooted classical values of humility and rationality. Spoken by Justice Clement, the wisest character in the play, it criticizes those who boast about their achievements as if they accomplished them entirely on their own. Clement compares such prideful men to tools—like a carpenter's square or tailor's needle—which play a part in creation but are not themselves responsible for the outcome. The message is that individuals are shaped by many factors—education, society, opportunity—and should not arrogantly claim all credit. This aligns with Jonson's broader satirical aim: to expose foolishness, especially in those ruled by vanity. Clement's wisdom provides a moral anchor, contrasting sharply with characters like Bobadill and Kitely, who are blinded by their self-importance. The quote promotes modesty and self-awareness, both key values in Jonson's comedic and moral vision.

2. "O, he is the courageous captain... stalks up and down like a walking lightning." — Wellbred (about Bobadill)

This line is a comically exaggerated description of Captain Bobadill, the archetypal "braggart soldier," who boasts endlessly about duels and wars he never actually fought. Wellbred's words are dripping with sarcasm, painting Bobadill as a fearsome warrior who "stalks" like "walking lightning"—a ridiculous image that parodies martial heroism. Jonson uses this to satirize the kind of false masculinity and shallow honour that were common in Elizabethan society. Bobadill represents a man dominated by the humour of pride and illusion, believing in his own grandiose lies. Wellbred, the clever observer, exposes him for what he is: a clownish impostor. The quote emphasizes a central theme of the play—appearance versus reality—and warns against placing value on empty boasts. Through characters like Bobadill, Jonson ridicules those who inflate themselves without merit, reinforcing the play's comedic yet moral critique of social pretension.

3. "A man must keep time in all." — Wellbred

This short line, spoken by Wellbred, carries a profound message about self-discipline and social intelligence. In the context of the play, it suggests that success in life and society depends on one's ability to act with proper timing—whether in speech, behaviour, or decision-making. Jonson's Every Man in His Humour is filled with characters who lack this balance: Kitely is consumed by jealousy, Bobadill by vanity, and Stephen by foolish ambition. These characters are ruled by their dominant "humours" or personality traits, leading them into absurd situations. Wellbred, on the other hand, acts with awareness and wit. His statement reflects Jonson's belief in moderation and reason as the key to good character. "Keeping time" is not just about punctuality—it's about knowing when and how to act, avoiding extremes. The quote reinforces the play's moral purpose: to expose the folly of those who act without thought and to praise those who live with awareness and restraint.

<u>Every man in his Humour</u> Short Questions and Answers

1. Name four Humours(Liquid) in human Body?

    These are;Phlegm, ,Blood,yellow bile and Black Bile.

2. Illustrate the role of Shakespeare in <u>Every man in his humour</u>?

    Critics emphasize on the fact that Shakespeare would have played the role of old knowell.

3. Define the meaning of Humour.

    It means something awkward in Man's disposition ,it can be a specific habit.

3. Name characters who try to copy the Bobadill's Oaths.

    Stephen and cob.

4. How many stories are described in this Drama ?

    it has 5 stories ,2 major and three minor.

5. Who is Country Gull?

Stephen is being called country Gul.We came to know that he is Edward cousin.

6.   What are the reasons Old knowell followed his son?

He wanted to see his son's actions and doings and wanted to investigate the whole situation for the betterment of his son.

7.   Who Disguises himself an Ex-soldier?

Brainworm, he did so,so that he would be able to convey message to Edward that his father is going to watch actions.

8.   Who is the wellbred Brother ?

Downright.

9.   Why does kitley Complain to Downright ?

She Complains to Downright that wellbred is breaking the peace of his home by bringing many friends.

10.   What is wellbred allegation about kitley's husband?

He says that kitely's husband is paying attention to Cob's wife Tib.

11.   Who is called Barggart?

This   name   is   given   to   Captain   Bobadill.who   shows Swordsmanship but he doesn't know anything about this.

12.   Who has the clothes of Downright?

Stephen ,he is the cousin of Edward Stephen picks up the Cloak .

13.   Justice Clement becomes angry at cob why?

When cob openly criticizes and Condemns tobacco-smoking at justice clement also becomes angry and rebuke to cob, because justice clement himself is a great champion of tobacco-smoking.

14. Describe Fight between Cob and Tib.

There is conflict between Cob and Tib .Kitely says to Cob that his house is being used by his wife as a brothel.Without any thinking,he beats her wife,and says that he would take her justice Clements's house.

15.   Who was the clerk of justice Clement ?

Formal is justice Clement's clerk .he somehow gets interested in Brainworm.

16.   Why Clements's clerk Formal is interested in Brainworm?

Formal is very interesting in Brainworm .Formal says to him that he would like to hear about his bravery stories.Formal likes when Braibworm is disguised as an exsoldier.

17.   Describe the Role of justice Clement in resolving the Complains ?

He played an important role in solving the problems . Almost every character problems he solved by his wit and Experience he had.

18.   What are the oldknowell's views about poetry?

According to Old knowell poetry is the hobby of idles.

19.   What kind of suggestions old knowell offers to his brother's Son?

Oldknwell says that his nephew Stephen Should learn wisdom and should practice the art of attaining prosperity .He also says not to spend too much money on the unnecessary things. Old knowell Christian name is Edward.

20. Old Knowell shocked when he read letter why?

When old knowell opens the letter and goes through it. He is shocked by the contents of the letter. Because the letter is written in frivolous manner.

21. What does letter refer to old knowell?

The Letter says that old knowell spend much of his time in counting the Green apricots growing on his trees.

22. What is the opinion of the letter writer, about apricots?

The writer of letter says that if he had been Old Knowell's son, he would have collected all the apricots and given to the young girls passing his house.

23. What kind of Book mattew holding in his hand?

Thomas kyd's book "the Spanish tragedy "He says that this book Contain a number of five speeches.

24. Who is Knowell?

He is a rich old man , his son name is Edward. He is against the poetry and the habit of hawking and hunting.

25. Who Burnt Stephen verses?

Stephen's verses are burnt under Clement's orders.

26. Who wrote letter to Edward?

Wellbred's wrote a letter to Edward.

27. Who buys the sword in the play?

Stephen buys the sword.

28. Who is Edward knowell?

He is Old knowell's son.He likes poetry and his father thinks that his son is wasting of his time. He likes the company of his Friend, Wellbred. He was the cousin of Stephen.

29. To whom Edward married?

Bridget.

30. Name the poem which Matthew has stolen .

It is 'Hero and Leander'.

31. Describe the character Sketch of Wellbred.

He is the friend of Edward, he enjoys being with friends but his father old knowell didn't like being with friends .

32. What kind of kitley's humour?

Her Humour is jealousy.

33. Write a few words about Dame Kitley.

She is the wife of Mr. Kitley.She likes her husband .She mistakenly doubt her husband because of the wellbred falsely information

34. Who was Country Gull? Few lines about Stephen.

Stephen ,he likes Hawking and Hunting. According to him,sports are studied better than Greek or Latin. He was the Cousin of Edward and Nephew of Old knowell.

35. Few lines about Oliver Cob.

He is a water-carrier and has great humour.He is being called cuckold by his wife many times in the play.

36. Who was the Tib?

She is the wife of Cob.she is interesting character and makes few humors situation .As she says to her husband cuckold,it also creates funny situation.

37. Character sketch of Justice Clement.

He is a city magistrate .He is an excellent good lawyer .He often likes tobacco. Clement hears the complains of society and then decides and give his judgment .

A. **What is a "viaticum"?**

Some of the characters in the play are concerned with the right of a person to be allowed their viaticum. The term is generally used by the Catholic Church and is also referred to as the Holy Communion a person receives just before they die. The practice was so important for the family of the dying person and for the priest that in some cases, when the dying person expired before a priest could arrive, food was put into the dead person's mouth. The reason why this was so important for many people is because they linked their salvation to the act of receiving the last rites. This gave them the assurance their soul will be accepted in heaven and thus not forced to suffer for eternity. The state of a person's soul is one of the major themes in the play and thus it is no surprise that the characters express an interest in the fate of their soul after death as well.

B. What are the "humors" mentioned in the play and why are they significant?

The humors are a theory from medieval and Renaissance thought. According to the humors theory, in every human body can be found four liquid elements which have to be in perfect balance with one another for a person to be healthy. Illnesses were considered as being the result of an excess or lack of humors and the doctors of the day tried to bring back the balance by using different methods such as blood-letting or excessive sweating. The four humors were blood, yellow bile, black bile and phlegm, and they was also linked with the personality traits a person had. Certain afflictions were linked with the excess of humors and it was believed that for example, someone who had an excess of black bile was depressed while someone who had an excess of yellow bile was extremely aggressive. This theory is also mentioned by many characters in the play as being the reason why many characters behave in one way or another.

C. How do Edward and Wellbred perceive Brainworm and his disguises?

Brainworm's many disguises are not annoying or cumbersome to Edward and Wellbred; rather, they are impressed with him. They see why he's doing what he's doing, that it works in their self-interest, and that it indicates a wit and adaptability that they also value. Matthew Kendrick suggests that Brainworm's behavior is "increasingly depicted as a form of skilled labor rather than as idleness or unwillingness to labor. In marked contrast to Knowell's moralistic condemnation, Edward and Wellbred express genuine respect for Brainworm's protean deception."

D. What are the various follies Jonson lampoons?

Jonson presents characters who embody the traits of hotheadedness, braggadocio, jealousy, and irrationality. Bobadil and Stephen and Matthew are quick to take offense even when there is none, and are desirous of fighting. Bobadil boasts of his prowess as a soldier but clearly has no skills. Matthew boasts of his skills as a poet but is proven a plagiarizer. Stephen is immature and volatile, and shows that he does not at all deserve to be Knowell's heir. Kitely's misplaced jealousy nearly destroys his relationship with his wife and leads him to doubt his trusted servant. Knowell's assumptions about his son are groundless and lead to fissures, albeit minor, in their relationship.

E. Why is Knowell so concerned for his son?

Knowell is not too different from many parents who assume that their child is associating with the wrong people, or behaving in deleterious ways. He thinks Wellbred and his associates are louche gallants, that they are not serious, that they are too given to games and smoking and carousing. He wants Edward to be a moral, upstanding young man. The issue is, of course, is that Knowell is old-fashioned and his advanced years preclude him from desiring to understand his son. He doesn't distinguish between youthful fun and legitimately bad behavior, and as Clement tells him blatantly, there's no real issue with Edward. By the end of the play it seems like Knowell has come to at least somewhat of an acceptance of this fact.

Long Questions and Answers

Q. Discuss everyman in his humor as a classical comedy.

Every Man in His Humour" is a classical comedy written by Ben Jonson, first performed in 1598. Here are some aspects that characterize it as a classical comedy:

Satirical Elements: Classical comedies often include satire, and "Every Man in His Humour" satirizes the prevalent humoral theory of the time. Humoral theory suggested that human behavior and health were governed by four bodily fluids or humors (blood, phlegm, yellow bile, and black bile), each associated with different personality traits.

Social Critique: The play critiques and mocks various social classes and types of people in Jacobean society. Characters are often exaggerated embodiments of their humors, such as the melancholic, the choleric, the sanguine, and the phlegmatic.

Stock Characters: Classical comedies frequently use stock characters who embody particular traits or stereotypes. Jonson's play employs these types effectively, creating recognizable characters like the jealous husband, the ambitious youth, the pretentious courtier, and the foolish country gull.

Intricate Plot: While the plot of "Every Man in His Humour" may not be as convoluted as later comedies, it still involves intricate interactions among characters driven by their humors. The plot revolves around the attempts of various characters to fulfill their desires and navigate social interactions, often resulting in comedic misunderstandings and reconciliations.

Language and Wit: Classical comedies emphasize verbal wit and wordplay, and Jonson is known for his clever use of language. The dialogue in "Every Man in His Humour" showcases Jonson's skill in crafting sharp exchanges and humorous repartee among characters.

Resolution and Morality: Like many classical comedies, "Every Man in His Humour" typically ends with a resolution that reaffirms social order or moral lessons. Characters often learn from their follies or mistakes, and harmony is restored by the end of the play.

Overall, "Every Man in His Humour" fits well into the tradition of classical comedy with its satirical portrayal of human behavior, use of stock characters, witty dialogue, and moralistic resolution. It reflects the social and moral concerns of its time while providing entertainment through its comedic elements.

Q: "Every Man in His Humour" as a comedy humour.

Every Man in His Humour is one of Jonson's best-known and most influential plays. Considered a comedy of intrigue, the play archives the efforts of a young, well-born man to wed his true love, although his well-intentioned father's tries to stop the wedding. Every Man in His Humour also famous in the theory of humours and is regarded as a major work of comic realism.

The main plot consists of three strands- the over enthusiastic father and his rakish son; the unreasonable misgiving of the Kitely family regarding the loyalty; the love intrigue between Edward and Bridget. These three elements have their separate unit.

The play opens with the miss-delivery of a letter addressed to Edward Knowell. It is written by Wellbred, friend of Edward. The letter is about the invitation to visit the Windmill Tavern. The letter finally reaches in the hands of Old Knowell. The letter rouses the suspicion of the father. He sets out to investigate the matter. The father always suspects that the son becomes very wasteful and derailed. Edward actually visits the city both to visit his friend, Wellbred, and to seek the hand of Bridget, his love who is from a lower economic and social class. But realizing that his father is following him and intent on damaging his attempts to wed Bridget, Edward begs the help of his father's clever servant, Brainworm, who assumes several masks to trick the elder Knowell and foil his pursuit.

Kitely, the victim of the second intrigue, is one of Jonson's most striking 'humours'. Jonson's intention is satiric comedy; he eliminates from Kitely all but the one idea of foolish jealousy, which, after the manner of 'humour', becomes an obsession, and ridiculously colors all his thoughts and behavior.

The third is the very thin love intrigue between Bridget and Edward Knowell. This is the one typically romantic aspect of the play. But Jonson naturally makes little of it. It is introduced in Act

IV Scene iii with no preparation; but it is slightly elaborated.

All the twists are finally resolved at Justice Clements's house. Kitely's jealousy and his wife's suspicion are found baseless. Brainworm unmasks his disguise. The wedding of Edward and Bridget is occurred. Old Knowell realizes his folly.

It is based upon the ancient theory of humours. The ancient and medieval universe was conceived to be composed of four elements. The four elements were combinations of four qualities- hot, cold, dry and moist. The earth was regarded as a combination of cold and dry qualities. Water was regarded of cold and moist qualities. Air was characterized as hot and moist qualities. Fire represented as hot and dry qualities.

Man's body was composed of earth and water. His soul is of air and water. The elements present in the human body were known as four humours. Each humour was responsible for peculiar physical and mental traits in the human personality.

This drama introduces us to a group of eccentric attitudes. Each of his character has his particular humour. Knowell's humour is he is excessively anxious and suspicious of the attitude of his son. Kitely's humour is his jealousy, which is humourous. The other characters come up with various eccentrics. Justice Cement is a crazy magistrate and he is fond of liquor. Stephen's humour is his melancholy mood. Edward and Wellbred's humours are their sense of intellectual superiority. Humour as the trait of absurdity, eccentricity or abnormality is perfectly portrayed.

Q. In the prologue of *Everyman in his Humour* Jonson says that his comedy is intended to show an image of the times. To what extent does the play succeed in this purpose?

Like ancient classical comedy, written by authors like Plautus and Terence, *Everyman in His Humour* reflects contemporary life. Jonson defined comedy as an imitation of life, as a mirror of the times, and as an image of truth. In this respect, Jonson's comedy is different from the romantic comedy of the time. The romantic dramatists did not mirror nature or life; the dealt with remote places; they idealized persons; they depict marvelous adventures and so on. The romantic satires did not attempt an orderly analysis of history or a rationalized imitation of the life of their own day. But the neo-classical comedy as represented by Jonson deals with real life, even though it exaggerates different aspects of that life in order to ridicule. This play definitely holds up a mirror to the life of the times, representing various aspects of it, and satirizing it to bring out the absurdities.

The habit of the people of that time to swear oaths, even when there was no need to do so, is clearly depicted in the play. Almost every character, even Justice Clement, swears oaths indiscriminately. Some characters in the play swear oaths to support every statement which they make. In fact these characters swear as a matter of routine, and they do so in a mechanical way.

The gallants of the time were greatly interested in hawking and hunting. Early in the play we find Stephen telling his uncle that hawking and hunting are being studied more earnestly than the Greek and the Latin languages. According to Stephen, nobody is fit to move in the company of the gallants without cultivating an interest in these sports. Duels too seems to have been very common in Jonson's time. Bobadill makes a reference to the great Caranza who had written a book on the subject of dueling, a book which contained all the rules and the guide-lines according to which duels are to be fought.

Tobacco smoking also seems to have been in fashion in those days. Bobadill, who is in the habit of smoking tobacco, grows eloquent in praise of it. Bobadill says that tobacco provides nourishment to the human system and that a man can live without food merely by smoking tobacco fo several days. According to him tobacco cures many ailments and diseases; and he describes it as the most sovereign and precious weed that ever the earth has offered to the use of man.

Moral standards in those days seem to have been rather loose and lax. After reading Wellbred's letter old Knowell says that this letter could have been written from a brothel, or from a hospital where patients suffering from venereal diseases. Later old Knowell deplores the fact that the parents of the time brought up their children without showing the least regard for moral values. In fact parents taught their children obscene jokes and bawdy songs. Fathers even took their sons to prostitutes in order to train them in the art of making love to their mistress. Similarly parents taught their sons the evil habit of gluttony and tried to make epicures of them. They also took pains to make their sons money minded and instructed them to make money by any means whatsoever.Certain tendencies which could be described as 'Humours', wre very much in fashion in those days. Melancholy was one such humour. Matthew describes melancholy as a fine humour, saying that trur melancholy breeds a perfectly fine wit. Thus Jonson succeeds in bringing before our minds the daily life of the London of the later years of the reign of Elizabeth and the early reign of James I.

The Origin and Development of English Drama

The Origin and Development of English Drama

The origin of English drama seems vague. There is no certain evidence proving its origin. However, it can be traced back from century of succeeding Norman Conquest to England on 1066. Many historians believe that drama came to England along with them. There was information that when the Roman where in England, they established vast amphitheatre for production some plays, but when they left, the theatre gone with them.

Originally, the term drama came from Greek word meaning "action" or "to act" or "to do". William J. Long argues that "drama is an old story told in the eye, a story put into action by living performers". Thus, drama is the form of composition design for performance in the theatre, in which the actors take role for certain characters, perform certain action and utter certain dialogues (Abrams and Harpham, 2015:95).

In England, drama had a distinctly religious origin from the church as the part of services. Apart from its origin, the Latin Church had condemned Roman theatre for many reasons. Thus, drama could not develop until tenth century when the church began to use dramatic elements as part of their services in the certain festival or ritual. The motives of the church began to use dramatics elements seem unclear. But, it was certain that the purpose was didactic, that is, to give deep understanding about the truth of their religion to the believer.

The oldest existing church drama was "Quem Quarritis" trope (whom are you seeking), when the three Marrys visited the empty tomb of Christ and met angel. Their conversation with angel consists of four sentences in Latin then adapted and performed by the clergy in very simple performance. This simple beginning gradually grew more elaborate. This drama called liturgical drama, in which the story simply taken from the scripture. The earlier play were given inside the church, the story were written by the clergy and performed by the clergy using Latin language. However, drama were not performed in all churches, only in certain cathedrals and monasteries where there were enough clergy to perform the plays.

From the liturgical, drama evolved to Miracle and Mystery play. In France, Miracle used to represent the life of the saints and Mystery used to represent any scene taken from the scripture. Meanwhile in England, there was no distinction between this two. The term Miracle play was used to represent any story taken from the scripture or the bible and the life of the saints.

The earliest recorded Miracle play in England was "Ludus Santa de Katherina", which performed in Dunstable around 1110. It was not known who wrote the original play, but the first version was prepared by the French school teacher, Geoffrey from St. Albans. The plays were given in Latin or French. The Miracle play attracted so many people and increased its popularity. The plays were before given inside the church began to move to the porch then to the churchyards. But when the plays began interfere the church services and had become too elaborate, the scandalized priest forbade the play in the church. By the thirteenth century, the Miracle play began move outside the church.

After the Miracle play move outside the church, the secular organization or town guilds began to take responsibility in its production. Few changes were made during this period. By the fourteenth and fifteenth century, the plays were given in vernacular pr local language. The actors were no longer clergy but the amateur actors which trained and selected carefully. The plays were given in the series of mansion in the town square. The plays were performed o moving platform called pageants and the act area called pletea. The stage were divide into three parts; hell, earth and heaven. Hell in the left side, earth in the centre and heaven in the right side. Usually the stages were identified by certain props. For instance, the head of dragon with red jaws or monstrous mouth with fire breathing represent hell where the devil characters will be dragged to the hell. The idea of salvation and damnation which later adopted in Dr. Faustus was inherited from this period. The costumes were distinguish in three realms; heaven, earth and hell. The heavenly characters such as God, angels, saints or certain Biblical character wore the church garments with certain accessories. The earthly characters wore the contemporary medieval garment appropriate to their rank. Meanwhile, for devil character wore black garments with wings, animals claws, beaks, horns or tails.

On 1311, the Council of Vienne revived the feat of Corpus Christi. This festival held in June every year and last for three or four days, sometimes extend to six days. The Miracle plays were presented in all large town city in England. It was arranged to exhibit the whole story from creation to the Day of Judgment in a cycle. There were four famous cycle existed in England. The York with 48 plays, the Chester with 25 plays, the Wakefield with 32 plays and the Coventry with 42 plays. During this religious period drama were written according to the Bible and no change was tolerated. This religious performances lasted till the sixteenth century.

The later development of drama was Morality play. it is a dramatization of personified abstraction generally vice against virtue. In these plays, the character were allegorical personified such as death, sin, good and bad angel, seven deadly sins, etc. The purpose of this drama was didactic, to give moral lesson to the audience. The morality plays generally ended with the virtue win against the evil. This play was marked by the introduction of personage called "vice", who was mischievous, comic and humorous character. Vice was the predecessor of the modern clown or jester. The examples of morality plays are "Everyman" and "The Castle of Perseverance". The introduction of Morality play also introduce so called "interlude". Interlude is the short version of morality play. Generally interludes were given during break of the scene. It was a short stage entertainment in a sense of humor and was considered as the forerunner of comedies. The example of interlude was "The Four P's" by John Heywood which performed around 1497.1

The final stage of the evolution of English drama was the artistic period. In this period, the purpose of the pay was not to point out a moral but to represent human life as it is. During this period, English drama was influenced by classical drama. The first comedy was "Ralph Roister Doister" written by Nicholas Udall on 1556. The play divided into acts and scenes and wrote in rhyming couplets. This first comedy had become the model and predecessor of English comedies. The first tragedy "Gorboduc" was written by Thomas Sackville and Thomas Northon around 1562. It was written in blank verse and divided into acts and scenes. After this era, the English drama developed gradually into regular form of drama which flourish during Elizabethan reign and which known till today.

Therefore, English drama gradually develop from the liturgical drama to Miracle and Mystery plays, continuously to Morality and interlude followed by the influence of classical model and finally evolve to the regular drama forms which known till today.

Few Important Topics to remember

1.Mystery Plays

History

Mystery Plays originated in the Middle Ages, during the twelfth century, from the lack of interest from the churchgoers in the typical church services and their ignorance of the Latin language. This problem prompted the elaboration of certain services. It began with subtle changes to the services for religious holidays such as Easter and Good Friday, that involved bringing down the cross for all to see; and expanded to the Christmas service with the scene of Christ's birth in the manger. One of the first liturgical performances was *Quem Quaeritis* ("Whom Seek Ye") in 925 Citation? . As the theatricals became more popular they were moved out of the church to accommodate the growing audience. During the thirteenth century Mystery plays gained less support from religious figures due to their questionable religious values, they started to be performed in the vernacular and were starting to drift away from being performed in the church. Once this happened and the performances were free from the church the strong religious themes started to disappear. In 1210 A.D. there was a ban of Mystery Plays by Pope Innocent III, which caused the plays began to performed in small town guilds,this act officially cut ties between the plays and the church and they were exclusively performed by town-guilds. With an ever growing audience to please, the town-guilds found that a perfect opportunity to showcase their works with the introduction of the Corpus Christi festival, in 1311, that takes place 57 days after Easter. The performances were grouped together and consisted of plays such as, Noah and the Flood, and The Creation of the World and the Fall of Adam. From these small groups came the four most prominent collections of mystery plays, the York cycle with 48 pageants, the Towneley plays with 32 pageants, the Chester cycle with 24 pageants, and the Wakefield (N-town) plays with 42 pageants. The term "Mystery" did not come from our term and the way it is used in present day. It was derived from the Latin word ministerium, meaning an association of clergy from different religious groups. This was the term used to describe the guilds which performed these plays, which is why is was used to name to describe the actual plays being performed. By the time of the end of the fifteenth century and the beginning of the Reformation, in England, the Mystery plays started to die down and were replaced in popularity by Morality plays.

Characteristics

Mystery plays were dramatizations of both the Old and New Testament miracles. Another popular topic was Christ and his crucifixion and resurrection. In the beginning of the popularity of Mystery plays the parts in the performance were played by clergymen and other members of the church. During their peak, Mystery plays were moved out of the church and performed on wagons and moved about the different towns. Due to the separation from the church the plays tended to have more of sarcastic tone to them and sometimes even went as far as mocking priests and monks, the people who had a big part in the creation of the plays. Another change that came with the separation of the church was the switch from clergymen as performers to members of guilds and craftsman. A huge aspect of Mystery plays was that they neglected to utilize the three unities; place, time, and action. Because of this the plays could represent any location or time and were not tied down by each story they were performing and could pose two time periods or locations together that are not cohesive. Also they did not limit their performances, they used technologies, such as trap doors and mechanisms to create the illusion of flying, to get the realest effect and please the audience.

One of the most widely known Mystery plays is *The Second Shepherd's Play*, which puts three shepherds at the birth of Christ in Bethlehem. It emphasizes the everyday life during the middle ages and juxtaposes the shepherd's story with that of Christ's, setting the secular and religious world side by side.

Some common Mystery Plays:

~ Birth of Jesus
~ The Wise Men
~ Flight into Egypt
~ The Second Shepherd's Play

2.Miracle plays

Miracle Plays, also called Saint's Plays, were plays dedicated to the lives of various saints, rather than Biblical events. Just like Mystery Plays the Miracle play originated to enhance the liturgical services, and were later separated from the church. They were switched to the English language, became less and less religious, and were performed in town festivals in the thirteenth century. Most Miracle plays are performed about either St. Nicholas or the Virgin Mary. The plays about St. Mary regularly involve her in the role of "deus ex machina" (god from the machine), there would usually be a problem that seems unsolvable and the characters call on the Virgin Mary to help. They were performed in Plain-an-gwarny (Cornish Medieval amphitheatre). During the sixteenth century there was a ban on Miracle Plays by King Henry VIII, some were destroyed, and after they soon began to fade away in popularity.

3.Morality Plays

History
Morality plays stemmed from Mystery and Miracle plays. It is the last in the trilogy of Vernacular drama. Typically, Morality plays tried to teach through a theatrical point of view. These plays were allegorical dramas that personified the moral values and abstract ideas to teach moral lessons. The plays were used to educate the masses on Christianity. It served better to learn when the information was presented in a theatrical fashion, as opposed to readings of the Bible. Moralities were popular during the fifteenth and sixteenth century in Medieval Europe as didactic, informative or educational, plays. "Quasi-professional groups of actors"

(Britannica; Morality Play) generally performed these plays, building off of their public rapport. Morality plays are still around in the 21st century. Many schools still have their students perform these plays during the holiday's as a school pageant.The most common and famous play is *Everyman*, an English version of the Dutch Play about the inevitability of death (Britannic, Middle English). With the wealth gained from the Renaissance, the traveling theaters were not needed due to the building of permanent theaters and the emergence of professional actors. This new era put an end to the Medieval drama, but it served as a great beginning to what we call drama today.

Characteristics

Morality plays are the result of Christian symbolism. Due to their roots, they were quite serious in the beginning but as time wore on the seriousness began to give way, and they began to gain characteristics from popular farce. "They are the intermediate step between liturgical to professional secular drama" (Britannica), while still having elements of each. The characters within the play themselves personify different moral qualities depending on the moral that is being taught. They have a focus primarily on a hero (Protagonist) whose inner weaknesses become the main conflict. Generally, the weaknesses are drawn out and antagonized by the Seven Deadly Sins (Antagonist) , that make the hero question not only himself but his standing with God. The Seven Deadly Sins for a point of reference are; Lust,Greed,

Gluttony, Envy, Anger, Pride and Sloth. Each Sin represents a different aspect that, as the Bible states, God will not forgive you for. Morality plays are based highly from a religious stand point in order to teach individuals about proper or true morals; right and wrong. To return back to the basic outline of a Morality play, the Hero then has the choice to take what he says to heart or strive for redemption and ask " The Four Daughters of God" (Mercy, Justice, Temperance, and Truth) to aid in his quest. The plays could more than likely be performed in under ninety minutes.

Some common Morality Plays:

~ The Castle of Perseverance (c. 1425)

~ Hickscorner

~ Everyman

Critically examine the contribution of "University Wits" to the growth of drama in the Elizabethan period.

The Elizabethan school of drama originated from a closely associated group of Oxford and Cambridge educated scholars. Regarded as the "mighty group of plannings who founded the English drama" by George Saintsbury, they came to be known as the 'University Wits'. The wits included Robert Greene, Thomas Kyd, Thomas Lodge, John Lyly, Christopher Marlowe, Thomas Nashe and George Peele, with Kyd being the only one who was not university educated. They held liberal views regarding God and morality and reshaped the native chronicle play and interlude in terms of its diversity and quality, thereby embodying the Renaissance influence on English culture and sensibility.

Through their educated and imaginative way of writing, the University Wits reformed the language used in drama and demonstrated a preference for tragedy over comedy, which was considered a lower form of dramatic art. They chose heroic themes, such as the lives of Mahomet and Tamburlaine, and gave them a heroic treatment using descriptive language, elaborate speeches, emotions, and violent incidents, often by way of blank verse.

Individual Contributions

Robert Greene is known for his powerful romantic settings and liberal use of blank verse in his comedies. Though weak in terms of characterization, his plays offered humor and imagination. His major plays include Friar Bacon and Friar Bungay, The Historie of Orlando Furioso and The Scottish Historie of James the Fourth.

Thomas Kyd used a well-constructed plot and forceful dialogues in his revenge play; for example, The Spanish Tragedy became popular due to its horrific plot, which included murder. He influenced Shakespeare and other Elizabethan dramatists like Webster.

Thomas Lodge, believed to have collaborated with Shakespeare on Henry VI, is famous for his prose romance, Rosalynde. His only original play is The Wounds of Civil War.

John Lyly, noted for his prose, also wrote plays that combined an intellectual tone with real comedy; his mixing of humor and romance served as an inspiration for Shakespeare. Lyly's important plays include Campaspe, Endymion and The Woman in the Moone.

Christopher Marlowe was the greatest of the University Wits, due to his significant contribution to English tragedy. For example, he replaced the Senecan motive of revenge with the theme of ambition. His concept of the tragic hero was marked by certain flaws, such as an overweening ambition. Marlowe used blank verse as the medium in his tragedies, which included Edward II, Tamburlaine The Great, The Jew of Malta and The Tragical History of Dr. Faustus.

Thomas Nashe exposed the social situations of the period through the use of satire in his plays. His Unfortunate Traveller, a prose tale, influenced the development of the English novel, while his most popular play is Summer's Last Will and Testament.

George Peele's plays are not only absurd and satirical but also romantic, the best ones being The Famous Chronicle of King Edward the First, The Old Wives Tale and The Love of King David and Fair Bethsabe. As a poet, he handled blank verse with ease and had a good sense of humor and pathos.

The contributions of the University Wits resulted in a radical transformation in Elizabethan drama due to a combination of artistic merit and intellectual arrogance (they ridiculed other playwrights without a university education or degree). They had a profound influence on William Shakespeare, who later redefined the English drama.

What is Interlude?

The word "interlude" directly translates to "between play" meaning, it is a break from the flow of a piece (whether music, a story, or a play).

An "interlude" in literary terms refers to a short, intervening episode, scene, or event that occurs between the main narrative or acts of a play. It often provides comic relief, commentary, or a break in the action, helping to maintain the audience's interest and offering a contrast to the primary story elements.

Example:

1. In Shakespeare's play "A Midsummer Night's Dream," the interlude of the mechanicals' play within the play serves as a humorous and lighthearted break from the romantic entanglements of the main plot. The comical performance by the amateur actors adds an element of farce and serves as a contrast to the more serious themes of love and enchantment.

2. British composer Benjamin Britten's "Sea Interludes."